UNDUE INFLUENCE AND VULNERABLE ADULTS

SANDRA D. GLAZIER
THOMAS M. DIXON
THOMAS F. SWEENEY

Cover design by Andrew Alcala.

Contents

About the Authors

Sandra D. Glazier is an equity shareholder at Lipson Neilson P.C., Bloomfield Hills, Michigan. She concentrates her practice in probate litigation, estate planning and administration, and family law. Sandy not only actively practices in these areas, she's also been engaged to act as a testifying or consulting expert. She also has served as a mediator in probate and family court cases. Sandy is active with the Oakland County Bar Association (OCBA), having held numerous leadership positions, and the ABA Real Property, Trust and Estate Law (RPTE) section, where she currently sits on the Trust & Estate Continuing Legal Education (TE CLE) committee. Sandy is a nationally recognized author in legal publications. She presents nationally on issues such as undue influence, ethical duties to vulnerable adults, defending fiduciaries, and the attorney-client privilege. She was awarded the OCBA's Distinguished Service Award; received Top Lawyer, Super Lawyer, Martindale-Hubbell AV Preeminent, and Accredited Estate Planner (AEP) designations; and was awarded *Trusts & Estates Magazine* Distinguished Author in Thought Leadership and *Bloomberg Tax* Estates, Gifts and Trusts Tax Contributor of the Year in 2018. For more background about Sandy, see https://lipsonneilson.com/attorney/sandra-d-glazier.

Thomas M. Dixon is an experienced trial lawyer, and he heads Clark Hill, PLC's Litigation Practice Group firmwide. Tom specializes in will, trust, estate, and probate litigation, and in complex commercial litigation. Tom has been continually recognized as a Michigan Super Lawyer in *Best Lawyers in America*, a Top Lawyer in *Crain's Detroit Business*, and a Top Lawyer in *DBusiness Magazine*. Tom also has received an AV Preeminent rating from Martindale-Hubbell. Tom has litigated cases involving wills, trusts, and probate estates, including cases involving claims of undue influence, lack of testamentary capacity, fraud, and duress. Tom has represented banks and other institutional fiduciaries, individual fiduciaries, families, other trustees and personal representatives, and beneficiaries in cases involving claims of fraud, negligence, and breach of fiduciary duty. Tom has litigated trust cases involving some of the largest private estates in Michigan. Tom also has litigated guardianship and conservatorship proceedings and claims of financial abuse of elderly persons. Tom has lectured nationally on the topic of undue influence and has co-authored numerous articles for national and Michigan publications. For more background about Tom, see https://www.clarkhill.com/people/thomas-m-dixon.

Thomas F. Sweeney was formerly a member of Clark Hill, PLC, in its Michigan offices. He now serves as counsel to the firm and focuses on estate planning, trust administration, and trust dispute resolution. Tom has lectured at the University of Michigan Law School and was an adjunct faculty member at Wayne State Law School, where he taught estate, gift, and generation-skipping taxation. He was a member of the Council of the Probate and Estate Planning section of the Michigan State Bar and formerly served as its chair. He has been recognized by *Best Lawyers in America* since 2003 and by Super Lawyers since 2006. Tom also has received an AV Preeminent rating. He has been a presenter at 16 of Michigan's Institute of CLE programs and has authored articles regarding various trust and tax law matters in the *Michigan Probate and Estate Planning Journal*. For more background about Tom, see https://www.clarkhill.com/people/thomas-f-sweeney.

Preamble

One may wish to heed the following quote from a recent U.S. Supreme Court opinion, which reflects that "[a]ll good trust-and-estate lawyers know that '[d]eath is not the end; there remains the litigation over the estate.'"[1] The number of estate plans that have come under attack on the premise that they are the product of undue influence appears to be escalating. While cases that involve the rich and famous make headlines, many more cases are brought in blended family scenarios or where dysfunctional relationships may be found to exist.

Elder abuse has been called "the crime of the 21st century."[2] Elder financial abuse is just one form of such abuse, and undue influence is a form of financial elder abuse. Elder financial abuse has been defined as the "misappropriation or abuse of financial control in a relationship where there is an expectation of trust, resulting in harm to the elderly victim." Also, "more than 200,000 scams and financial abuse cases targeting the elderly are reported to authorities every year, and most experts agree that's just the tip of the iceberg." Estimates "show $1.17 billion in damages are reported to authorities, but the real figure likely dwarfs that amount when factoring in unreported elder fraud."[3]

This book is not intended to be a survey or an all-inclusive resource on elder financial abuse or undue influence. However, it is our sincere desire that this book provide readers with a global understanding of undue influence, and how to identify it, plan for its possibility, litigate it, and address issues related to it.

While this book primarily is geared toward estate planners and probate litigators, it may provide a greater understanding of issues relating to

---

[1] Sveen v. Melin, 138 S. Ct. 1815, 1818–1819, 201 L. Ed. 2d 180, 86 USLW 48392 (2018) (citing Ambrose Bierce, 8 THE COLLECTED WORKS OF AMBROSE BIERCE: NEGLIGIBLE TALES, ON WITH THE DANCE, EPIGRAMS 365 (1911)).

[2] Kristen M. Lewis, *The Crime of the 21st Century: Elder Financial Abuse*, 28 PROB. & PROP. 11–15 (2014).

[3] Paul Bischoff, *The United States of Elder Fraud: How Prevalent Is Elder Financial Abuse in Each State?* COMPARITECH (Apr. 17, 2019), https://www.comparitech.com/blog/vpn-privacy/elder-fraud-by-state/.

capacity, the attorney's role, and the process known as "undue influence." As such, we hope that other professionals—including financial planners, trust administrators, and health care providers—who serve vulnerable individuals derive benefit from its contents, as well.

This book does not constitute legal advice. It represents a collaborative effort by the authors to provide an overview and better understanding of a variety of issues that often are associated with rendering services when diminished capacity and undue influence may be a concern.

Much thanks goes to our colleague Thomas E. F. Fabbri, Esq., for his research efforts on other matters, which provides some of the source material cited in this book.

Introduction[1]

A brilliant and accomplished man suffers injuries in an accident. He is being cared for by a woman who is a former nurse. This woman worships, adores and admires him. She attends to all his needs. While he lacks mobility and is unable to attend to even his most basic needs (such as food preparation, toileting, and transfers) and he requires significant assistance, his mind is crisp and clear. His sense of humor remains intact. His ability to formulate a plan of action and engage in conduct with the expressed goal of implementing it is evident. Anyone observing him would have no doubt that he has his wits about him and is fully competent. He suffers no cognitive limitations or impairments. His female "help mate," at times, reminds him that he better hope that nothing ever happens to her (and anyone looking at his face knows that he believes her when she says it).

It is obvious that he has full knowledge of just how isolated and dependent he truly is. She coos such things to him as "[s]ush, darling, trust me, it's for the best, G-d I love you." She tells him "[y]ou've got a lot of recovering to do. There's nothing to worry about. You'll be just fine." She tells him "I'm your number one fan" and how brilliant he is. She assures him that she has contacted the appropriate healthcare providers and obtained the best medical advice possible. She makes special food just for him. She says things like: "you poor dear thing"; "let me help you"; "comfy?"; "it breaks my heart to see you like this"; and, "I have faith in you my darling." She knows everything about him. Her admiration of him is long standing and apparent. One might even say her concern over him is obsessive. She keeps a picture of him in a prominent location in her home. She intones how she has saved his life and is working to

---

[1] This introduction is adapted from an article previously published by BNA: Bloomberg BNA, Sandra D. Glazier, Esq., Thomas M. Dixon, Esq., & Thomas F. Sweeney, Esq., *What Every Estate Planner Should Know About Undue Influence: Recognizing It, Insulating/Planning Against It . . . And Litigating It*, TAX MANAGEMENT MEMORANDUM (2015).

nurse him back to health. There are, at times, interchanges of dialogue between them, which contain words of respect, caring and concern.

Is he competent? Absolutely. There is no doubt that he knows and understands his situation. One could easily surmise that he knows the objects of his bounty, extent of his estate and is of sound mind. Were he to do so, there would be no question that he has sufficient capacity to execute an estate-planning instrument.

However, despite these apparently loving and respectful interchanges of dialogue, those privy to the backstory are fully cognizant that this relationship is one based upon fear, vulnerability and dependency. But without access to, or the utilization of, an independent individual who might meet with the man in private and instill confidence sufficient for him to trust that what he communicates will not be disclosed back to the woman, an outsider might only see a loving caring woman who attends to the man's every need. To the outside world the impact of the man's vulnerabilities, dependency and fear, as well as the true story behind the situation, might not be apparent.

Does this scenario sound familiar? It comes from the 1990 movie, *Misery*, based upon the novel by Stephen King. As a viewer, one is privy to the nuances of the relationship and able to make independent observations. However, in the typical undue influence case, such nuances are conducted outside the purview of others – in privacy and in secret. If the character, Paul Sheldon, were to die, discovery of the true circumstances of the relationship might be lost. To the viewer, there is no doubt that Paul Sheldon's burning of the sole copy of his newest manuscript and writing of a new one that suits the demands of his caregiver, Annie, are the direct result of undue influence. We see it. We understand it. We know it to be the undeniable truth because through the director's eyes we have a front row seat. But if you did not see it, had not experienced it, if it had been more subtle and nuanced, and if Paul Sheldon had died and never escaped Annie's clutches, how would you be able to identify it?

Turning from fiction to reality, and perhaps further down the capacity spectrum, a different example can be found in the saga of musician Brian Wilson of the Beach Boys fame, recently recounted in the movie *Love & Mercy* (2014). Imagine Brian Wilson, a youthful musical genius in the 1960s, writing hit song after hit song to lead his band the Beach Boys to fame and fortune. Now, imagine Wilson 20 years later, a broken, vulnerable man, damaged by drugs, alcohol, and recurring mental illnesses, living as a recluse under the control of a therapist/guardian who abuses that fiduciary relationship for personal gain.

What is significant about this real-life story is the number of indicia ("red flags") that point to undue influence present in this story that are common to many other situations of undue influence, including:

- A vulnerable adult (an elderly, infirmed, or disabled person)
- Undue influence effected as a process over time, rather than as a single event
- Family and friends believing that addressing the victim's issues may be a lost cause
- Perpetrator's complete control of the victim's life under the guise of 24-hour psychiatric therapy
- Use of medication to deny the victim the ability to take independent action
- Isolation of the victim away from family and friends
- Isolation of the victim from historical or perhaps other professional advisors
- Isolation of the victim from the world at large
- Restriction of the victim's communication via telephone, mail, or other means
- Use of chaperones to routinely accompany the victim when not in isolation
- Perpetrator's use of the victim's home as his own
- Perpetrator making himself a business partner of the victim
- Perpetrator making the victim (and others) question the victim's own abilities and thereby enhancing dependency
- Transfer of substantial funds to the perpetrator, allegedly as reasonable compensation
- Modification of the victim's will to make the perpetrator the primary beneficiary
- Abuse of the fiduciary relationship of the therapist and patient for personal benefit
- Abuse of the relationship of guardian and ward for personal benefit

While the list of suspicious circumstances in the Brian Wilson case was long (and ultimately exposed during his lifetime, via a chance conversation at an automobile dealership visited by Brian and his chaperones to purchase a new car for Brian, and which led to Brian's escape from this abusive relationship), the same is not necessarily apparent or existent in other situations where undue influence is present (and perhaps differently nuanced or more subtle).

In Brian's case, while sitting in the front seat of a new car as the saleswoman explained the car's features outside the hearing of chaperones, Brian was able to write on her business card that he was frightened, lonely, and afraid. This eventually led to his family learning about his abusive guardian; they were able to take legal action to end it. In Brian Wilson's situation, he was able to escape the abusive control that was exerted by his guardian/therapist, and the therapist was removed as guardian and lost his license. Brian returned to his musical work, and several years later, he married the saleswoman. In many instances, the victim does not escape, and it is up to the victim's family to address these issues after the victim's death.

The question posed by this book is not the entertainment value of the aforementioned situations but rather, whether in addressing a Paul Shelton, a Brian Wilson, or a situation somewhere else along a spectrum of behaviors, why is understanding this process so important to estate planners?

CHAPTER 1

Ethical Considerations When Representing Vulnerable Adults[1]

Age-related issues, including diminished capacity, can be a significant indicator of the potential vulnerability of a client to undue influence, and also an indicator that our population as a whole is aging.

The Alzheimer's Association reports that:

> Millions of Americans have Alzheimer's or other dementias. As the size and proportion of the U.S. population age 65 and older continue to increase, the number of Americans with Alzheimer's or other dementias will grow. This number will escalate rapidly in coming years, as the population of Americans age 65 and older is projected to nearly double from 48 million to 88 million by 2050. The baby boom generation has already begun to reach age 65 and beyond, the age range of greatest risk of Alzheimer's; in fact, the first members of the baby boom generation turned 70 in 2016.[2]

---

[1] Portions of this chapter were adapted from two articles published by BNA: Sandra D. Glazier, Esq., *Capacity and Ethical Considerations When Representing Vulnerable Adults*, 43 TAX MANAGE. ESTATES GIFTS TRUSTS J. (2018); and Bloomberg BNA, Sandra D. Glazier, Esq., Thomas M. Dixon, Esq., & Thomas F. Sweeney, Esq., *What Every Estate Planner Should Know About Undue Influence: Recognizing It, Insulating/Planning Against It . . . And Litigating It*, TAX MANAGEMENT MEMORANDUM (2015).

[2] Alzheimer's Association, *2017 Alzheimer's Disease Facts and Figures*, 13 ALZHEIMERS. DEMENT. 325–373 (2017).

To put the prevalence of Alzheimer's disease—which is only one form of dementia—in perspective, a 2014 report indicates that in 2010, one in nine people aged 65 or older suffered from Alzheimer's disease (or 11 percent of this population) and one-third of all people aged 85 or older (or 32 percent of this population) had Alzheimer's.[3] Further, as of 2014, it was estimated that 5.2 million persons of all ages had Alzheimer's.[4]

It logically follows that as our population ages, so does our client base. It is therefore incumbent upon the lawyer to be cognizant of issues that confront the clients we serve. Clients who have cognitive impairments are vulnerable to elder abuse. Such abuse can include, but is not necessarily limited to, financial exploitation.[5]

The National Council on Aging reports that:

> Approximately 1 in 10 Americans aged 60+ have experienced some form of elder abuse. Some estimates range as high as 5 million elders who are abused each year. One study estimated that only 1 in 14 cases of abuse are reported to authorities.[6]
>
> In almost 60% of elder abuse and neglect incidents, the perpetrator is a family member. Two thirds of perpetrators are adult children or spouses.[7]
>
> Recent studies show that nearly half of those with dementia experienced abuse or neglect.[8]

The 2015 True Link Report on Elder Financial Abuse placed losses experienced by the elderly as a result of all forms of elder financial abuse at a staggering $36.48 billion per year.[9]

Today, the youngest members of the "greatest generation" are 94 years old, the youngest members of the "silent generation" are 73, and the

---

[3] Alzheimer's Association, *2014 Alzheimer's Disease Facts and Figures*, 10 ALZHEIMERS. DEMENT. e47–e92, at e54 (2014).

[4] *Id.* at e54.

[5] *What Is Elder Abuse?* NATIONAL COUNCIL ON AGING, Home Page > Public Policy & Action > Elder Justice>Elder Abuse Facts, https://www.ncoa.org/public-policy -action/elder-justice/elder-abuse-facts.

[6] *Id.*

[7] *Id.*

[8] *Id.*

[9] *The True Link Report on Elder Financial Abuse 2015*, TRUE LINK FINANCIAL (January 2015), at 1, http://documents.truelinkfinancial.com/True-Link-Report-On-Elder -Financial-Abuse-012815.pdf.

"baby boomer generation" started to turn 70 in 2016. Members of these aging generations would be considered vulnerable adults under current legislation,[10] without consideration of additional potentially compounding factors. In addition to age, how friendly the individual historically was, and mental impairment (such as dementia or Alzheimer's disease) are two of the (numerous) factors that can make an individual vulnerable to elder abuse.[11]

The Elder Law and Special Needs section of the New York State Bar Association (NYBSA) created an FAQ resource due to the widespread and growing problems of elder abuse, and in support of the NYBSA's belief that attorneys are effectively positioned to identify and address incidents of elder abuse in clients and potential clients.[12] As estate planners, we often find ourselves on the front lines of dealing with this potentially devastating issue. Being able to identify, as counsel for a vulnerable adult, the indicia of undue influence, its processes, and the potential for litigation, is critical to the delivery of competent advice and appropriate service to our clients.

Some have defined elder abuse as:

> an action or lack of appropriate actions, which causes harm, risk of harm, or distress to an individual 60 years or older and occurs:
> a. within a relationship where there is an expectation of trust; or
> b. when the targeted act is directed towards an elder person by virtue of age or disabilities.[13]

The adverse impact of financial elder abuse is not limited to a loss of funds. A single episode of abuse can tip the precarious scales of an otherwise self-sufficient older person. The worry, fear, embarrassment, and other ramifications of being a victim of elder abuse can be magnified in the elderly. As a consequence, a single incident of mistreatment can trigger a downward spiral that leads to loss of independence, serious complicating illness, and even death.

---

[10] *See, e.g.,* 42 U.S.C. § 1397j to 1397m(5) (2018); Financial Industry Regulatory Authority (FINRA) Manual, r. 4512, 2165 (effective February 5, 2018); *and* Economic Growth, Regulatory Relief, and Consumer Protection Act, S.2155, 115th Congress (2017–2018), Title III § 303 (2018).

[11] *True Link Report on Elder Financial Abuse, supra* note 9, at 19–23.

[12] https://www.nysba.org/Sections/Elder/Elder_Abuse_FAQ.html.

[13] *Id.*

According to a five-year mortality rate study conducted across five categories of substantiated elder abuse (which included caregiver neglect, physical abuse, emotional abuse, financial exploitation, and poly-victimization), elderly adults who were subjected to caregiver neglect and financial exploitation had the lowest survival rates.[14]

The 2015 *True Link Report on Elder Financial Abuse* also reported that an estimated 954,000 seniors were skipping meals as a result of financial abuse.[15] The results of these studies should set off alarm bells among lawyers and financial advisors. The studies show that financial elder abuse is as dangerous for our clients as caregiver neglect (and more deadly than even physical abuse).

Elder abuse has been labeled "the crime of the 21st century."[16] Undue influence is just one form of such abuse.

Some say that they will know elder abuse, will be able to identify undue influence, and will recognize signs of deteriorating cognition when they see it. Even those who believe they are fully cognizant of the issues might benefit from greater training and education on these topics. The importance of such training and enhanced understanding has recently been recognized in a variety of forums.

In 2011, actor Mickey Rooney testified before Congress and urged it to do something about elder abuse.[17] During that hearing, Rooney commented that if elder abuse could happen to him, it could happen to anyone. He recalled being fearful, told to shut up, and denied food and medicine if he challenged his stepson (who was the individual he had entrusted with his finances). Rooney poignantly indicated that elder abuse can take many forms, including physical, emotional, and financial abuse.

It appears that the U.S. Congress and some states have finally begun to focus on this important area.

---

[14] Five-year all-cause mortality rates across five categories of substantiated elder abuse occurring in the community, Jason Burnett, PhD, Shelley L. Jackson, PhD, Arup K. Sinha, MS, Andrew R. Aschenbrenner, BS, MS, Kathleen Pace Murphy, PhD, Rui Xia, PhD, & Pamela M. Diamond, PhD, JOURNAL OF ELDER ABUSE & NEGLECT Vol. 28, Issue 2 (2016).

[15] *True Link Report on Elder Financial Abuse*, *supra* note 9, at 2.

[16] Kristen M. Lewis, *The Crime of the 21st Century: Elder Financial Abuse*, 28 PROB. & PROP. 11–15 (2014).

[17] Tom Cohen, *Mickey Rooney Tells Senate Panel He Was a Victim of Elder Abuse*, CNN (Mar. 2, 2011), http://www.cnn.com/2011/SHOWBIZ/03/02/rooney.elderly.abuse/index.html.

FEDERAL STATUTES AND DEFINITIONS

In 2018, amendments to the Public Health and Welfare Act via the Elder Justice Act[18] attempted to address issues of elder abuse.

Section 1397j of the Elder Justice Act (2018)[19] defines an "elder" as "an individual age 60 or older." The Act attempts to address "abuse" that inflicts physical or psychological harm or deprivation of goods or services that are necessary to meeting the essential needs of an individual and avoidance of physical or psychological harm.[20] It indicates that Adult Protective Services (APS) is responsible for investigating reports of adult abuse, neglect, and exploitation made to APS.[21] The Act defines "exploitation" as the "fraudulent or otherwise illegal, unauthorized, or improper act or process of an individual, including a caregiver or fiduciary, that uses the resources of an elder for monetary or personal benefit, profit, or gain, or that results in depriving an elder of rightful access to, or use of, benefits, resources, belongings or assets."[22]

Important to the application of the Act are the terms "fiduciary" and "caregiver." For purposes of this Act, "fiduciary" is defined as:

> (A) . . . a person or entity with the legal responsibility—
> > (i) to make decisions on behalf of and for the benefit of another person; and
> > (ii) to act in good faith and with fairness; and
> (B) includes a trustee, a guardian, a conservator, an executor, an agent under a financial power of attorney or health care power of attorney, or a representative payee.[23]

For purposes of this Act, the term "caregiver" means:

> . . . an individual who has the responsibility for the care of an elder, either voluntarily, by contract, by receipt of payment for care, or as a result of the operation of law, and means a family member or other individual who provides (on behalf of such individual or of a public or private agency, organization, or institution)

---

[18] 42 U.S.C. §§ 1397 (j) to 1397(m) (5) (2018).

[19] 42 U.S.C. § 1397(j) (5).

[20] 42 U.S.C. § 1397(j) (1).

[21] 42 U.S.C. § 1397(j) (2)(A).

[22] 42 U.S.C. § 1397(j) (8).

[23] 42 U.S.C. § 1397(j) (9).

compensated or uncompensated care to an elder who needs supportive services in any setting.[24]

While the Elder Justice Act is more general in its application, on February 5, 2018, the Financial Industry Regulatory Authority (FINRA) amendment to Rule 4512 and a new rule, Rule 2165, became effective. These rules are intended to address situations where the broker has a reasonable concern that a vulnerable client is being or may be subjected to financial exploitation. For purposes of the FINRA rules, the vulnerable client is referred to as a *Specified Adult*, which is:

> (A) a natural person age 65 or older; or (B) a natural person age 18 and older who the member reasonably believes has a mental or physical impairment that renders the individual unable to protect his or her own interests.[25]

FINRA Rule 2165 defines *financial exploitation* as:

> (A) the wrongful or unauthorized taking, withholding, appropriation, or use of a Specified Adult's funds or securities; or
> (B) any act or omission by a person, including through the use of a power of attorney, guardianship, or any other authority regarding a Specified Adult, to:
>> (i) obtain control, through deception, intimidation or undue influence, over the Specified Adult's money, assets or property; or
>> (ii) convert the Specified Adult's money, assets or property.[26]

FINRA, therefore, explicitly recognizes that even a person imbued with the power to transact business with regard to a client's account may be engaged in financial exploitation. When there is a reasonable basis to suspect that financial exploitation is taking place, the broker may freeze the account on a temporary basis and alert others so that additional action to protect the client may take place. Because these rules may affect our clients, it can be helpful for estate planners to keep abreast of legislative

---

[24] 42 U.S.C. § 1397(j) (3).
[25] FINRA Rule 2165(a) (1).
[26] FINRA Rule 2165(a) (4).

actions and other initiatives intended to protect the elderly. More importantly, given the staggering statistics regarding elder abuse occasioned at the hands of vulnerable adults' family members and trusted advisors, it is imperative that estate planners be cognizant of and vigilant to indicia of undue influence and financial abuse as they engage in representation of vulnerable clients. Estate planners also need to understand their ethical duties and responsibilities when representing vulnerable clients.

On May 24, 2018, the Economic Growth, Regulatory Relief, and Consumer Protection Act[27] included a provision entitled "Immunity from Suit for Disclosure of Financial Exploitation of Senior Citizens." This provision essentially provides immunity from civil or administrative proceedings to trained individuals who are employed in supervisory, compliance, or legal roles (at credit unions, depository institutions, investment advisors, broker dealers, insurance companies, and transfer agencies) for disclosures made in good faith and with reasonable care relative to suspected financial exploitation of a senior citizen. The Act specifies that these individuals shall receive training in a number of areas, including but not limited to common signs that financial exploitation of a senior citizen may be occurring. The Act does not mandate reporting (nor does it set forth the action to take when financial abuse is reasonably suspected). However, the bill may facilitate protective action by eliminating concerns that reporting might be considered a breach of the financial institution's obligation to keep a client's information confidential when disclosure is required to address the suspected financial exploitation of seniors. Perhaps even more importantly, the training required under the Act may result in greater and more effective scrutiny of suspicious transactions.

ETHICAL RESPONSIBILITIES OF ATTORNEYS

Given the apparent increase in elder abuse (whether via awareness or occurrence or both),[28] some states have also undertaken initiatives

---

[27] Economic Growth, Regulatory Relief, and Consumer Protection Act, Title III § 303.

[28] *See* Rebecca C. Morgan, J.D., Pamela B. Teaster, Ph.D., & Randolph W. Thomas, M.A., *A View from the Bridge: A Brief Look at the Progression of Cases of Elder Financial Exploitation Prosecutions*, *in* STETSON UNIVERSITY COLLEGE OF LAW LEGAL STUDIES RESEARCH PAPER SERIES Research Paper No. 2018–2 (2017).

in an attempt to battle abuse of the elderly and other vulnerable adults.[29,30,31,32] But what are our responsibilities as attorneys?

---

[29] In early 2018, San Diego County, California, developed a "Blueprint" for addressing abuse of elderly and other vulnerable adults. The Blueprint attempts to address abuse encountered by persons over age 65, as well as any person between 18 and 64 who has physical or mental limitations that restrict his or her ability to carry out normal activities or to protect his or her rights. The Blueprint defines a caretaker as any person who has the care, custody, or control of, or who stands in a position of trust with, an elder or dependent adult, whether or not the person is paid. The Blueprint addresses the importance of training dispatch and patrol units to recognize signs of abuse, and in dealing with Alzheimer's and other forms of dementia. It notes that in an encounter, caregivers should be interviewed separately because in some situations the caregiver might be the abuser. The Blueprint stresses the importance of getting adult protective services involved in certain situations. Even prosecutors are encouraged to obtain ongoing training and education in the field of elder and dependent adult abuse. Among the mandatory reporters referenced in the Blueprint are persons who provide care, health practitioners, and all officers and employees of financial institutions. See *San Diego County Elder and Dependent Adult Abuse Blueprint 2018,* https://www.sdcda.org/helping/elder-abuse-blueprint.pdf. The Blueprint was in apparent response to law enforcement investigations of more than 3,000 claims of abuse of elders aged 65 years and older and a 39 percent increase in the elder abuse cases filed by the county's District Attorney's Office and the San Diego City Attorney's Office. Adult Protective Services received 14,741 referrals between 2016 and 2017; financial abuse was the most common form of abuse in the county's confirmed cases. *See Initiative to Better Protect Seniors from Elder Abuse,* COUNTY NEWS CENTER (March 1, 2018), https://www.countynewscenter.com/initiative-to-better-protect-seniors-from-elder-abuse.

[30] On March 22, 2018, West Virginia Attorney General Patrick Morrisey announced that the state had formed an elder abuse litigation and prevention unit. *West Virginia launches elder abuse litigation and prevention unit,* WVNS TV (Mar. 23, 2018), http://www.wvnstv.com/west-virginia-news/west-virginia-launches-elder-abuse-litigation-and-prevention-unit/1073667078.

[31] On June 1, 2018, Louisiana's governor signed "Granny cam" legislation into law. *See "Granny Cam" Nursing Home Bill Signed Into Law by Louisiana Governor,* CBS NEWS (June 1, 2018), https://www.cbsnews.com/news/granny-cam-nursing-home-bill-signed-into-law-by-louisiana-governor-john-bel-edwards. The law enacted under Louisiana HB 218 does not address the ability (or inability) to provide such protections to the elderly who continue to reside at home (or in a facility other than a nursing home). The ability of a guardian to authorize remote observation and recording might prove to be both a blessing and a curse. A cam might be used as a means of remote "chaperoning," which could inhibit the type of communication necessary to alert others that financial exploitation or undue influence is occurring or has occurred. Other states are considering similar statutes.

[32] In 2018, Louisiana also adopted Act No. 434 (HB 503). Like the Economic Growth, Regulatory Relief, and Consumer Protection Act, the Act provides financial

Although the Model Rules of Professional Conduct (MRPC)[33] have not been adopted verbatim in every state, they may be instructive for the purposes of helping the lawyer assess the lawyer's ethical responsibilities and considerations when engaged in the representation of vulnerable adults. Of additional aid in the lawyer's quest to balance the needs of a client with the lawyer's ethical responsibilities and considerations are the American College of Trust and Estate Counsel (ACTEC) Commentaries.[34] (Despite the existence of these valuable reference materials, one should always consider and generally give deference to a pertinent jurisdiction's adopted rules of professional conduct and any available ethics opinions in that jurisdiction.)

In Michigan, it generally is recognized that:

> [i]n the nature of law practice, . . . conflicting responsibilities are encountered. Virtually all difficult ethical problems arise from conflict between a lawyer's responsibilities to clients, to the legal system, and to the lawyer's own interest in remaining an upright person while earning a satisfactory living. The Rules of Professional Conduct prescribe terms for resolving such conflicts. Within the framework of these rules many difficult issues of professional discretion can arise. Such issues must be resolved through the exercise of sensitive professional and moral judgment guided by the basic principles underlying the rules.[35]

---

institutions with immunity and guidelines for taking protective action when it is reasonably suspected that an individual over the age of 60 or otherwise defined as a person subject to the Adult Protective Services Act is being financially exploited. The Act defines "financial exploitation" to include acts taken in a representative capacity through a trust, power of attorney, or other means, including but not limited to obtaining control over or depriving an eligible adult from the ownership, use, benefit, or possession of his money, assets, or property by deception, intimidation, or undue influence.

[33] *MRPC*, for purposes of this book, refers to the American Bar Association (ABA) Model Rules of Professional Conduct, in effect as of December 28, 2017, https://www.americanbar.org/groups/professional_responsibility/publications/model_rules_of_professional_conduct.html.

[34] In 2016, the ACTEC Commentaries (5th ed. 2016) was published by the American College of Trust and Estate Counsel Foundation. Some of the recent revisions to the ACTEC Commentaries reflect a change in attitudes and perspectives with regard to the MRPC in the realm of estate planning.

[35] MICH. PROF'L CONDUCT R., *Preamble* (April 28, 2017).

IDENTIFYING THE CLIENT

At the outset, it is important to identify who the client is. When dealing with an elderly or otherwise vulnerable client, it is not uncommon for a family member to make the initial contact. Such contact may be common when Medicaid planning is involved. However, if you are engaged to draft documents for a vulnerable client, it remains important to remember that the vulnerable individual is the client and not the family member who contacted you. It is also important to recognize that contact by a family member (as opposed to by the client) may be indicia of possible undue influence. In fact, in some states, procurement is an element of the presumption of undue influence.[36] Consequently, it can be helpful to make and maintain a record of the initial contact (including references to who made the contact and the content of the communication). In addition, to the extent possible, encourage all further contact to be directly engaged in with the client.

The attorney should encourage family members who are not clients (for purposes of that particular estate planning engagement) to wait outside when the attorney meets with the client. For some, this can be a difficult conversation, especially when other family members are clients under separate engagements (such as when the attorney provides intergenerational representation or business representation for a family business).[37] Being able to meet with the client away from others, whose mere presence might interfere with the free flow of information and a frank discussion of the client's desires and circumstances, is extremely important.

Paragraph 4 to the preamble to the Michigan Rules of Professional Conduct makes this provision:

> In all professional functions a lawyer should be competent, prompt and diligent. *A lawyer should maintain communication with a client concerning the representation.* A lawyer should keep in confidence information relating to representation of a client except so far as disclosure is required or permitted by the Rules of Professional Conduct or other law.[38]

---

[36] *See* Illinois Pattern Jury Instructions § 200 *Will Contest* ¶ C.1.a. at 2, 3, § 200.03 *Will Contest—Undue Influence Based Entirely on Unrebutted Presumption Arising from Fiduciary Relationship,* http://illinoiscourts.gov/CircuitCourt/CivilJuryInstructions/default.asp.

[37] Using the ABA publication *Why Am I Left in the Waiting Room?: Understanding the Four C's of Elder Law Ethics* can be helpful. *See* https://www.americanbar.org/products/inv/brochure/211008886.

[38] MICH. PROF'L CONDUCT R., *Preamble* at ¶ 4 (emphasis added).

COMMUNICATIONS WITH A CLIENT WHO HAS DIMINISHED CAPACITY

Even when the client faces cognitive challenges, MRPC 1.14(a) requires the lawyer to maintain as normal a lawyer-client relationship as possible:

> (a) When a client's capacity to make adequately considered decisions in connection with a representation is diminished, whether because of minority, mental impairment or for some other reason, the lawyer shall, as far as reasonably possible, maintain a normal client-lawyer relationship *with the client.*[39]

Comments to MRPC 1.4 expound on the lawyer's responsibilities when the client suffers from diminished capacity:

> [1] The normal client-lawyer relationship is based on the assumption that the client, when properly advised and assisted, is capable of making decisions about important matters. When the client is a minor or suffers from a diminished mental capacity, however, maintaining the ordinary client-lawyer relationship may not be possible in all respects. In particular, a severely incapacitated person may have no power to make legally binding decisions. Nevertheless, a client with diminished capacity often has the ability to understand, deliberate upon, and reach conclusions about matters affecting the client's own well-being. For example, children as young as five or six years of age, and certainly those of ten or twelve, are regarded as having opinions that are entitled to weight in legal proceedings concerning their custody. So also, it is recognized that some persons of advanced age can be quite capable of handling routine financial matters while needing special legal protection concerning major transactions.
>
> [2] The fact that a client suffers a disability does not diminish the lawyer's obligation to treat the client with attention and respect. *Even if the person has a legal representative, the lawyer should as far as possible accord the represented person the status of client, particularly in maintaining communication.*
>
> [3] *The client* may wish to have family members or other persons participate in discussions with the lawyer. When necessary to assist in the representation, the presence of such persons generally does

---

[39] MRPC 1.14(a) (emphasis added).

not affect the applicability of the attorney-client evidentiary privilege. Nevertheless, *the lawyer must keep the client's interests foremost* and, except for protective action authorized under paragraph (b), *must look to the client, and not family members, to make decisions on the client's behalf.*

[6] In determining the extent of the client's diminished capacity, the lawyer should consider and balance such factors as: the *client's ability* to articulate reasoning leading to a decision, variability of state of mind and ability to appreciate consequences of a decision; the substantive fairness of a decision; and the consistency of a decision with the known long-term commitments and values of the client. In appropriate circumstances, the lawyer may seek guidance from an appropriate diagnostician.[40]

ASSESSING THE CLIENT'S CAPACITY

As indicated earlier, it is incumbent upon the lawyer to ascertain whether the client has sufficient capacity to engage in a proposed transaction. In doing so, the lawyer is not required to perform standardized psychological or neurological tests.[41] In fact, it is recommended that lawyers *not* engage in clinical assessments of a client unless they are professionally trained to engage in such testing.[42] It also is noteworthy that tests such as the Mini-Mental Status Exam (MMSE) and neurological assessments or orientation may not be reflective of whether a client has or does not have sufficient capacity.[43]

Instead, the lawyer should carefully observe the client and consider factors like those identified by the 1993 National Conference on Ethical Issues in Representing Older Clients (relying, in part, on an article by Peter Margulies):

---

[40] MRPC 1.14 *Client with Diminished Capacity – Comment*, cmt. 1, 2, 3, 6 (emphasis added).

[41] The ABA indicates that while lawyers should:

> . . . engage in the legal assessment of capacity and should do so in a systematic manner, for a variety of reasons . . ., it is generally not appropriate for attorneys to use more formal clinical assessment instruments, such as the MMSE . . . . Lawyers generally do not have the education and training needed to administer these tests. Many factors must be taken into consideration when administering and interpreting psychological tests.

ABA COMMN. ON L. & AGING & AM. PSYCHOLOGICAL ASSN., ASSESSMENT OF OLDER ADULTS WITH DIMINISHED CAPACITY: A HANDBOOK FOR LAWYERS, at 21 (2005).

[42] *Id.* at 3.

[43] *Id.* at 3.

1. *The client's ability to articulate reasoning leading to a decision.* The client should be able to state the basis for his or her decision. The stated reasons for the decision should be consistent with the client's overall stated goals and objectives.
2. *Variability of state of mind.* Margulies defines this factor as the extent to which the individual's cognitive functioning fluctuates.
3. *Ability to appreciate consequences of a decision.* For example, does a client recognize that without a given medical decision, he or she may physically decline or even die, or that without a legal challenge to an eviction, he or she may be without a place to live.
4. *The substantive fairness of the decision.* Margulies maintains that while lawyers normally defer to client decisions, a lawyer nonetheless cannot simply look the other way if an older individual or someone else is being taken advantage of in a blatantly unfair transaction. To do so could defeat the very dignity and autonomy the lawyer seeks to enhance, and thus fairness is one element to balance. Of course, judging fairness risks the interjection of one's own beliefs and values, and so caution is required. Yet, the reality is that when the desired legal plan conforms to conventional notions of fairness—e.g., equitable distribution of assets among all children—or the plan is consistent with the lawyer's long-standing knowledge of the client and family, then capacity concerns wane proportionately. Capacity may be diminished but adequate for a legal transaction deemed to be very low risk in the context of conventional fairness.
5. *The consistency of a decision with the known long-term commitments and values of the client.* The decision normally should reflect the client's lifelong or long-term perspective. This will be easier to determine if the lawyer-client relationship is long-standing. At the same time, individuals can change their values framework as they age. The distinction is important.
6. *Irreversibility of the decision.* This factor is listed in the Margulies article but not in the Comment to Rule 1.14. Margulies notes that "the law historically has attached importance to protecting parties from irreversible events," and that "doing something that cannot be adjusted later calls for caution on the part of the attorney."[44]

In essence, the lawyer generally observes and assesses the client's cognitive, emotional, and behavioral functioning in initially determining whether the client has sufficient capacity to engage in the proposed estate planning

---

[44] ABA, A HANDBOOK FOR LAWYERS, *supra* note 42, at 18, 19.

transaction.[45] If questions remain after the lawyer performs their own assessment, the lawyer may either consult with a qualified professional[46,47] or, with the client's consent, have a more extensive assessment performed by a qualified professional.[48] Even if a referral to a qualified professional occurs, it remains the lawyer's responsibility to determine, in the exercise of independent judgment, whether the client has sufficient capacity to engage in the proposed transaction.[49]

Within the realm of "decision-making capacity" and "rational" or "free will" decision-making, there may be some important crossovers between legal and psychological analysis.[50] Things such as "priming" have been recognized by social psychologists as subliminal motivations to unconsciously influence behavior, and perhaps even influence working memory and executive functions.[51]

---

[45] *Id.* at 23–26.

[46] Sometimes, an attorney will seek a private consultation with a clinician to discuss and clarify specific capacity issues before proceeding further with representation. Disclosure of the attorney's concerns is private, at least at this stage of the process, and it does not involve the client. The Comment to Rule 1.14(b) provides explicit recognition of such external consultations, indicating that it is proper for attorneys to seek guidance from an "appropriate diagnostician" in cases where clients demonstrate diminished capacity. *Id.* at 31.

[47] Does the consultation trigger the need for additional ethical considerations? The ABA Joint Commission indicates that:

> ... one possible interpretation of the rule and comment is that, since consultation with an appropriate clinician is a very minimal protective action, the threshold for meeting the trigger criteria in Rule 1.14(b) is correspondingly low, thereby justifying very limited disclosure of otherwise confidential information. Unfortunately, authoritative resolution of the question is lacking. The lawyer needs to use good judgment and limit information revealed to what is absolutely necessary to assist with a determination of capacity. Whenever possible, the lawyer should seek to consult the assessor informally without identifying the client. In that case, the question of consent does not arise. The consultation is simply professional advice to the lawyer. *Id.* at 34.

[48] *Id.* at *iii.* If a referral is made to a qualified professional for assessment of capacity, it may be helpful to provide the professional with the legal standard to be applied to the proposed transaction.

[49] *Id.* at 33, 34.

[50] *See* Dominic J. Campisi, Evan D. Winet, & Jake Calvert, *Undue Influence: The Gap Between Current Law and Scientific Approaches to Decision-Making and Persuasion,* 43 ACTEC L. J. 359 (2018).

[51] *Id.* at 361 (citing John A. Bargh, *Our Unconscious Mind,* Sci. Am. 34–37 (2014)).

IF DIMINISHED CAPACITY IS BELIEVED TO BE PRESENT

MRPC 1.14 provides:

> (b) When the lawyer reasonably believes that the client has diminished capacity, is at risk of substantial physical, financial or other harm unless action is taken and cannot adequately act in the client's own interest, the lawyer may take reasonably necessary protective action, including consulting with individuals or entities that have the ability to take action to protect the client and, in appropriate cases, seeking the appointment of a guardian ad litem, conservator or guardian.
>
> (c) Information relating to the representation of a client with diminished capacity is protected by Rule 1.6. When taking protective action pursuant to paragraph (b), the lawyer is impliedly authorized under Rule 1.6(a) to reveal information about the client, but only to the extent reasonably necessary to protect the client's interests.[52]

Comment 5 to MRPC 1.14 illustrates what may constitute appropriate action by the lawyer when a client with diminished capacity may be at risk of harm unless action is taken:

> [5] . . . Such measures could include: consulting with family members, using a reconsideration period to permit clarification or improvement of circumstances, using voluntary surrogate decision-making tools such as durable powers of attorney or consulting with support groups, professional services, adult-protective agencies or other individuals or entities that have the ability to protect the client. In taking any protective action, the lawyer should be guided by such factors as the wishes and values of the client to the extent known, the client's best interests and the goals of intruding into the client's decision making autonomy to the least extent feasible, maximizing client capacities and respecting the client's family and social connections.[53]

Consequently, just as brokers are now required to do under FINRA Rule 4512, perhaps lawyers might consider: (1) inquiring whether there

---

[52] MRPC 1.14(a) and (b).
[53] MRPC 1.14 *Client with Diminished Capacity - Comment*, cmt. 5.

is a family member or another trusted individual whom the client would like the lawyer to contact if concerns about the client later arise, and (2) obtaining authorization for such contact to occur should circumstances merit the same.

However, it merits caution and consideration before the lawyer takes action. Even barring specific authorization, the ACTEC Commentaries to MRPC 1.14 reflect that while there may be an implied authority to disclose otherwise confidential information and take protective action under the circumstances identified in MRPC 1.14, the lawyer must nonetheless consider the potential implications of such action and the risks and substantiality of harm:

> [I]n deciding whether others should be consulted, the lawyer should also consider the client's wishes, the impact of the lawyer's actions on potential challenges to the client's estate plan, and the impact on the lawyer's ability to maintain the client's confidential information. In determining whether to act and in determining what action to take on behalf of a client, the lawyer should consider the impact a particular course of action could have on the client, including the client's right to privacy and the client's physical, mental and emotional well-being. In appropriate cases, the lawyer may seek the appointment of a guardian ad litem, conservator or guardian or take other protective action.[54]
>
> . . . For the purposes of this rule, the risk of harm to a client and the amount of harm that a client might suffer should both be determined according to a different scale than if the client were fully capable. In particular, the client's diminished capacity increases the risk of harm and the possibility that any particular harm would be substantial. If the risk and substantiality of potential harm to a client are uncertain, a lawyer may make reasonably appropriate disclosures of otherwise confidential information and take reasonably appropriate protective actions. In determining the risk and substantiality of harm and deciding what action to take, a lawyer should consider any wishes or directions that were clearly expressed by the client during his or her competency. Normally, a lawyer should be permitted to take actions on behalf of a client with apparently diminished capacity that the lawyer reasonably believes are in the best interests of the client.[55]

---

[54] ACTEC COMMENTARIES, *ACTEC Commentary on MRPC 1.14*, at 160 (5th ed. 2016).
[55] *Id.* at 160, 161.

Michigan Rules of Professional Conduct comments on MRPC signify caution:

> If the lawyer seeks the appointment of a legal representative for the client, the filing of the request itself, together with the facts upon which it is predicated, may constitute the disclosure of confidential information which could be used against the client. If the court to whom the matter is submitted thereafter determines that a legal representative is not necessary, the harm befalling the client as the result of the disclosure may be irreparable.

* * *

> [D]isclosure of the client's disability can adversely affect the client's interests. For example, raising the question of disability could, in some circumstances, lead to proceedings for involuntary commitment. The lawyer's position in such cases is an unavoidably difficult one. The lawyer may seek guidance from an appropriate diagnostician.[56]

Additional ACTEC commentaries on MRPC 1.7 further illuminate considerations under MRPC 1.14 relative to clients with diminished capacity:

> [A] lawyer may take reasonable steps to protect the interests of a client the lawyer reasonably believes to be suffering from diminished capacity, including the initiation of protective proceedings. See ACTEC Commentary on MRPC 1.14 (Client with Diminished Capacity). Doing so may create a conflict of interest between the lawyer and the client. The client might, for example, oppose the protective action being taken by the lawyer and consider it a breach of the duty of loyalty. In such a circumstance, the lawyer is entitled to continue to take protective action, but where possible, should call the court's attention to the client's opposition and ask that separate counsel be provided to represent the client's stated position if the client has not already retained such counsel. A lawyer who is retained on behalf of the client to resist the institution of a protective action may not take positions that are contrary to the client's position or make disclosures contrary to MRPC 1.6 (Confidentiality of Information).[57]

---

[56] MICH. PROF'L CONDUCT R., cmt. at 1.14 *36 (April 28, 2017).
[57] ACTEC COMMENTARIES § 1.7 at 108.

WHAT IF ONE SUSPECTS ELDER ABUSE?

If one suspects elder abuse, further action may be required. In some jurisdictions, if the lawyer suspects that elder abuse has occurred (whether such abuse is physical or economic in nature), reporting or other action by the lawyer may be required. ACTEC commentary on MRPC 1.14 reflects:

> Elder abuse has been labeled "the crime of the 21st century,"[58] and the federal and state governments are responding with legislation and programs to prevent and penalize the abuse. The role and obligations of lawyers with respect to elder abuse varies significantly among the states. Some states have made lawyers mandatory reporters of elder abuse. *See, e.g.*, Tex. Hum. Res. Code § 48.051(a)–(c) (2013) (Texas); Miss. Code Ann. § 43-47-7(1)(a)(i) (2010) (Mississippi); Ohio Rev. Code Ann. § 5101.61(A) (2010) (Ohio); A.R.S. § 46-454(B) (2009) (Arizona); Mont. Code Ann. § 52-3-811 (2003) (Montana) (exception where attorney-client privilege applies to information). Other states have broad mandatory reporting laws that do not exclude lawyers. *See, e.g.*, Del. Code Ann. Tit. 31, § 3910. The exception to the duty of confidentiality in MRPC 1.6(b)(6), which allows disclosure to comply with other law, should apply, but disclosure would be limited to what the lawyer reasonably believes is necessary to comply. In states where there is no mandatory reporting duty of lawyers, a lawyer's ability to report elder abuse where MRPC 1.6 may restrict disclosure of confidentiality would be governed by MRPC 1.14 in addition to any other exception to MRPC 1.6 (such as when there is a risk of death or substantial bodily harm). In order to rely on MRPC 1.14 to disclose confidential information to report elder abuse, the lawyer must first determine that the client has diminished capacity. If the lawyer consults with other professionals on that issue, the lawyer must be aware of the potential mandatory reporting duties of such professional and whether such consultation will result in reporting that the client opposes or that would create undesirable disruptions in the client's living situation. The lawyer is also required under MRPC 1.14 to gather sufficient information before concluding that reporting is necessary to protect the client. *See* NH Ethics Committee Advisory Opinion #2014-15/5 (The Lawyer's Authority to Disclose Confidential Client Information to Protect a Client from Elder Abuse or Other Threats of Substantial Bodily Harm). In cases

---

[58] MRPC 1.14 (citing Lewis, *supra* note 16, at 161, 162).

where the scope of representation has been limited pursuant to Rule 1.2, the limitation of scope does not limit the lawyer's obligation or discretion to address signs of abuse or exploitation (consistent with Rules 1.14 and 1.6 and state elder abuse law) in any aspect of the client's affairs of which the lawyer becomes aware, even if beyond the agreed-upon scope of representation.[59]

In some states, the failure to engage in mandatory reporting of suspected elder abuse can subject the mandatory reporter to criminal implications, such as the conviction of a misdemeanor.[60]

CAPACITY AND DEFINING THE LAWYER'S ETHICAL RESPONSIBILITIES

As can be discerned from a review of the ethical rules and commentaries cited, the issue of diminished capacity plays an integral role in defining the duties imposed upon lawyers.

An additional ethical conundrum may arise when the client is a new client, relating to the (potential) client's capacity to even engage the lawyer. The level of capacity required to contract (or engage the lawyer's services) can be greater than the capacity required to engage in the planned transaction. Therefore, it is important that the lawyer understand and evaluate whether the client might have been subjected to undue influence or another form of abuse, as well as whether the client has the requisite capacity to hire the lawyer and engage in the proposed estate planning transactions.

Assuming the client has the requisite capacity to engage the lawyer, the obligation to assess capacity does not end there. The lawyer then needs to assess whether the client has the requisite capacity to engage in the planned transaction.

CONFLICTS IN REPRESENTATION

Even if the lawyer determines that the client has all of the requisite capacities identified here, have all of the lawyers' ethical duties been satisfied? Perhaps not.

---

[59] ACTEC COMMENTARIES § 1.14 at 161, 162.
[60] For an example, see Georgia Code § 30-5-4 and § 30-5-8(a) (2) (2015).

Beyond the ethical duties imposed regarding the representation of clients with diminished capacity, the lawyer must analyze (as they must do with any client) whether any conflicts of interest exist, and whether any (actual or potential) conflicts identified may be waived. However, some conflicts of interest are so serious that even the provision of "informed consent" will not suffice in permitting the lawyer to undertake or continue the representation.[61]

Waiver itself perhaps contemplates yet another level of capacity—that which is required to provide "informed consent." In this regard, "informed consent" represents the agreement by a person to a proposed course of conduct after the lawyer has communicated adequate information and explanation about the material risks of and reasonably available alternatives to the proposed course of conduct.[62]

If the lawyer represents (or is requested to represent) a couple or various members of the same family, it is incumbent upon the lawyer to determine if a possible or actual conflict of interest exists.[63]

---

[61] ACTEC COMMENTARIES § 1.7 at 104.

[62] *Id.* at 105.

[63] In the estate planning arena, the existence of an improperly addressed conflict of interest can prove fatal to the enforceability of the plan. In Haynes v. First National State Bank of New Jersey, 87 N.J. 163, 432 A.2d 890, 23 A.L.R.4th 347 (N.J. 1981), where the decedent utilized her daughter's lawyer to drastically change her estate plan during a period when the decedent was dependent and reliant upon her daughter, the presumption of undue influence was not only applied, but the burden imposed to rebut the presumption in light of the attorney's ethical duties when a conflict of interests appeared to exist required the proponent of the estate planning documents to rebut the presumption with clear and convincing evidence that the instruments were indeed reflective of the decedent's intent. In Haynes, the court found that:

> [A] conflict of interest, moreover, need not be obvious or actual to create an ethical impropriety. The mere possibility of such a conflict at the outset of the relationship is sufficient to establish an ethical breach on the part of the attorney. Even where the representation of two clients has become a routine practice on the part of the bar generally, when the latent conflict becomes real, the attorney must fully disclose all material information and, if need be, extricate himself from the conflict by terminating his relationship with at least one party.
>
> Accordingly, it is our determination that there must be imposed a significant burden of proof upon the advocates of a will where a presumption of undue influence has arisen because the testator's attorney has placed himself in a conflict of interest and professional loyalty between the testator and the

What if an existing client asks the lawyer to engage in estate planning for a vulnerable individual? ACTEC Commentaries reflect that:

> [a] lawyer should exercise particular care if an existing client asks the lawyer to prepare for another person a will, trust, power of attorney or similar document that will benefit the existing client, particularly if the existing client will pay the cost of providing the estate planning services to the other person. The lawyer would, of course, need to communicate with the other person and decide whether to undertake representation of that person as a new client, along with all the duties such a representation involves, before agreeing to prepare such a document. If the representation of both the existing client and the new client would create a significant risk that the representation of one or both clients would be materially limited, the representation can only be undertaken as permitted by MRPC 1.7(b). In any case, the lawyer must comply with MRPC 1.8(f) (Conflict of Interest: Current Clients: Specific Rules)

---

beneficiary. In view of the gravity of the presumption in such cases, the appropriate burden of proof must be heavier than that which normally obtains in civil litigation. The cited decisions which have dealt with the quantum of evidence needed to dispel the presumption of influence in this context have essayed various descriptions of this greater burden, *viz:* "convincing," "impeccable," "substantial," "trustworthy," "candid," and "full." Our present rules of evidence, however, do not employ such terminology. The need for clarity impels us to be more definitive in the designation of the appropriate burden of proof and to select one which most suitably measures the issue to be determined. Only three burdens of proof are provided by the evidence rules, namely, a preponderance, clear and convincing, and beyond a reasonable doubt. The standard in our evidence rules that conforms most comfortably with the level of proofs required by our decisions in this context is the burden of proof by clear and convincing evidence. Hence, the presumption of undue influence created by a professional conflict of interest on the part of an attorney, coupled with confidential relationships between a testator and the beneficiary as well as the attorney, must be rebutted by clear and convincing evidence.

Applying these principles to this case, it is clear that attorney Buttermore was in a position of irreconcilable conflict within the common sense and literal meaning of DR 5–105. In this case, Buttermore was required, at a minimum, to provide full disclosure and complete advice to Mrs. Dutrow, as well as the Cotsworths, as to the existence and nature of the conflict and to secure knowing and intelligent waivers from each in order to continue his professional relationship with Mrs. Dutrow. Even these prophylactic measures, however, might and should consider cautioning both clients of the possibility that the existing client may be presumed to have exerted undue influence on the other client because the existing client was involved in the procurement of the document.[64]

In the context of multigenerational planning, it may be possible to meet ethical responsibilities through a knowing waiver and with separate engagements.[65,66] However, when the conflict (or potential conflict) exists between spouses, the lawyer may not be able to engage in representation of both clients, especially when one spouse wishes the lawyer to persuade

---

not have overcome the conflict, nor have been sufficient to enable the attorney to render unimpaired "independent professional judgment" on behalf of his client. Any conflict, of course, could have been avoided by Buttermore simply refusing to represent Mrs. Dutrow. But, Buttermore was apparently insensitive or impervious to the presence or extent of the professional conflict presented by these circumstances. He undertook none of these measures to eliminate the dual representation or overcome the conflict. Consequently, a strong taint of undue influence was permitted, presumptively, to be injected into the testamentary disposition of Mrs. Dutrow.

Accordingly, the attorney's conduct here, together with all of the other factors contributing to the likelihood of wrongful influence exerted upon the testatrix, has engendered a heavy presumption of undue influence which the proponents of the will must overcome by clear and convincing evidence.

Haynes, id. at 181–184 (internal citations omitted).

[64] ACTEC COMMENTARIES § 1.7 at 102.

[65] ACTEC COMMENTARIES on MRPC 1.7 reflects that:

> . . . some experienced estate planners undertake to represent related clients separately with respect to related matters. Such representations should only be undertaken if the lawyer reasonably believes it will be possible to provide impartial, competent and diligent representation to each client and even then, only with the informed consent of each client, confirmed in writing. *See* ACTEC Commentaries on MRPC 1.0(e) (Terminology) (defining informed consent) and MRPC 1.0(b) (Terminology) (defining confirmed in writing). The writing may be contained in an engagement letter that covers other subjects, as well.

ACTEC COMMENTARIES § 1.7 at 103.

[66] *See also* Sandra D. Glazier & Martin M. Shenkman, *Joint/Dual Representation: Add Protections to Your Retainer Agreements to Reflect Challenges Involved,* TRUSTS & ESTATES (July 20, 2017), https://www.wealthmanagement.com/estate-planning /jointdual-representation.

or advocate for the other spouse to engage in a particular course of conduct.[67]

ACTEC Commentaries caution lawyers about attempting to represent spouses as individuals via separate engagements while still representing both:

> In that context, attempting to represent a husband and wife separately while simultaneously doing estate planning for each, is generally inconsistent with the lawyer's duty of loyalty to each client. Either the lawyer should represent them jointly or the lawyer should represent only one of them. See generally PRICE ON CONTEMPORARY ESTATE PLANNING, section 1.6.6 at page 1059 (2014 ed).[68]

When the lawyer represents both the vulnerable individual and his/her spouse or is engaged in multigenerational representation, assessing the ability of the client who might have diminished capacity (or who is otherwise vulnerable) to provide informed consent to waive conflicting interests, especially where the planning involved contemplates gifting or other forms of divestment, can place the lawyer in an ethical quandary. This may be particularly true when Medicaid planning is involved, given that the net result may be the impoverishment of one client for the benefit of another.

Even if the client prefers to provide the benefit of their assets to another and ultimately rely upon government assistance (such as Medicaid), the client who might have diminished capacity may need to be able to not only understand that the plan will result in the permanent reduction of the assets that they control, but that reliance upon Medicaid may do the following:

1. Adversely affect the resources, facilities, and level of care available to them.
2. Result in future disruptions in accommodations or facilities, if the facility they initially enter does not qualify for Medicaid or if they are hospitalized for a period of time such that their bed at a Medicaid-qualified facility is lost and no other bed at the same facility is then available.
3. For couples who move to the same senior care/senior living campus so that they can remain together, utilization of an irrevocable trust

---

[67] *Id.*

[68] ACTEC COMMENTARIES § 1.7 at 102, 103 (citing generally JOHN R. PRICE, PRICE ON CONTEMPORARY ESTATE PLANNING § 1.6.6 at 1059 (2014)).

that's solely for the benefit of the community spouse (SBO) may result in the ultimate separation of the spouses at a time when neither can easily be transported to visit the other.

4. Result in the little extras that make life more comfortable not being available, because there are no guarantees that the family member to whom a significant gift is provided will maintain and utilize those funds for the benefit of the vulnerable adult (as such is the very nature of an irrevocable gift).

5. Make benefits available to the client unpredictable, given changing political positions, regimes and stated intentions to limit or otherwise cut "entitlement" programs.

When someone other than the vulnerable client originates the idea to make lifetime gifts, create an irrevocable trust, or engage in Medicaid planning, the lawyer will have to navigate and assess these concerns:

- Ethical responsibilities
- The client's vulnerabilities (to potential undue influence and to other forms of financial abuse)
- The client's capacity
- The potential for client conflict
- The client's ability, if conflicts are identified (whether actual or potential), to engage in a knowing and voluntary waiver

If the attorney is engaged by the client's agent (e.g., acting under a durable power of attorney with authority to gift property or modify the client's estate plan in order to engage in Medicaid planning), additional ethical considerations may come into play:

> The lawyer retained by a person seeking appointment as a fiduciary or retained by a fiduciary for a person with diminished capacity, including a guardian, conservator or attorney-in-fact, stands in a lawyer-client relationship with respect to the prospective or appointed fiduciary. A lawyer who is retained by a fiduciary for a person with diminished capacity, but who did not previously represent the person with diminished capacity, represents only the fiduciary. Nevertheless, in such a case the lawyer for the fiduciary owes some duties to the person with diminished capacity. See ACTEC Commentary on MRPC 1.2 (Scope of Representation and Allocation of Authority Between Client and Lawyer). If the lawyer represents the fiduciary, as distinct from the person with diminished capacity,

and is aware that the fiduciary is improperly acting adversely to the person's interests, the lawyer may have an obligation to disclose, to prevent or to rectify the fiduciary's misconduct. See MRPC 1.2(d) (Scope of Representation and Allocation of Authority Between Client and Lawyer) (providing that a lawyer shall not counsel a client to engage, or assist a client, in conduct that the lawyer knows is criminal or fraudulent).

* * *

Whether the person with diminished capacity is characterized as a client or a former client, the client's lawyer acting as counsel for the fiduciary owes some continuing duties to him or her. See Ill. Advisory Opinion 91-24 (1991) (summarized in the Annotations following the ACTEC Commentary on MRPC 1.6 (Confidentiality of Information). If the lawyer represents the person with diminished capacity and not the fiduciary, and is aware that the fiduciary is improperly acting adversely to the person's interests, the lawyer has an obligation to disclose, to prevent or to rectify the fiduciary's misconduct.

. . . A conflict of interest may arise if the lawyer for the fiduciary is asked by the fiduciary to take action that is contrary either to the previously expressed wishes of the person with diminished capacity or to the best interests of such person, as the lawyer believes those interests to be. The lawyer should give appropriate consideration to the currently or previously expressed wishes of a person with diminished capacity.[69]

THE IMPORTANCE OF THESE ISSUES FROM THE ESTATE PLANNER'S PERSPECTIVE

Why might these issues be of such great importance when confronting allegations or concerns relating to undue influence? Besides the ethical considerations identified, the importance of the existence of competent independent counsel and advice, especially when defending against a claim of undue influence, should not be underestimated.

Black's Law Dictionary defines the term *independent* as "not dependent; not subject to control, restriction, modification, or limitation from a given outside source." The term *independent advice* is defined as "advice given

---

[69] ACTEC COMMENTARIES § 1.14 at 162, 163.

confidentially by a person in a fiduciary capacity."[70] MRPC 2.1 provides further guidance on what independent advice entails when it indicates that "in representing a client, a lawyer shall exercise independent professional judgment and render candid advice. In rendering advice, a lawyer may refer not only to law but also to other considerations such as moral, economic, social, and political factors that may be relevant to the client's situation.

The importance of such independent competent legal advice is discussed at greater length in chapter 7. Suffice it to say, preservation of this potential defense can be of great import, thereby buttressing the need for estate planners to have a sufficient understanding of the various factors that may affect whether the advice they might provide will be viewed as both "independent" and "competent."

While estate planning for those clients who are clearly competent and fully functioning adults rarely requires significant or further inquiry as to the client's competency or vulnerability to exploitation, estate planning for vulnerable adults may require additional care and an initial screening by the lawyer. In some instances, where potential vulnerability factors exist, a more extensive inquiry and even psychological or neurological evaluation may be merited.

As the population in the United States ages, there will be an increased need for estate planning attorneys to pay careful attention to the needs and potential vulnerabilities of this client base. According to a recent report by the Alzheimer's Association, by 2030, 20 percent of the U.S. population will be over 65, and this segment of the population is at the greatest risk of suffering from the type of cognitive impairments that might be classified as falling along the dementia spectrum.[71]

The preparation of an estate plan normally involves several documents that may include, but not be limited to, a will, revocable trust, power of attorney (usually durable), and health care authorization (usually referred to as patient advocate designation, advance directive, and/or durable power of attorney for health care). Also part of the estate plan may be beneficiary designations for life insurance contracts, annuity contracts, and retirement plans or retirement accounts, as well as for deeds of conveyance and assignments of personal property. In addition, more sophisticated estate plans may include one or more irrevocable trusts and the creation of

---

[70] THE LAW DICTIONARY (featuring BLACK'S LAW DICTIONARY, 2d ed. 1910), https://thelawdictionary.org/independent.

[71] Alzheimer's Association, *2014 Alzheimer's Disease Facts and Figures, supra* note 3, at e57.

closely held business entities such as partnerships, limited liability companies, and corporations.

The lawyer meeting with a client who is a vulnerable adult needs to be alert to determine the potential existence of any issues involving diminished cognition or client vulnerabilities, even though in many cases there may be no overt evidence of either. Particularly, in an initial meeting with a vulnerable adult, attention should be given to an informal screening of the cognition and vulnerability to exploitation based on a more extensive dialogue with the client. If vulnerabilities are identified, heightened concern may be merited. This might include clients whose environment alone justifies greater inquiry and documentation (i.e., a client who has evidence of physical dependency or where the meeting takes place in a nursing home, foster care, or hospital-like setting).

If there are any initial concerns identified by the lawyer, it may be for the lawyer to reflect such concerns and any additional inquiry made by the lawyer in his/her notes. Even in those cases where the lawyer previously represented the vulnerable adult and that client was previously determined to have sufficient capacity and did not appear otherwise vulnerable, the lawyer should assess whether there have been changes in the client's condition, or evidence of any diminished cognition or increased vulnerability since the prior engagement. If such changes become apparent during the interview process, further inquiry might then be merited. In screening a vulnerable adult for diminished cognition, the lawyer should have an understanding of the indicia of dementia (which may be viewed as an important vulnerability factor) and an understanding that dementia has a spectrum that may start with forgetfulness or memory loss, which might appear long before lack of capacity becomes an issue.[72]

As will be discussed in further detail in chapter 2, in assessing a vulnerable adult client's level of cognition for purposes of determining capacity, the lawyer should recognize that there are different levels of capacity required for different documents. While "testamentary capacity" as defined by applicable statute or case law is the standard for wills and often for revocable trusts, the requisite standard for powers of attorney, health care powers, irrevocable trusts, beneficiary designations, deeds of conveyance, and other contractual undertakings will likely require satisfaction of a somewhat higher standard.

---

[72] See chapter 2 for a detailed discussion of the dementia spectrum. *See also* Robert B. Fleming, *Dealing with the Aging Client*, in 53rd Annual Probate and Estate Planning Institute, Institute of Continuing Legal Education 24–3 to 24–5 (2013).

The standard of capacity applied by medical personnel for making a medical decision, while potentially analogous, may not be identical to that required for estate planning documents. Further, a determination that the individual can make their needs known, remain involved in discussions relating to their own care, or be sufficiently oriented (i.e., alert [awake] and oriented to the extent of knowing his name, location, and the time) also does not satisfy the standard of "testamentary capacity," much less the somewhat different standards for certain other estate planning documents. Consequently, when a client is a vulnerable adult, the lawyer should satisfy himself that the applicable standards of capacity have been met based upon the lawyer's screening. If after an initial assessment the lawyer has concerns regarding the client's capacity, those concerns should be documented in the lawyer's notes. In addition, the lawyer, as part of his undertaking to protect the client, should consider the extent to which appropriate additional steps might be required to confirm that the client has sufficient capacity to execute the contemplated estate planning documents. In cases where cognition issues are transient, such as those resulting from a temporary illness, accident, or medical procedure, such concern might dissipate with the client's recovery over the passage of time.

OBSERVATION OF RISK FACTORS

While lawyers are not omniscient, the careful documentation of observations can be an important defense mechanism to the preservation of the client's estate plan. The documentation of the lawyer's screening process and analysis, when dealing with an estate planning client who is a vulnerable adult, may prove crucial to establishing the "independence" of counsel as opposed to merely being tasked with being a "scrivener" who fails to exercise independent judgment.[73]

---

[73] Documenting such observations, so that they can be accurately and more fully retrieved following the passage of time between the execution and challenge of an instrument, can prove to be extremely important to defending the validity of an instrument. This can be especially true when the client is suffering from mild or even moderate dementia, given the possibility for vacillation in cognitive functioning from day to day, or even hour to hour. As a consequence, the attorney's testimony (and that of other contemporaneous witnesses to execution) may prove as important as that of medical professionals, especially if the medical professionals were not present at the execution or did not evaluate the decedent in close proximity to the time of the execution. See *In re* Bednarz Trust, 2009 Mich. App. LEXIS 1349 (Mich. Ct.

Things that the lawyer may wish to document in their notes when concerns about vulnerability exist include but are not limited to:

- Who made the initial contact for the appointment?
- Who referred the client to the lawyer?
- Was there a prior attorney involved with the client's plan, and why has the client decided to change attorneys?
- If the change desired by the client represents a deviation from prior estate planning documents, inquire and note the client's rationale for the change.
- Note how the client arrived for the appointment—did a family member or care provider bring them?
- If the client had any notable physical limitations, note them.
- Note any other "red flags" or "suspicious circumstances."
- You might wish to note how the client appeared (e.g., perfectly coifed or disheveled).
- Consider noting actual language or quotes from the client regarding the client's estate planning desires by the use of quotation marks.
- Ask open-ended questions, and if the client is unable to easily communicate, reflect the manner in which information was elicited. Be sure to ask questions that would reflect whether the client was providing false positive or false negative responses.
- Try to determine and note whether there are any individuals upon whom the client is already reliant or dependent and the extent of those dependencies.
- Document whether the client has any health conditions or is taking any medications that might affect the client's cognition or level of dependency.
- Note information provided by the client that demonstrated the client had sufficient capacity (e.g., members of the client's family and the general extent of the client's estate).
- Note any concerns (e.g., word finding problems, slow in providing responses, hard of hearing, vision issues, need for the lawyer to repeatedly answer the same question or repetition of information that might indicate memory issues or other indications of lapses of memory).

App. June 16, 2009) (citing Bradford v. Vinton, 59 Mich. 139, 154, 26 N.W.401 (1886)). *See also* MICH. R. EVID. (MRE) 701.

- Note the date of the meeting, the location (if outside the lawyer's office), and how long the meeting took.
- To the extent advice was rendered, it might be helpful to reflect at least some of the advice provided topically.

After analysis, the lawyer may have concerns that indicia of exploitation are present (such as when the client has testamentary capacity but appears to be vulnerable due to possible diminished cognition, physical infirmity, or dependency on others for many activities of daily living). If so, the lawyer should assess and document whether there are other circumstances that satisfied the lawyer's concern. The lawyer should take note of the facts that he believes support the conclusion that the plan was generated by and represented the unfettered will of the client. The lawyer should document circumstances that he believes support such conclusions.

In evaluating whether there are potential indicia of undue influence, Peisah, et al., note numerous risk factors that may predispose an individual to undue influence.[74] While there is no exhaustive list of risk factors, red flags, or suspicious circumstances, Bennett Blum, M.D., has listed over 30 circumstances that he identifies as "red flags" or "suspicious circumstances."[75] These include but are not limited to the following:

1. The identified victim's susceptibility or vulnerability to influence (including, among other things, issues related to age, physical or mental deterioration, emotional state, education, or finances)
2. A confidential relationship between the supposed perpetrator and identified victim
3. A beneficiary's active involvement or participation in procuring the legal instrument in question

---

[74] Carmelle Peisah, Sanford I. Finkel, Kenneth Shulman, Pamela S. Melding, Jay S. Luxenberg, Jeremia Heinik, Robin J. Jacoby, Barry Reisberg, Gabriela Stoppe, A. Barker, Helen Cristina Torrano Firmino, & Hayley I. Bennett, *The Wills of Older People: Risk Factors for Undue Influence, for* INTERNATIONAL PSYCHOGERIATIC ASSOCIATION TASK FORCE ON WILLS AND UNDUE INFLUENCE, 21 INT. PSYCHOGERIATR., 7–15, 10, 11 (2009).

[75] Bennett Blum, M.D., *Undue Influence - Suspicious Circumstances*, BENNETT BLUM, M.D. INC. (n.d.), http://www.bennettblummd.com/undue_influence_suspicious _circumstances.html; Bennett Blum, M.D., *Undue Influence – More Suspicious Circumstances*, BENNETT BLUM, M.D. INC. (n.d.), http://www.bennettblummd.com /undue_influence_more_suspicious_circumstances.html.

4. Secrecy concerning the existence of the transaction or legal changes, or the events occurring in haste
5. Lack of independent advice related to that transaction or new legal document
6. Changes in the identified victim's attitude toward others
7. Discrepancies between the identified victim's behavior and previously expressed intentions
8. The unjust or unnatural nature of the terms of the transaction or new legal instrument (new will, new trust, etc.)
9. Anonymous criticism of other potential beneficiaries made to the identified victim
10. Suggestion, without proof, to the identified victim that other potential beneficiaries had attempted to physically harm him or her
11. Withholding mail
12. Limiting telephone access
13. Limiting visitation
14. Limiting privacy when victim is with others (conduct generally known as "chaperoning")
15. Discussion of transaction at an unusual or inappropriate time
16. Consummation of the transaction at an unusual place
17. Use of multiple persuaders against a single vulnerable person
18. Demand that the business be finished at once
19. Extreme emphasis on the consequences of delay
20. Obtaining a lawyer for the victim
21. Using victim's assets, such as property, money, credit cards, etc.
22. Becoming conservator, trustee, beneficiary, executor, etc.
23. Obtaining access to bank accounts
24. Obtaining access to safety deposit boxes
25. Having the victim name the perpetrator on power of attorney forms
26. Isolating the testator and disparaging family members
27. Mental inequality between the decedent and the beneficiary
28. Reasonableness of the will or trust provision
29. Presence of the beneficiary at the execution of the will
30. Presence of the beneficiary on those occasions when the testator expressed a desire to make a will
31. Recommendation by the beneficiary of a lawyer to draw the will
32. Knowledge of the contents of the will by the beneficiary prior to execution
33. Giving instructions on preparation of the will by the beneficiary to the lawyer drawing the will
34. Securing witnesses to the will by the beneficiary

The ability of the estate planning lawyer to identify and be cognizant of such indicia so that they might then conduct an enhanced screening of the client's vulnerabilities, potential susceptibility to exploitation, and ability to generate an independently created plan may prove important. As a result, several circumstances should initially be considered:

a. Is the client vulnerable to influence based on diminished cognition, physical condition, emotional state, financial circumstances, isolation from pertinent information, relatives and friends, and dependence on others?

b. Are persons other than the client involved in the estate planning process, particularly if they are not the client's natural objects of his or her bounty? These include a cohabitating adult family member, a caregiver, a more distant family member such as a nephew or niece, a friend or neighbor, a suitor, or a professional such as an attorney, accountant, clergy, doctor, or investment advisor. Did such persons arrange for the appointment with the lawyer?

c. Is there a confidential or fiduciary relationship between the client and another person involved in the estate planning process?

d. Do the client's estate planning goals reflect a significant departure from a pattern in prior estate planning documents?

e. Is there a formerly trusted family member who is no longer trusted? Is there a significant change in the client's attitude toward former beneficiaries?

f. Is there family conflict present between siblings or a spouse and the client's descendants?

g. Have you been retained after dismissal of a prior long-standing estate planning attorney who is still actively practicing?[76]

PRACTICE GUIDELINES WHEN CAPACITY MAY BE AN ISSUE

If any concerns regarding vulnerability to exploitation remain, these should be documented in the lawyer's notes. In addition, the lawyer, as part of undertaking to protect the client, should then consider what appropriate additional steps might be undertaken to protect the client or the intended plan.

For concerns that relate to capacity, what should a lawyer do if, based on the initial screening, the lawyer has doubts whether the client has sufficient

---

[76] Peisah, *The Wills of Older People, supra* note 75, at 1, 10, 11; Blum, *Undue Influence.*

capacity to validly execute any of the proposed estate planning documents? The following suggestions to a lawyer in this situation may fall within the purview of MRPC 1.14, which authorizes a lawyer to ". . . take other protective action with respect to a client when the lawyer reasonably believes the client cannot adequately act in the client's own interest."[77]

- First, if the level of apparent cognitive impairment appears substantial to the lawyer, based on the spectrum of dementia, some professional medical review might be suggested to the client. In some cases, the administration of the so called mini-mental exam (MME) administered by the client's physician as part of a routine examination might be sufficient to resolve the concern.[78]
- Second, if the MME is not satisfactorily passed, a referral to a qualified health care provider might be appropriate for a more complete clinical examination. This may involve the submission of the individual to examination by a psychiatrist, geriatric psychiatrist, neurologist, or speech pathologist who is trained to assess cognitive functioning. Such an examination should include the ". . . usual features of medical and psychiatric history, mental status, and cognitive examination, as well as the specific issues relevant to testamentary capacity. . . ."[79]
- Third, if the lawyer's assessment (and any subsequent examinations deemed appropriate) confirms that the client has sufficient capacity to execute the estate planning instruments, it is a good practice to make sure that the documents are provided to the client in advance of the appointment when they are to be executed. Providing the documents to the client in advance provides the client with adequate time to digest and process the contents of the instruments and to formulate and ask any questions the client might have regarding the impact of the instruments or meaning of language that might be otherwise unclear to the client. If the client has vision issues, it may be important to ascertain that an independent individual (or the lawyer) read the document to the client paced in a manner intended to facilitate comprehension and understanding.

---

[77] MRPC 1.14.

[78] Examples of both a Standardized Mini Mental State Examination (SMMSE) and a separate Global Deterioration Scale (GDS), provided by the Alzheimer Drug Therapy Initiative for physician use, can be viewed at www2.gov.bc.ca/assets/gov/health/health-drug-coverage/pharmacare/newsletters/news16-003.pdf.

[79] K.I. Shulman, C. Peisah, R. Jacoby, J. Heinik, & S. Finkel, *Contemporaneous Assessment of Testamentary Capacity*, 21 INT. PSYCHOGERIATR. 433–9, at 5 (2009).

- Fourth, it may be advisable to have the estate planning instruments executed in the presence of independent (and to the extent possible, professional) witnesses. As part of the witnessing and execution process, it is recommended that the lawyer review pertinent provisions of the document orally with the client, preferably with the witnesses present, and have a dialogue with the client to elicit factual support evidencing the elements of testamentary or other capacity required for the particular estate planning documents. When a client is a vulnerable adult, it may be important for both the lawyer and witnesses to create and retain notes regarding the execution.
- Fifth, if after proceeding through one or more of the foregoing steps, the lawyer is still concerned, based on the lawyer's dialogue with the client and/or actions taken or not taken, that the client lacks sufficient capacity to execute one of more of the estate planning documents, the lawyer should so advise the client of his concerns and decline to participate in the execution of any document where the lawyer isn't satisfied that sufficient capacity is present. If the client has capacity to execute some of the estate planning documents that will operate independently of the documents where the level of capacity is insufficient, the lawyer can, however, proceed with the execution of those documents where evidence of sufficient capacity does exist in the manner described in the preceding steps and elect not to proceed with regard to those documents where capacity remains questionable.

GUIDELINES WHEN VULNERABILITY MAY BE AN ISSUE

What about the client who has sufficient capacity but who appears vulnerable to exploitation? What should the lawyer do when faced with a client who is vulnerable and now wishes a change that is clearly contrary to previously stated estate planning desires? The following quotation in a *Michigan Bar Journal* article sheds some light on the challenge faced by a lawyer in responding to this question. It identifies that the lawyer "should pay careful attention to the possibility of exploitation or undue influence by the proposed agent. Dementia can add a layer of misunderstanding or confusion that either disguises exploitation or misinterprets innocent behavior as wrongdoing."[80]

---

[80] Beth A. Swagman & Caroline M. Dellenbusch, *An Overview of Dementia and Competency*, MICH. BAR J., November 2014, at 26, 29.

As in the case of determining capacity, the following suggestions are believed to also fall within the gambit of steps permitted under the auspices of MRPC 1.14, which directs a lawyer to "take other protective action with respect to a client when the lawyer reasonably believes the client cannot adequately act in the client's own interest"[81]:

- First, the lawyer's responsibility is to the client, and the lawyer's efforts should be directed to ascertaining the client's actual estate planning goals, free of any possible elements of undue influence (as well as free of fraud or duress). It may be that despite the existence of certain vulnerabilities or other indicia, in addition to the lawyer's initial concerns, there is in fact no undue influence, fraud, or duress.
- Second, the lawyer should insist on meeting with the client in the absence of any other person who may benefit from any particular disposition of property in their lifetime or at death. It may also be important to exclude any agent or representative of a person who might benefit from the instrument or plan. Multiple meetings may provide additional guidance and confirmation of the client's estate planning goals. It is advisable for the lawyer to create and preserve notes of all discussions with the client.
- Third, including a client's disinterested third-party professional advisors in a meeting with the client may be helpful in providing additional insights and confirmation regarding the client's estate planning intentions. Again, it is advisable that the lawyer create and retain notes of these meetings.
- Fourth, if isolation from information or family and friends becomes apparent, with the client's permission, the lawyer might engage in actions intended to breach the isolation. This might include obtaining authorization for provision of key financial documents to the client from advisors and financial institutions, or accommodations intended to provide important contact with the client or lawyer. It is advisable for the lawyer to confirm the client's perspective with regard to such information during the estate planning process. Again, it is recommended that the lawyer create and retain notes of any discussions involving family, friends, or the client's independent advisors, as well as with regard to any subsequent communications engaged in with the client during the planning process after receipt of such information.

---

[81] MRPC 1.14.

- Fifth, a medical examination by a qualified psychiatrist, geriatric psychiatrist, psychologist, or other relevant health care provider may be useful if concerns remain after one or more of the prior steps have been taken.
- Sixth, if estate planning documents are to be executed, as indicated in the section relating to capacity, the instruments should be provided to the client in advance, either for him to read and review or to be read to him by the lawyer or another independent person.
- Seventh, when the lawyer is satisfied that the estate planning documents reflect the client's intent, it is advisable to have the estate planning instruments executed in the presence of independent (and to the extent possible, professional) witnesses. As part of the witnessing and execution process, it is recommended that the lawyer review pertinent provisions of the document orally with the client, preferably with the witnesses present, and have a dialogue with the client to elicit factual support evidencing the elements of testamentary or other capacity required for the particular estate planning documents. When a client is a vulnerable adult, it is recommended that both the lawyer and witnesses create and retain notes regarding the execution.
- Eighth, no beneficiary should be present in the room during the execution and witnessing of the instruments.
- Ninth, if after proceeding through one or more of the preceding steps, the lawyer still has concerns that the proposed plan may be the product of undue influence, it is recommended that the lawyer advise the client of his concerns and decline to take further action to assist in the execution of the suspect estate planning documents. It is further recommended that the lawyer create and retain notes regarding the lawyer's concerns and the foregoing actions that emanated as a result.

Because lawyers are engaged in a "service" profession, they often attempt to accommodate a client's desires. They may placate a client's expressions that the lawyer take shortcuts or otherwise give short shrift to concerns that the lawyer has raised. It remains important for estate planning lawyers to remember that they are engaged to document a client's estate planning desires. They are also to engage in conduct and draft documents under practice parameters in order to enhance the enforceability of the instruments created for the client's benefit. At times, having discussions that are blunt and frank with the client about why additional steps and safeguards are being recommended may convince the client of the merit of such efforts because they increase the likelihood that the client's estate planning objectives are met.

Evidence that the lawyer exercised independent judgment and provided independent advice, as opposed to merely acting in the capacity of a "scrivener," may, under certain circumstances, become the single most important body of evidence that the instrument was duly executed while the individual possessed the requisite capacity, and that such instrument represented the individual's intent (as opposed to the supplanted intent of another). Consequently, evidence of true independence of counsel, coupled with documentation of the efforts engaged in by the estate planning lawyer to assess the client's capacity and unfettered intent, may well be the most effective and best defense to a subsequent attack premised on lack of capacity or a claim of undue influence on the enforceability of the estate planning documents.

CHAPTER 2

To Understand Undue Influence, One Needs to Understand Capacity[1]

To be unduly influenced, one must have capacity to engage in the transaction. "Undue influence in the procurement of a will . . . is a ground for contesting a will 'separate and distinct from the ground of testamentary incapacity; for while testamentary incapacity implies the want of intelligent mental power, undue influence implies the existence of a testamentary capacity subjected to and controlled by a dominant influence or power.'"[2] While lack of capacity and undue influence often are pled together, as a basis for setting aside an instrument or transaction, generally if one lacks sufficient capacity to engage in the contested transaction, the action will be deemed void *ab initio* because the grantor lacked the requisite capacity. Conversely, a person who has the requisite capacity may nonetheless be vulnerable (for a variety of reasons) to the influence of others. If that influence is "undue," or if the transaction is the result of "fraud" or "duress," the transaction (rather than being void) may be set aside.

Each state has its own set of definition(s) for capacity. Depending upon what type of instrument is involved, the definition of what is required for

---

[1] Portions of this chapter were adapted from two articles published by BNA: Sandra D. Glazier, Esq., *Capacity and Ethical Considerations When Representing Vulnerable Adults*, 43 TAX MANAGE. ESTATES GIFTS TRUSTS J. (2018); and Bloomberg BNA, Sandra D. Glazier, Esq., Thomas M. Dixon, Esq., & Thomas F. Sweeney, Esq., *What Every Estate Planner Should Know About Undue Influence: Recognizing It, Insulating/ Planning Against It . . . And Litigating It*, TAX MANAGEMENT MEMORANDUM (2015).

[2] *In re* Estate of Danford, 550 S.W.3d 275, 281 (Tex. Ct. App. – Houston 2018) (citing Rothermel v. Duncan, 369 S.W.2d 917, 922 (Tex. 1963)).

capacity to exist also can vary. Courts generally will presume that the requisite level of capacity exists. As a result, a challenger has the burden of proving the testator, settlor, transferor, or donor lacked capacity.[3]

Examples of where the definition of capacity may differ include but are not limited to the capacity to execute or make a will, revocable trust, power of attorney, medical or advanced directive, gift, irrevocable trust, deed, or contract, or to provide informed consent for a medical procedure, marry, designate a beneficiary, create a joint account, or even drive.[4] "The law regarding capacity is full of fine distinctions: capacity to marry is one thing,[5] the capacity to enter into a contractual relation is another, and the capacity to execute a will still another."[6] It's "never wise to think that categories that were developed by doctors to aid in the treatment of patients can, with ease, be transferred to legal contexts."[7]

Therefore, it is important that the lawyer understand and evaluate whether the client might have been subjected to undue influence, fraud, duress, or another form of abuse, as well as whether the client has the requisite capacity to hire the lawyer and engage in the proposed estate planning transactions.

While a diagnosis of dementia may reflect the existence of cognitive issues such as diminished capacity and vulnerabilities, it does not necessarily mean that a client lacks the capacity to hire the lawyer or engage in estate planning transactions.

The dementia spectrum has been described as having five levels:[8]

    a. *Mild cognitive impairment.* The person may experience memory problems but is able to live independently. This person should have sufficient capacity to execute the customary estate planning documents.

---

[3] *In re* Powers Estate, 375 Mich. 150, 158, 134 N.W.2d 148, 151 (1965); *in re* Sprenger's Estate, 337 Mich. 514, 521, 60 N.W.2d 436, 440 (1953); *in re* Vollbrecht Estate, 26 Mich. App. 430, 434, 182 N.W.2d 609, 612 (1970).

[4] ABA COMMN. ON L. & AGING & AM. PSYCHOLOGICAL ASSN., ASSESSMENT OF OLDER ADULTS WITH DIMINISHED CAPACITY: A HANDBOOK FOR PSYCHOLOGISTS, at 52–102 (2008).

[5] See discussion about the law compared to reality in the courtroom, Stephen L. Elkins, *Exploitative Marriages in Michigan: "To Love and to Honor Until Death Does Its Part,"* MICH PROB & TR LJ, Winter 2014, at 29–32.

[6] Robert B. Fleming, *Dealing with the Aging Client,* in 53rd ANNUAL PROBATE AND ESTATE PLANNING INSTITUTE, INSTITUTE OF CONTINUING LEGAL EDUCATION 24–3 to 24–5 (2013).

[7] *Id.* at 24–4 to 24–7.

[8] *Id.* at 24–3, 24–4.

b. *Mild dementia.* The person may experience impaired memory and thinking skills. The person may no longer be able to live completely independently and may require assistance with some instrumental activities of daily living (IADLs)[9] and activities of daily living (ADLs).[10] The person might become confused when in public. This person usually will have sufficient capacity to execute the customary estate planning documents.

c. *Moderate dementia.* The person may experience severe memory loss and difficulty communicating. The person cannot live alone and needs help with most IADLs and ADLs. The person needs assistance if out in public. The capacity of such a person to execute the customary estate planning documents likely will be slipping away and will be lost by the time severe dementia occurs.

d. *Severe dementia.* The person may experience severe problems with communication and incontinence, and they require constant care. The person needs hands-on assistance with all ADLs and is unable to perform any IADLs. This person likely will lack sufficient capacity to execute any estate planning documents.

e. *Profound dementia.* This person is usually bedridden and has insufficient capacity to execute any estate planning document.[11]

Lawyers need to understand the legal standards for the specific transaction contemplated. "The definition of 'diminished capacity' in everyday legal practice depends largely on the type of transaction or decision under consideration."[12] While there are deviations and distinctions between the

---

[9] IADLs include managing finances, handling personal transportation, shopping, preparing meals, using telephone and communication devices, and performing housework. *See* Caring.com, *Family Caregiver Basics | A Practical Guide,* https://www.caring.com/caregivers/family-caregivers/.

[10] *Id.* ADLs include feeding, toileting, selecting proper attire, grooming, maintaining continence, dressing, bathing, walking, and transferring.

[11] Fleming, *supra* note 6, at 24–3 to 24–5. In the medical arena, the Charles F. and Joanne Knight Alzheimer Disease Research Center (Knight ADRC) at Washington University in St. Louis, Missouri, developed what it calls the Clinical Dementia Rating (CDR) Dementia Staging Instrument as an aid to defining a patient's level of dementia impairment. Under this rating system, there are only four classified levels of dementia impairment: very mild dementia, mild dementia, moderate dementia, and severe dementia. *See* https://knightadrc.wustl.edu/cdr/cdr.htm.

[12] ABA COMMN. ON L. & AGING & AM. PSYCHOLOGICAL ASSN., ASSESSMENT OF OLDER ADULTS WITH DIMINISHED CAPACITY: A HANDBOOK FOR LAWYERS, at 5 (2005).

various standards for capacity, in this book, the focus is on the general capacity precepts relating to testamentary, contractual, and donative capacity.

Because the lawyer must first determine whether the client has the capacity to hire him, initially the lawyer will need to determine whether the client has sufficient contractual capacity. Courts, when determining an individual's capacity to execute a contract, "generally assess the party's ability to understand the nature and effect of the act and the business being transacted." If the act or business is "highly complicated, a higher level of understanding may be needed to comprehend its nature and effect, in contrast to a very simple contractual arrangement."[13]

In Michigan, to enter into a business contract or settlement agreement, or to open a bank account or change insurance policy beneficiaries, persons must "generally possess 'sufficient mind' to understand in a reasonable manner the nature and effect of the act in which the person is engaged."[14]

To some, this may seem a nominal standard. However, it is generally perceived to require greater capacity than that which is required to create a will or a revocable trust.

Assuming the client has the requisite capacity to engage the lawyer, the obligation to assess capacity does not end there. The lawyer then needs to assess whether the client has the requisite capacity to engage in the planned transaction. While exploring all standards of capacity is beyond the scope of this book, lawyers may nonetheless wish to refer to other sources that might provide guidance on capacity requirements,[15] as well as to statutory and case law standards that are established in the jurisdiction where the transaction is proposed. However, to provide an understanding of some of the considerations covered in this book, generalized references to capacity standards include:

> The ability to create and execute a will is generally one of the lowest standard of capacity.[16] Typically, the testator at the time of executing a will must have capacity to know the natural objects

---

[13] *Id.* at 6 (internal citations omitted).

[14] Persinger v. Holtz, 248 Mich. App. 499, 503, 639 N.W.2d 594, 597 (2001) (citing *In re* Erickson 202 Mich. App. 329, 332, 508 N.W.2d 181(1993)).

[15] *See* ABA, A HANDBOOK FOR LAWYERS, *supra* note 13; ABA, A HANDBOOK FOR PSYCHOLOGISTS, *supra* note 4; *and* ABA COMMN. ON L. & AGING & AM. PSYCHOLOGICAL ASSN., JUDICIAL DETERMINATION OF CAPACITY OF OLDER ADULTS IN GUARDIANSHIP PROCEEDINGS (2006).

[16] The capacity to marry may be considered the lowest. See *In re* Marriage of Greenway, 217 Cal. App. 4th 628, 639, 158 Cal. Rptr. 3d 364 (2013).

of his or her bounty, to understand the nature and extent of his or her property, and to interrelate these elements sufficiently to make a disposition of property according to a rational plan. The terminology that the testator must be of "sound mind" is still commonly used. The test for testamentary capacity does not require that the person be capable of managing all of his or her affairs or making day-to-day business transactions.[17]

The Uniform Trust Code (UTC)[18] reflects that the capacity to make a revocable trust is the same as that which is required to make a will.[19] However, some trusts created to qualify individuals for Medicaid benefits or for tax planning (in order to take advantage of an individual's annual gift or lifetime exemptions) are irrevocable in nature. The standard for such trusts may require that the grantor meet a higher capacity standard. While the UTC does not specifically set forth the standard of capacity required for an irrevocable trust, the commentary to UTC § 601 reflects that the differentiation in capacity standards are in recognition that *revocable* trusts are now commonly utilized as will substitutes:

> The revocable trust is used primarily as a will substitute, with its key provision being the determination of the persons to receive the trust property upon the settlor's death. To solidify the use of the revocable trust as a device for transferring property at death, the settlor usually also executes a pourover will. The use of a pourover will assures that property not transferred to the trust during life will be combined with the property the settlor did manage to convey. Given this primary use of the revocable trust as a device for disposing of property at death, the capacity standard for wills rather than that for lifetime gifts should apply . . . .
>
> The Uniform Trust Code does not explicitly spell out the standard of capacity necessary to create other types of trusts, although Section 402 does require that the settlor have capacity. This section includes a capacity standard for creation of a revocable trust because of the uncertainty in the case law and the importance of the issue in modern estate planning. No such

---

[17] ABA, A HANDBOOK FOR LAWYERS, *supra* note 13, at 5.
[18] In this book, *UTC* refers to the Uniform Trust Code as revised or amended in 2010 by the NATIONAL CONFERENCE OF COMM'RS ON UNIFORM STATE LAWS.
[19] *See* UTC § 601. *See also* UTC § 402, cmt. at 60.

uncertainty exists with respect to the capacity standard for other types of trusts. To create a testamentary trust, the settlor must have the capacity to make a will. *To create an irrevocable trust, the settlor must have the capacity that would be needed to transfer the property free of trust.* See generally Restatement (Third) of Trusts § 11 (Tentative Draft No. 1, approved 1996); Restatement (Third) of Property: Wills and Other Donative Transfers § 8.1 (Tentative Draft No. 3, approved 2001).[20]

Consequently, the requisite capacity for the creation of an *irrevocable* trust may be more akin to that required for donative capacity than what is required to create a will, or even to enter into a contract. Donative capacity has been identified to require:

> . . . an understanding of the nature and purpose of the gift, an understanding of the nature and extent of property to be given, a knowledge of the natural objects of the donor's bounty, and an understanding of the nature and effect of the gift. Some states use a higher standard for donative capacity than for testamentary capacity, *requiring that the donor knows the gift to be irrevocable and that it would result in a reduction in the donor's assets or estate.*[21]

Other levels (or standards) of capacity also may be involved in effectuating the plan intended by a client. To execute a deed of conveyance, a person must have "sufficient mental capacity to understand the business in which he was engaged, to know and understand the extent and value of his property, and how he wanted to dispose of it, and to keep these facts in his mind long enough to plan and effect the conveyances in question without prompting and interference from others."[22]

In a recent case of first impression, the Michigan Court of Appeals addressed the effectiveness of a proxy provided at a time when the grantor was alleged to have lacked sufficient capacity or, in the alternative, was the product of undue influence.[23] In *Menhennick Family Trust*,[24] Ilean Menhennick's son obtained her proxy. The proxy shifted what had been fractured rights

---

[20] UTC § 601, cmt. at 100, 101 (emphasis added).

[21] ABA, A HANDBOOK FOR LAWYERS, *supra* note 13, at 6 (emphasis added).

[22] *Persinger*, at 893.

[23] *See* Menhennick Family Trust, 326 Mich. App. 504, 927 N.W.2d 741 (2018).

[24] *Id.*

to voting control resting with her son. Once the son had voting control, he was able to modify operational control via amendment of the family's closely held business operating agreements and issue additional stock to himself, which also vested absolute voting control in that son. The court held:

> Whether a person was mentally competent is determined by a preponderance of the evidence. Generally, "whatever a person may lawfully do, if acting in his own right and on his own behalf, he may lawfully delegate to an agent." However, in order to do so, the person "must be free to enter into a valid contract of agency." "The test of mental capacity to contract is whether the person in question possesses sufficient mind to understand in a reasonable manner the nature and effect of the act in which the person is engaged." A person is too mentally unsound to contract if "the person had no reasonable perception of the nature or terms of the contract." A person may be incapable of conducting business successfully and still be mentally competent.[25]

During the trial, testimony was elicited from Ilean's treating physician and other family members that reflected she had difficulty following directions to do basic and simple tasks, she could not recall three words after one minute, and she had been diagnosed with moderate dementia. Ilean had difficulty placing calls and would talk, at times, to people who were not there. While Ilean recalled signing some documents, her conversations were vague, she could not interact in a complex conversation, and she was incapable of complex thought. She also suffered from severe memory impairment. Her doctor testified that she would not have been able to understand business complexities. While Ilean could clearly sign her own name, engage in some level of conversation, and perhaps understand that by signing the proxy she would not have to attend the shareholder's meeting, her doctor testified that she would not have been able to understand the business ramifications of signing the proxy. Further, the court found it unpersuasive that Ilean had signed a durable power of attorney and patient advocate (medical directive) six months earlier because her condition had deteriorated over that six-month period and the nature of the documents were different. The court held that it need not address whether the proxy was the result of undue influence once it found that Ilean lacked the mental capacity to understand the nature of the

---

[25] *Id.* (internal citations omitted).

proxies signed; the proxies were, therefore, void *ab initio*, and the transactions resulting from the exercise of power granted thereunder were vacated.[26]

With regard to durable financial powers of attorney and the potential ramifications that might be attendant to them, at least one court recognized that:

> . . . requiring the principal of a power of attorney to be mentally competent at the time of its execution advances important public policy concerns. We are hard pressed to conceive of a more effective and efficient means by which to devastate and destroy the estate of a vulnerable person than through a durable general power of attorney. Sanctioning the execution of a power of attorney by a mentally incompetent principal would give license to those who have the power or inclination to coerce, cajole, or dupe such a person into effectively relinquishing rights to their property, finances, and other assets with minimal effort. Considering the nature, breadth, and consequences of a power of attorney, public policy interests are served by the requirement that the principal have the ability to engage in thoughtful deliberation and use reasonable judgment with regard to its formation.[27]

While the standard for making informed medical decisions may be a consideration, the standard for creating a durable medical power of attorney (like that of a proxy) differs from that required for the actual medical decision itself and is, instead, likely akin to that required to contract (discussed earlier).

It therefore is incumbent upon the lawyer to ascertain and satisfy himself or herself that the client has the requisite capacity, and to notate the file with regard to observations, especially when addressing a transaction that involves a client who might be considered a vulnerable adult.

---

[26] *Id.*

[27] *Persinger*, at 506–507.

CHAPTER 3

What Is Undue Influence?[1]

To understand undue influence, one needs to understand that undue influence is "not a one-time act; it involves a pattern of manipulative behaviors to get a victim to do what the exploiter wants, even when the victim's actions appear to be voluntary or are contrary to his or her previous beliefs, wishes, and actions."[2] Undue influence "occurs as the result of a process, not a one-time event."[3] These types of cases are very fact-dependent. At times, the tactics used may be "similar to brainwashing techniques used by cults and hostage takers. There are also parallels to domestic violence, stalking, and grooming behaviors used by some sexual predators."[4] Consequently, a thorough understanding of the facts leading up to (and sometimes after) the execution of an instrument at issue and the relationship between the individual and the influencer is needed.[5] A general rule is that:

> [u]ndue influence is not exercised openly, but, like crime, seeks secrecy in which to accomplish its poisonous work. It is largely a matter of inference from facts and circumstances surrounding the testator, his character and mental condition, as shown by the

---

[1] Adapted from an article previously published by BNA: Bloomberg BNA, Sandra D. Glazier, Esq., Thomas M. Dixon, Esq., & Thomas F. Sweeney, Esq., *What Every Estate Planner Should Know About Undue Influence: Recognizing It, Insulating/Planning Against It . . . And Litigating It*, TAX MANAGEMENT MEMORANDUM (2015).

[2] Bonnie Brandle, Candice J. Heisler, & Lori A. Stiegel, *The Parallels Between Undue Influence, Domestic Violence, Stalking, and Sexual Assault*, 17 J. ELDER ABUSE NEGL. 37 (2005).

[3] *Id.* at 39.

[4] *Id.*

[5] *Id.*

evidence, and the opportunity possessed by the beneficiary for the exercise of such control.[6]

Undue influence "may be insidious and not in front of witnesses, but fair inferences can be drawn from the facts."[7]

CLINICAL VS. LEGAL PERSPECTIVE

From a "clinical" versus "legal" perspective, it has been found that the more risk factors or "red flag" indicia of undue influence that are found to exist, the more likely it is that undue influence is occurring or has occurred.[8] These indicia are discussed in greater detail in chapters 1, 2, and 4.

As indicated in chapter 2, regardless of the applicable standard for capacity, for undue influence to occur, the person influenced must have the capacity to engage in the transaction, or the transaction would generally be considered void *ab initio*. Consequently, competency and undue influence are mutually exclusive.[9] Every victim of undue influence was, by definition, competent (even though lack of capacity and undue influence may be pled in the alternative as a basis for invalidating an instrument, and experts often are asked to opine on both testamentary capacity and the vulnerability to undue influence). While reduced cognition may be a factor in many undue influence cases (due to the existence of fertile ground for susceptibility and vulnerability to influence that it can create), it is not a necessary element.

WHAT IS UNDUE INFLUENCE?

So, what is undue influence? It is not "undue" to persuade, suggest, ask, recommend, or even attempt to guilt a person into taking action, as long as such conduct does not abuse the relationship or otherwise supplant the will of the individual. In the most general sense, influence is "undue" if

---

[6] Walts v. Walts, 127 Mich. 607, 611, 86 N.W. 1030, 1031 (1901).

[7] *In re* Paquin's Estate, 328 Mich. 293, 303, 43 N.W.2d 858, 862 (1950). *See also In re* Persons Estate, 346 Mich. 517, 532, 78 N.W.2d 235, 243 (1956).

[8] Carmelle Peisah, Sanford I. Finkel, Kenneth Shulman, Pamela S. Melding, Jay S. Luxenberg, Jeremia Heinik, Robin J. Jacoby, Barry Reisberg, Gabriela Stoppe, A. Barker, Helen Cristina Torrano Firmino, & Hayley I. Bennett, *The Wills of Older People: Risk Factors for Undue Influence, for* INTERNATIONAL PSYCHOGERIATIC ASSOCIATION TASK FORCE ON WILLS AND UNDUE INFLUENCE, 21 INT. PSYCHOGERIATR., at 7, 10 (2009).

[9] *In re* Estate of Danford, 550 S.W.3d 275, 281 (Tex. Ct. App. – Houston 2018).

that persuasion abuses the relationship.[10] Undue influence may be exerted by improper threat, but more generally it takes the form of unfair persuasion in the context of a relationship that is thereby abused. Influence thus becomes undue as a function of the relationship.[11,12]

It is often said that to establish undue influence, it must be shown that the individual was subjected to threats, misrepresentation, undue flattery, fraud, or physical or moral coercion sufficient to overpower volition, destroy free agency, and impel the grantor to act against his inclination and free will.[13] While a claim of undue influence may involve elements of fraud, duress, or misrepresentation, each of these elements need not be present. Such elements, in and of themselves, may be separate causes of action, with differing burdens and proofs from those associated with an undue influence claim. Undue influence is said to consist of "persuasion carried to the point of overpowering the will, or such a control over the person in question as prevents him from acting intelligently, understandingly, and voluntarily, and in effect destroys his free agency and constrains him to do that which he would not have done if such control had not been exercised."[14] Moreover, not all influence is undue.

> [I]nfluences to induce testamentary disposition may be specific and direct without becoming undue as it is not improper to advise, persuade, solicit, importune, entreat, implore, move hopes, fears, or prejudices or to make appeals to vanity, pride, sense of justice, obligations of duty, ties of friendship, affection, or kindred, sentiment of gratitude or to pity for distress and destitution, although such will would not have been made but for such influence, so long as the testator's choice is his own . . ..[15]

To constitute undue influence, a person's mind "must be so controlled or affected by persuasion or pressure, artful or fraudulent contrivances, or by the insidious influences of persons in close confidential relations with

---

[10]   *See* Kar v. Hogan, 399 Mich. 529, 537, 251 N.W.2d 77, 79 (1976).

[11]   *Walts*, 127 Mich. at 611.

[12]   The existence of such relationship does not have to mean that voidable transactions relate only to those where the influencer or members of his family benefit. It has been extended to charities (and others) with which the influencer is involved or represents. *See* Estate of Edel, 182 Misc. 2d 878, 700 N.Y.S. 664 (Sur. Ct. 1999).

[13]   *In re* Peterson, 193 Mich. App. 257, 259–260, 483 N.W.2d 624, 625 (1991).

[14]   *Kar*, 399 Mich. at 554 (Levin, J., dissenting) (quoting from 2 BLACK, RESCISSION AND CANCELLATION § 237 at 676, 677 (2d ed. 1929)).

[15]   *In re* Spillette Estate, 352 Mich. 12, 17–18, 88 N.W.2d 300, 303 (1958).

him, that he is not left to act intelligently, understandingly, and voluntarily, but subject to the will or purpose of another."[16]

Therefore, what becomes important in an undue influence case is to establish that the free agency of the person influenced was taken from him (or her) or destroyed, and in its place the will of another person was substituted.[17] "Motive, opportunity, or even ability to control, in the absence of affirmative evidence that it was exercised, is not sufficient."[18] "Evidence showing only an opportunity to influence and a substantial benefit under the will does not show the exercise of undue influence."[19] Further, undue influence cannot be inferred merely from acts of kindness.[20,21]

MODELS THAT ADDRESS THE PSYCHOLOGICAL PROCESS OF UNDUE INFLUENCE

Because undue influence is essentially a psychological process, various models have been developed in the psychological community to assist in assessing the likelihood of undue influence, including:[22]

- IDEAL[23]
- Cult model[24]

---

[16] Peacock v. DuBois, 105 So. 321, 322 (Fla. 1925).

[17] *Kar*, 399 Mich. at 554 (Levin, J., dissenting).

[18] *In re* Estate of Erickson, 202 Mich. App. 329, 331, 508 N.W.2d 181, 183 (1993).

[19] Holland v. Holland, 277 Ga. 792, 793, 596 S.E.2d 123 (2004) (citing Quarterman v. Quarterman, 268 Ga. 807(2), 493 S.E.2d 146 (1997)).

[20] *In re* Langlois Estate, 361 Mich. 646, 650, 106 N.W.2d 132, 134 (1960).

[21] *But see* Dominic J. Campisi, Evan D. Winet, & Jake Calvert, *Undue Influence: The Gap Between Current Law and Scientific Approaches to Decision-Making and Persuasion*, 43 ACTEC L. J. 359, 372 (2018) (citing Kelly v. First State Bank of Princeton, 81 Ill. App. 3d 402, 414 (Ill. App. Ct. 1980)), despite the court's reluctance to find that such acts represent coercive behavior in the context of family interactions.

[22] Bennet Blum, *Undue Influence – Behavioral Models* (2012) http://www .bennettblummd.com/undue_influence_models.html.

[23] The IDEAL model was developed by Bennett Blum, M.D. IDEAL stands for **I**solation, **D**ependency, **E**motional manipulation and/or **E**xploitation of a vulnerability, **A**cquiescence, and **L**oss.

[24] The Cult model, also known as the "Thought Reform Model," was developed by Margaret Thaler Singer, Ph.D. This model emphasizes social influence conditions that include isolation, fostering a siege mentality, dependency, a sense of powerlessness, manipulation of fears and vulnerabilities, and keeping the victim unaware and uninformed.

- SCAM[25]
- SODR[26]
- The Undue Influence Wheel[27]

These models (and factors identified in them) are discussed in greater detail in chapters 1 and 4. The models are identified here because not only is there a degree of overlap among the models that generally are recognized within the psychological community, but some of these factors have now also been codified into a statutory definition of undue influence.[28]

A STATUTORY DEFINITION OF UNDUE INFLUENCE

In 2014, California codified its new definition of undue influence.[29] This definition was intended to "supplement the common law meaning of undue influence without superseding or interfering with the operation

---

[25] The SCAM model was developed by Dr. Susan Bernatz, Ph.D. This model builds on the work of Singer and Blum but also includes factors that contribute to a victim's "susceptibility." and the model addresses the issue of "active procurement" of the legal or financial transaction. SCAM stands for **S**usceptibility, **C**onfidential Relationship, **A**ctive Procurement, and **M**onetary Loss.

[26] SODR stands for **S**usceptibility of the supposed victim, **O**pportunity for the exertion of undue influence, **D**isposition to exert undue influence, and **R**esult of such undue influence.

[27] The Undue Influence Wheel is sometimes referred to as the Brandle/Heisler/ Stiegel model. The model was developed by Bonnie Brandle, Candice J. Heisler, and Lori A. Stiegel. The Undue Influence Wheel primarily addresses financial exploitation and highlights the typical perpetrator tactics, which include (1) isolating the victim from others and information, (2) creating fear, (3) preying on vulnerabilities, (4) creating dependencies, (5) creating lack of faith in one's own abilities, (6) inducing shame and secrecy, (7) performing intermittent acts of kindness, and (8) keeping the victim otherwise unaware.

[28] In Daniel A. Plotkin, James E. Spar, & Howard L. Horwitz, *Assessing Undue Influence*, 44 J. Am. Acad. Psychiatry Law (2016), http://jaapl.org/content/44/3/344, the authors view the adoption of Cal. Prob. Code § 86 and Cal. Welf. & Inst. Code § 15610.70 as important in helping to define the role of the mental health professional expert in identifying undue influence, which most often lies in addressing the question of the testator's vulnerability to undue influence and often ventures into territory usually addressed by the trier of fact.

[29] Cal. Prob. Code § 86, adopting the same meaning as Cal. Welf. & Inst. Code § 15610.70.

of that law."[30] This new definition reflects that undue influence generally is "excessive persuasion that causes another person to act or refrain from acting by overcoming that person's free will and results in inequity."[31] California's statute now also enumerates factors to consider in determining whether undue influence has occurred, including:

1. The victim's vulnerability, evidence of which may include "incapacity, illness, disability, injury, age, education, impaired cognitive function, emotional distress, isolation or dependency, and whether the influencer knew or should have known of the alleged victim's vulnerability."

2. The influencer's apparent authority, evidence of which may include "status as a fiduciary, family member, care provider, health care professional, legal professional, spiritual advisor, expert, or other qualification."

3. The influencer's conduct, evidence of which may include "(a) Controlling necessaries of life, medication, the victim's interactions with others, access to information, or sleep; (b) Use of affection, intimidation, or coercion; (c) Initiation of changes in personal or property rights, use of haste or secrecy in effecting those changes, effecting changes at inappropriate times and places, and claims of expertise in effecting changes."

4. The equity of the challenged result, evidence of which may include "the economic consequences to the victim, any divergence from the victim's prior intent or course of conduct or dealing, the relationship of the value conveyed to the value of any services or consideration received, or the appropriateness of the change in light of the length and nature of the relationship. . . . Evidence of an inequitable result, without more, is not sufficient to prove undue influence."[32]

However, there is no requirement that all four of the previously referenced factors be present for a court to find that undue influence has

---

[30] A.B. 140, Chapter 668, Legislative Counsel's Digest (Cal. 2013–2014), http://leginfo.legislature.ca.gov/faces/billTextClient.xhtml?bill_id=201320140AB140.

[31] Cal. Welf. & Inst. Code § 15610.70(a).

[32] Michael LaMay, *Undue Influence Defined: New Statutory Definition and Recent Case Law*, Contra Costa Lawyer Online (April 2014), http://cclawyer.cccba.org/2014/04/undue-influence-defined-new-statutory-definition-and-recent-case-law/ (citing Cal. Welf. & Inst. Code § 15610.70(a) (1)-(4)).

occurred. This has led some to opine that the need to consider the identified factors is important from an evidentiary perspective.[33]

An important aspect of the California statute is the recognition that decision-making capacity (and, presumably, vulnerability to undue influence) can be impaired in older adults without apparent cognitive impairment.[34]

The factors identified in the models (and in the California statute) are not all inclusive, nor do they necessarily create a presumption that undue influence has occurred.

---

[33] *See* H.L. Horwitz, *California's New Statutory Definition of Undue Influence: Modernization or Game Changer?* 19 Cal. Trusts Estates Q. 11–18 (2013).

[34] Plotkin, *Assessing Undue Influence, supra* note 27 (citing P.A. Boyle, R.S. Wilson, & L. Yu, et al., *Poor Decision Making Is Associated with an Increased Risk of Mortality Among Community-Dwelling Older Persons Without Dementia*, 40 Neuroepidemiology 247–52 (2013); N.L. Denburg, D. Tranel, & A. Bechara, *The Ability to Decide Advantageously Declines Prematurely in Some Normal Older Persons*, 43 Neuropsychologia 1099–1106 (2005)). *See also* Horwitz, *id.*

CHAPTER 4

Evidence of Undue Influence[1]

Being able to evaluate whether there are signs of possible undue influence is important. Therefore, it can be helpful for planners and litigators alike to be able to identify "indicia" or "red flags," such as those identified in chapters 1 and 3, which could indicate that undue influence may be present. The presumption of undue influence will be discussed at greater length in chapters 6 and 7. The presumption is not the only way to prove that undue influence may have occurred; if the presumption has not or cannot be established to create a *prima facie* case of undue influence, it otherwise may be necessary to prove that undue influence has occurred.[2]

While the presumption generally arises out of a relationship of trust, such relationships are not an element, per se, of undue influence. It is possible for undue influence to exist regardless of whether all the elements of the presumption have been met.[3] Furthermore, because "sufficient" evidence may be presented by the proponent to rebut the presumption, prudence dictates that the challenger not plan on merely relying upon the presumption to prevail.

---

[1] Adapted from an article previously published by BNA: Bloomberg BNA, Sandra D. Glazier, Esq., Thomas M. Dixon, Esq., & Thomas F. Sweeney, Esq., *What Every Estate Planner Should Know About Undue Influence: Recognizing It, Insulating/Planning Against It . . . And Litigating It*, TAX MANAGEMENT MEMORANDUM (2015).

[2] *In re* Estate of Mikeska, 140 Mich. App. 116, 121, 362 N.W.2d 906, 909 (1985).

[3] *Id.*

DIRECT VS. CIRCUMSTANTIAL EVIDENCE

In general, all evidence, both direct and circumstantial, that bears upon the question of undue influence should be admitted.[4] A party may use circumstantial evidence to show undue influence, but the evidence must do more than raise a mere suspicion.[5] Because (as discussed further later) undue influence cases tend to require a longitudinal analysis of the evidence, in such cases, "[e]vidence showing acts of undue influence at a date subsequent to the execution of the will is competent, in connection with other facts and circumstances, in support of the charge of undue influence exerted at the earlier date."[6]

RELEVANT EVIDENCE

But, what is relevant? "Relevant evidence" has been defined as evidence that has any tendency to make the existence of any fact that is of consequence to the determination of the action more probable or less probable than it would be without the evidence.[7] The term "any" indicates that the merest tendency will suffice, which represents a low threshold. This evidentiary rule encourages the admission of arguable relevant evidence proffered and indicates that if reasonable minds could differ about the relevance of a particular item of evidence, it should be considered relevant. Evidence may be relevant because it is direct evidence of the event sought to be proved ("direct evidence"). Alternatively, evidence may be relevant because it is of a quality that leads to an inference that a probable event did or did not occur ("circumstantial evidence"). Generally, all relevant evidence is admissible unless it is excluded by the U.S. Constitution, by a pertinent state Constitution, or by another applicable statute or rule of evidence.[8]

IMPORTANCE OF CIRCUMSTANTIAL EVIDENCE IN UNDUE INFLUENCE LITIGATION

Due to the very nature of undue influence cases, it is recognized that the evidence in such cases is largely circumstantial in nature:

---

[4] *In re* Loree's Estate, 158 Mich. 372, 376, 122 N.W. 623, 624 (1909).

[5] *In re* Willey's Estate, 9 Mich. App. 245, 257, 156 N.W.2d 631, 638 (1967).

[6] Leffingwell v. Bettinghouse, 151 Mich. 513, 518, 115 N.W. 731, 733 (1908).

[7] MICH. R. EVID. (MRE) 401. *See also* FED. R. EVID. (FRE) 401.

[8] Because the attorney-client privilege may be of particular importance in this regard, chapter 12 has been devoted to this issue.

Undoubtedly, circumstantial evidence may be relied on by [challengers] to show undue influence. . . . However, to carry the question to the jury, such circumstantial evidence must be of considerable probative force and, quite clearly, must do more than raise a mere suspicion.[9]

To establish undue influence it must be shown that the grantor was subjected to threats, misrepresentation, undue flattery, fraud, or physical or moral coercion sufficient to overpower volition, destroy free agency and impel the grantor to act against his inclination and free will.[10]

In general, all evidence, both direct and circumstantial, that bears upon the question of undue influence will be deemed admissible: "[A]ll evidence which tends to prove or disprove the main contention that this will was procured by . . . undue influence . . . should be admitted."[11] Moreover, "the evidentiary rules and procedures in probate law strike a balance between honoring a testator's actions while addressing situations where those actions were wrongfully taken. 'Safeguarding freedom of disposition requires the court to invalidate a disposition that was not volitional because it was procured by undue influence.'"[12]

The Restatement (Third) of Property: Wills and Other Donative Transfers § 8.3 cmt. e. explains the use of circumstantial evidence in undue influence cases:

In the absence of direct evidence of undue influence, circumstantial evidence is sufficient to raise an inference of undue influence if the [challenger] proves that (1) the donor was susceptible to undue influence, (2) the alleged wrongdoer had an opportunity to exert undue influence, (3) the alleged wrongdoer had the disposition to exert undue influence, and (4) there was a result appearing to be the effect of undue influence.[13]

Courts also have recognized that indirect proof of undue influence should be allowed due to the difficulty of developing direct proof in such

---

[9] *In re* Willey's Estate, 9 Mich. App. at 257.

[10] *In re* Estate of Karmey, 468 Mich. 68, 75, 658 N.W.2d 796, 799 (2003).

[11] *In re* Loree's Estate, 158 Mich. at 376.

[12] Archer v. Anderson, 556 S.W.3d 228, 235, 61 Tex. Sup. Ct. J. 159 (2018) (internal citations omitted).

[13] RESTATEMENT (THIRD) OF PROP.: WILLS AND OTHER DONATIVE TRANSFERS § 8.3 cmt. e.

claims. Direct evidence and circumstantial evidence of undue influence are both admissible, although direct evidence is less common than circumstantial evidence because of the secretive nature of undue influence. Therefore, in undue influence cases, "[t]he case must be determined generally upon circumstantial evidence. This is necessarily so by reason of the secret and insidious means by which such influence is usually exercised":[14]

> A challenger may prove undue influence by establishing the existence of certain indicators which might be considered Circumstantial Evidence that a confidential relationship may have been abused and the decedent's decision-making process corrupted. Circumstances are deemed "suspicious" based upon a review of the totality of the facts and not any one fact in isolation of others. The Restatement (Third) of Property (Wills & Don. Trans) Section 8.3 cmt. h, provides that: In evaluating whether suspicious circumstances are present, all relevant factors may be considered, including: (1) the extent to which the donor was in a weakened condition, physically, mentally, or both, and therefore susceptible to undue influence; (2) the extent to which the alleged wrongdoer participated in the preparation or procurement of the will or will substitute; (3) whether the donor received independent advice from an attorney or from other competent and disinterested advisors in preparing the will or will substitute; (4) whether the will or will substitute was prepared in secrecy or in haste; (5) whether the donor's attitude toward others had changed by reason of his or her relationship with the wrongdoer; (6) whether there is a decided discrepancy between a new and previous wills or will substitutes of the donor; (7) whether there was a continuity of purpose running through former wills or will substitutes indicating a settled intent in the disposition of his or her property; and (8) whether the disposition of the property is such that a reasonable person would regard it as unnatural, unjust, or unfair, for example, whether the disposition abruptly and without apparent reason disinherited a faithful and deserving family member.[15]

As previously stated, because undue influence is indeed a process and not a single event, a longitudinal view and approach to the evidence often

---

[14] *In re* Loree's Estate, 158 Mich. at 378.
[15] RESTATEMENT (THIRD) OF PROP.: WILLS AND OTHER DONATIVE TRANSFERS § 8.3 cmt. h.

is warranted. Therefore, evidence both before and after the execution of the instrument in question will be deemed relevant. In this regard, even evidence of undue influence that occurred after the date on which the testator made his or her will is relevant and admissible as tending to show a continuance of undue influence.[16]

INDICIA OF UNDUE INFLUENCE

Because of the circumstantial nature of many undue influence cases, it can be important to understand—whether you are an estate planner or a litigator—some of the recognized indicia of possible undue influence. While there is no all-inclusive or exhaustive list of indicia of undue influence, there are some generally recognized indicia. There are common overarching themes to these indicia, but because there is no exhaustive list nor one universally recognized source material, various models have been identified in this book to assist practitioners in understanding the variety of circumstances that might raise concerns that further inquiry may be merited. Even when some of these factors are found to exist such that vulnerability to undue influence may be present, the existence of such vulnerabilities will not necessarily be determinative that undue influence occurred.

In 2008, the Psychogeriatric Association's subcommittee of an international task force identified from a "clinical" perspective some common factors that might alert an expert to the risk of undue influence:[17]

> (i) [S]ocial or environmental risk factors such as dependency, isolation, family conflict and recent bereavement; (ii) psychological and physical risk factors such as physical disability, deathbed wills, sexual bargaining, personality disorders, substance abuse and mental disorders including dementia, delirium, mood and paranoid disorders; and (iii) legal risk factors such as unnatural provisions in a will, or a provision not in keeping with previous wishes of

---

[16] *See* Walts v. Walts, 127 Mich. 607, 610, 611 86 N.W. 1030, 1031 (1901). *Also see Leffingwell,* 151 Mich. *and In re* Vhay's Estate, 225 Mich. 107, 108, 195 N.W. 674 (1923).

[17] Carmelle Peisah, Sanford I. Finkel, Kenneth Shulman, Pamela S. Melding, Jay S. Luxenberg, Jeremia Heinik, Robin J. Jacoby, Barry Reisberg, Gabriela Stoppe, A. Barker, Helen Cristina Torrano Firmino, & Hayley I. Bennett, *The Wills of Older People: Risk Factors for Undue Influence, for* INTERNATIONAL PSYCHOGERIATIC ASSOCIATION TASK FORCE ON WILLS AND UNDUE INFLUENCE, 21 INT. PSYCHOGERIATR., at 7–15, 10, 11 (2009).

the person making the will, and the instigation or procurement of a will by a beneficiary.[18]

The subcommittee found that undue influence was more likely to occur:

(i) [w]here there is a special relationship in which the testator invests significant trust or confidence in another; (ii) where there is relative isolation (whether due to physical factors or communication difficulties) which limit free flow of information and allows subtle distortion of the truth: and, (iii) where there is vulnerability to influence through impaired mental capacity or emotional circumstances (such as withholding of affection, or persuasion on grounds of social, cultural or religious convention or obligation).[19]

In regard to the "special relationship," an elderly cognitively impaired person might be adversely influenced by a person who was (1) a cohabiting family member, such as an adult child; (2) a non-resident child; (3) a helpful neighbor or friend; (4) a formal or informal care provider; (5) a more distant family member; (6) a "suitor" who may or may not become a de facto partner or spouse, and who generally is significantly younger and cognitively intact; or, (7) professionals such as attorneys, clergy, doctors, accountants, or police officers.[20] It is even possible for multiple people to be involved in the "influence" process.[21]

Where an individual is cognitively or emotionally vulnerable, influence that is "less coercive" might be determined to be "undue."[22] By way of example, ". . . a person in the last days or hours of life may have become so weak and feeble that very little influence will be sufficient to bring about the desired result."[23]

Some social circumstances might actually enhance the possibility of undue influence. These include (1) sequestration and isolation of the impaired person such that outside contact is inhibited, (2) previously trusted individuals might no longer be favored or trusted by the cognitively

---

[18] *Id.* at 7.
[19] *Id.* at 10.
[20] *Id.* at 10.
[21] *Id.* at 10.
[22] *Id.* at 8.
[23] *Id.* at 8 (citing Wingrove v. Wingrove (1885) LR 11 PD 81, 82–83).

impaired decedent, (3) family conflict, and (4) physical or psychological dependency on a person who renders care.[24]

Psychological factors that might enhance the possibility of adverse influences include (1) loneliness, (2) sexual bargaining, (3) emotional vulnerability to the influence of others, (4) highly "medicalized" or acute care settings, (5) family dynamics that feed on a sense of guilt, martyrdom, anxiety, or fear of abandonment, (6) mourning and grief associated with the loss of a powerful relationship, (7) persons who are excessively dependent, (8) chemical dependency, (9) a myriad of mental disorders, such as delirium, dementia, chronic schizophrenia, paranoia, or depression, or (10) other cognitive impairments.[25]

Other factors may increase an individual's vulnerability to undue influence. These factors could include such things as other adverse life events, inexperience, naiveté, being a trusting person, lacking knowledge about financial matters, being fearful, being uninformed, loneliness, isolation, immigration status, inability to speak English, or exhaustion.[26] "Under the right circumstances anyone can be unduly influenced."[27]

It may be important to note that while certain cognitive impairments that create fertile ground for suspicious or paranoid ideation may make an individual more amenable to undue influence, it may also protect them from such influence.[28] Consequently, a person's suspicions (founded or otherwise) that people are trying to take advantage of them might, in certain circumstances, counteract attempts to unduly influence that individual.

Some key terms to consider when reviewing materials about "risk factors" are:

- *Vulnerability*, which can relate to the individual's age, mental, or physical condition.[29]

---

[24] *Id.* at 10.

[25] *Id.* at 11, 12.

[26] Bonnie Brandle, Candice J. Heisler, & Lori A. Stiegel, *The Parallels Between Undue Influence, Domestic Violence, Stalking, and Sexual Assault*, 17 J. ELDER ABUSE NEGL. 37, 39 (2005).

[27] *Id.*

[28] Peisah, *The Wills of Older People, supra* note 17, at 13.

[29] The National Academy of Sciences published a comprehensive study regarding the decline of mental ability as part of the aging process. *See* Dominic J. Campisi, Evan D. Winet, & Jake Calvert, *Undue Influence: The Gap Between Current Law and Scientific Approaches to Decision-Making and Persuasion*, 43 ACTEC L. J. 359, 372 (2018) (citing Dan G. Blazer, et al., eds., *Cognitive Aging: Progress in Understanding*

- *Isolation*, which need not be imposed by another, but may be the natural result of technological or other challenges or other conditions.
- *Lack of independent advice or counsel*, which can be the result of, among other things, who contacted, arranged for, and communicated with the lawyer, and whether counsel breached a duty of loyalty to the individual. It can include even whether counsel took sufficient steps to ensure the capacity of the individual and the independence of the plan that was generated.
- *Conduct of the beneficiary*, which may relate to patterns of behavior or the actions of the beneficiary before, during, and after the execution of the instrument.

The ABA Commission on Law and Aging and the American Psychological Association (APA) interdisciplinary task force recognized that there are some factors that may create a predisposition for financial exploitation. Per *A Handbook for Psychologists* ("the Psychologist Handbook"), generated by the task force,[30] these may include such factors as:

- Advanced age (over age 75)
- Unmarried, widowed, or divorced
- Organic brain damage
- Cognitive impairment
- Physical, mental, or emotional dysfunction (especially depression)
- Recent loss of a spouse or divorce
- Living with or dependent on an abuser
- Living alone
- Social isolation
- Estrangement from children
- Financial independence, with no designated financial caretaker
- In the middle- or upper-income bracket
- Taking multiple medications
- Frailty
- Fear of change in living situation

---

and Opportunities for Action, COMM. ON PUB. HEALTH DIMENSIONS OF COGNITIVE AGING, INST. OF MED. OF THE NAT'L ACADS. (April 2015) *and* Mary Joy Quinn, et al., *Developing an Undue Influence Screening Tool for Adult Protective Services*, 29 J ELDER ABUSE & NEGL. 57–185 (2016).

[30] ABA COMMN. ON L. & AGING & AM. PSYCHOLOGICAL ASSN., ASSESSMENT OF OLDER ADULTS WITH DIMINISHED CAPACITY: A HANDBOOK FOR PSYCHOLOGISTS, at 52–102 (2008).

- Implied promise by perpetrator to care for elderly person if funds or material goods are transferred
- Being elderly and subject to deception (misrepresentation or concealment of information for selfish gain)
- Being elderly and subject to intimidation (perpetrator induces dependency with fear of rejection if demands are not met, or creates fear by threat of physical or emotional harm or abandonment)

The Psychologist Handbook also points to certain characteristics of persons who might exploit the elderly. The characteristics may include but are not limited to any number of the following:

- Caregiving relationship to the elderly person
- Instilling a sense of helplessness and dependency
- Isolation of the elderly person from family members and other social contacts
- Presentation of self as a protector of the elderly victim while isolating them from others
- Enhancement of inadequacies and diminished self-worth in victim, making him or her more vulnerable
- History of multiple unstable relationships
- Falsified credentials or embellishment of personal power, role, or position
- Opportunistic
- Psychologically dysfunctional
- Predatory
- Antisocial, with little regard for rights of others
- Methodically identifies victims and establishes power and total control over them
- Gains control of assets through deceit, intimidation, and psychological abuse

The Psychologist Handbook also describes certain signs and symptoms that are suggestive of undue influence, such as:

- Elderly person's actions are inconsistent with past long-standing values and beliefs.
- Older person makes sudden changes in financial management that enriches one individual.
- Elderly person changes his will or disposition of assets, belongings, property, and directs assets toward one who is not a natural "object of his bounty."

- Caretaker dismisses previous professionals and directs the elderly person to new ones (e.g., bankers, stockbrokers, lawyers, physicians, realtors).
- Elderly person is isolated from family, friends, community, and other stable relationships.
- Non-family caretaker moves into the home or takes control of elderly person's daily schedule.
- Older person directs income flow to caretaker.
- Will, living will, or power of attorney or trust is altered, with new caretaker or friend as beneficiary/executor/power holder/trustee.
- Elderly person develops a mistrust of family members, particularly about financial affairs, with this view supported by new friend, acquaintance, or caretaker.
- Older person finds new caretaker, who guarantees lifelong care if he or she gives the caretaker his or her assets.
- Elderly person is in a relationship that is characterized by power imbalance between parties, with caretaker assuming restrictive control and dominance.
- Caretaker or friend accompanies the elderly person to most important transactions, not leaving him or her alone to speak for himself or herself.
- Elderly person increasingly is helpless, frightened, or despondent, feeling that only the caretaker can prevent his or her further decline.
- Elderly person sees acquaintance or caretaker as exalted, with unusual powers or influence.
- Legal risk factors such as unnatural provisions in a will or provisions are not in keeping with previously expressed wishes of the person making the will, and the instigation or procurement of a will by a beneficiary (commonly referred to as "active procurement").

MODELS THAT ADDRESS SOME OF THE PSYCHOLOGICAL FEATURES OF UNDUE INFLUENCE

As alluded to in earlier chapters, various recognized models have been established to assist in understanding, analyzing, and developing the requisite factual basis pertinent to undue influence cases. A working knowledge of these models may assist the litigator in the development of themes and strategies in the case. Five of these models were identified in chapter 3. Two of those models, the IDEAL and SODR models, are discussed here in more detail.

The IDEAL Model

The IDEAL model, promoted by Dr. Bennett Blum, is just one of the prominently developed and marketed models relating to the "indicia" or "red flags" of undue influence. Dr. Blum identifies and explains the IDEAL acronym:[31]

Isolation – This refers to isolation from pertinent information, friends, relatives, or usual advisors. Causes can include medical disorders, a history of poor relationships with others, perpetrator interference, geographic changes (e.g., travel) and technological isolation (e.g., loss of telephone service or of the ability to communicate in that fashion).

Dependency – This refers to dependence on the perpetrator, such as for physical support, emotional factors, or for information.

Emotional manipulation or exploitation of a weakness – This often is manifested as a combination of promises and threats regarding either issues of safety and security or companionship and friendship. Perpetrators sometimes make use of a victim's weakness or vulnerabilities. It is not unusual to encounter cases in which, for example, a perpetrator provides alcohol to an alcoholic or has him execute documents, despite knowing that the victim is mentally impaired due to the acute or long-term effects of alcohol. Or, a perpetrator might have a vision-impaired person sign a legal document, or misrepresent documents and their consequences to the cognitively impaired individual.

Acquiescence – This refers to the victim's apparent consent or submission. The act is not truly voluntary but is instead the product of inaccurate, misleading, or deceptive information that is believed due to the victim's impairments or relationship with the perpetrator.

Loss – This refers to damages, such as *inter vivos* financial loss.[32]

---

[31] Bennet Blum, *Undue Influence Models – IDEAL* (2012) http://www.bennettblummd .com/undue_influence_ideal_model.html.

[32] "Loss" can also refer to the loss of one's unencumbered ability to dispose of all or part of one's property as he or she sees fit. As such, a change in dispositive provisions (whether in estate planning documents, beneficiary designations, or the creation of remainder interests) can satisfy the "loss" element. *See* People v. Owsley, 2013 IL. App. (1st) 111975, 996 N.E.2d 118, 374 Ill. Dec. 671 (2013).

According to leading forensic psychiatric experts Dr. Sanford Finkel and Dr. Bennett Blum, the more "red flag indicia"[33] or "suspicious circumstances"[34] of undue influence, the more likely undue influence might be found to have occurred. This might be akin to the analogy that "where there is smoke there is fire" or the proverb that "if it walks like a duck, quacks like a duck, and looks like a duck, it must be a duck."

The SODR Model

A 2010 study[35] that essentially adopted the SODR model formed the premise (at least in part) for the enactment of California's statutory definition of undue influence when it was found that:

> . . . [d]espite wide variations in the context and circumstances in which [undue influence] and coercive persuasion in general have been explored, the elements of [undue influence] are remarkably similar in each and can be reduced to four salient factors: susceptibility (of the victim), opportunity (of the influencer), disposition (of the influencer), and result.[36]

In addition, the neuropsychological paradigm included in California's Due Process in Competency Determination Act,[37] which focuses on alertness, attention, information processing, thought processes, short-term and working memory, problems with comprehension, and the ability to modulate mood and effect also may provide some assistance in assessing the potential existence of cognitive issues that might make an individual more vulnerable to undue influence.[38]

---

[33] Peisah, *The Wills of Older People, supra* note 17.

[34] Peisah, *The Wills of Older People, supra* note 17; Blum, *supra.*

[35] Mary Joy Quinn, Lisa Nerenberg, et al., *Undue Influence: Definitions and Applications*, report for THE BORCHARD FOUNDATION CENTER ON LAW & AGING (March 2010).

[36] Daniel A. Plotkin, James E. Spar, & Howard L. Horwitz, *Assessing Undue Influence*, 44 J. AM. ACAD. PSYCHIATRY LAW 344–351 (September 2016), http://jaapl.org /content/44/3/344.

[37] CAL. PROB. CODE § 810–813.

[38] *See* Dominic J. Campisi, Evan D. Winet, & Jake Calvert, *Undue Influence: The Gap Between Current Law and Scientific Approaches to Decision-Making and Persuasion*, 43 ACTEC L. J. 362, 363 (2018).

A study on the psychology of persuasion identified several (additional) categories of tactics that persuaders may employ to effect undue influence for financial gain.[39] Among the tactics identified, generally applicable to estate planning situations, are "reciprocity," "commitment and consistency," "authority," and the creation of or taking advantage of "false memories":

Reciprocity: The "reciprocity" principle entails creating a debt of gratitude. While courts are reticent to apply this principle in family dynamics, it has been found that "[i]f kindness and affection result in overcoming the testator's free agency and leave the will that of the beneficiary rather than the testator, then such constitutes undue influence."[40]

Commitment and consistency: When the "commitment and consistency" process is used, persuaders exploit the internal and interpersonal pressures often felt by individuals to justify and stand by decisions once made. Here, the persuader makes it easy for the victim to make a commitment. This tactic can be successful even with persons described as "strong-willed" or "stubborn." Once such individuals make a commitment, they tend to stick to it. Therefore, after the commitment that benefits the persuader is made, the victim is encouraged to follow through. In addition, by using this process, a "stubborn" individual may be persuaded to adopt negative perceptions of others and the belief that others are undeserving of an inheritance. Once the victim incorporates such beliefs as "facts," the "commitment and consistency" principle can make it difficult to overcome such perceptions and convince the victim that the contrary may be true.[41]

Authority: Most people have a respect for authority and a disinclination to defy authority. When the "authority" process is used, the persuader attempts to clothe himself with the trappings of authority or to recruit others, including professionals, to aid and abet the persuader, whose authority (on its own or by such affiliation) benefits the persuader's efforts for financial gain. This process abuses the perception of authority, whether that perception is created by title, education, or attire. In the context of estate planner, the

---

[39] *Id.* at 371–380 (citing the psychological study by Robert B. Cialdini, *Influence: The Psychology of Persuasion*).

[40] Kelley v. First State Bank of Princeton, 81 Ill. App. 3rd 402, 414 (Ill. App. Ct. 1980), 401 N.E.2d 247, 256 (1980).

[41] Campisi, *Undue Influence, supra* note 37, at 373, 374.

persuader "will often take steps to place himself in control of the testator's finances or estate plan and then represent to the testator that he must sign off on modification or transactions because they are necessary. . . ."[42] This process abuses the trust that the victim has placed in others.

False memories: Without being ageist, studies have indicated that the elderly may be more vulnerable than capable adults to the creation of false memories, which can be induced by repetitive efforts of a predator to reframe the elder's relationship with family members or other previously favored individuals or institutions.[43]

OTHER CONSIDERATIONS

The existence of a significant number of these "circumstances" or "indicia" may well be persuasive that "probable cause" for a contest exists, as well as indicative that influence has been exerted. Nonetheless, it is equally important to remember that undue influence cases are extremely fact-specific, and the existence of a single countervailing factor may significantly affect the outcome of the case. Therefore, the mere existence of such "red flags" or indicia is not necessarily determinative that the influence was "undue" such that the will of an individual has been supplanted by another. Moreover, a single mitigating or countervailing fact may be sufficient to establish the independence of the plan created.

In the development of one's pre-trial, discovery, and trial strategies, a thorough understanding of the indicia and potential impact of cognitive deficits, dependency, and impairments on the facts and circumstances of your case is paramount. Again, because cognitive impairments may not result in a lack of capacity, the tedious effort of understanding such impairments (to the extent they exist) in a particular case can be very important.

---

[42] *Id.* at 377, 378.
[43] *Id.* at 367, 368.

CHAPTER 5

Fraud and Duress Are Different Than Undue Influence

A contestant challenging a will, trust, beneficiary designation, gift, or other transfer of property often pleads the contest on multiple grounds. These grounds may include claims of undue influence, fraud, and duress. Courts have long recognized that there is a distinction between undue influence and fraud.[1] While duress is a separate cause of action,[2] in these types of cases, lawyers and courts often both misapply the term "duress" to conduct that technically does not fit within the legal definition of "duress." In common usage, the term "duress" often has a broader meaning that is similar to "coercion" or "coercive persuasion." However, it is the distinct legal meaning of the word that applies to a claim that an instrument or action was executed under "duress." Nonetheless, attorneys and courts use the term "duress" to describe coercive conduct in support of undue influence that may not meet the legal definition of the term "duress."

As in the case of undue influence, a challenge based on fraud or duress is dependent on the testator, settlor, transferor, or donor having sufficient capacity to execute the instrument or the action being challenged. If such capacity does not exist, the instrument or action is void *ab initio*, regardless of whether fraud or duress exists.

---

[1] Howe v. Palmer, 80 Mass. App. Ct. 736, 956 N.E.2d 249 (2011); Peffer v. Bennet, 523 F2d 1323 (10th Circ. 1975); *In re* Johnson's Estate, 326 Mich. 310; 40 N.W.2d 163 (1949); *In re* Chinsky's Estate, 150 Misc. 274, 288 N.Y.S. 666 (Sur. Ct. 1934); Gockel v. Gockel, 66 S.W. 867, 92 A.L.R. 784 (Mo 1933); Worth v. Pierson, 208 Iowa 353 (1929); Stolle v. Kanetzky 259 S.W. 657 (1924 Tex. Civ. App. – Austin); Murphy v. Hoagland, 32 Ky. L. Rep. 839, 101 S.W. 303 (1908).

[2] Estate of McKenna, 500 S.W.3d 850 (Mo. App. E.D.) (2016).

FRAUD

The essential elements of fraud are (1) a material representation, (2) the representation is false, (3) the representation is known to be false or is made recklessly without any knowledge of its truth as a positive assertion, (4) the representation is made with the intention that the other party would act on it, (5) the other party acts based on the representation, and (6) the other party is damaged by relying on the representation.[3]

To establish fraud in the inducement of a will, one court has identified six elements that should be proved:

1. Willful false statements were made to the testator.
2. The statements were made by a beneficiary under the will that was induced.
3. The statements were intended to deceive the testator.
4. The testator was actually deceived.
5. The statements actually induced the testator to make a will.
6. The testator would not have made the induced will absent the false statements.[4]

With respect to wills (which should be equally applicable to trusts, beneficiary designations, and other donative transfers), three circumstances have been identified as encompassing most fraud claims:

1. The testator, settlor, transferor, or donor may make a devise or gift or take another action, the motive for which is induced by deceit, either on the part of the devisee, transferee, or donee, or on the part of a third person.
2. The testator, settlor, transferor, or donor signs an instrument without reading it or it was not read to such person, which contains a transfer of property which the testator, settlor, transferor, or donor is unaware of.
3. The testator, settlor, transferor, or donor is prevented or dissuaded through fraudulent misrepresentation from making or amending a will, trust, or other instrument, or from taking or not taking any donative action.[5]

---

[3] Beuschel Trust v. Beuschel, 2014 WL 6679306 (Mich. App. Nov 25 2014), at 4 (citing with approval Zaremba Equipment, Inc v. Harco National Insurance Company, 280 Mich. App. 16, 38, 39, 761 N.W.2d 151, 165, *lv. denied*, 495 Mich. 947 (2014)).

[4] Himmelfarb v. Greenspoon, 411 A.2d 979, 983 (App. D.C. 1980) (citing WILLIAM HERBERT PAGE, 1 A TREATISE ON THE LAW OF WILLS § 179, at 353 (1941)).

[5] Joseph Warren, *Fraud, Undue Influence, and Mistake in Wills*, 41 HARVARD LAW REV. 309 1 (1928).

Although fraud and undue influence are not identical and are distinct causes of action, they are closely associated; elements of fraud sometimes are part of an undue influence case. However, "[u]ndue influence does not embrace every species of fraud."[6] Misrepresentation is an essential element of fraud, but misrepresentation is not an essential element of undue influence.

Fraud has been described as consisting of the use of false statements or other deceptions for the purpose of defrauding another person. Although undue influence is a species of fraud and misrepresentations may be used in the commission of undue influence, undue influence may be exercised without any actual fraud being committed.[7] An alleged victim of deceit may have acted voluntarily without having that victim's free will subjugated to the will of the alleged perpetrator.[8] In describing the difference between undue influence and fraud, one court has stated that "fraud deceives the mind whereas undue influence overpowers it."[9] Misrepresentation also can be an important element in an undue influence case when it is used to substitute the free will of the alleged victim with the free will of the alleged perpetrator. As in the case of duress, attorneys and courts sometimes use the word "fraud" to describe conduct that may not meet the technical legal meaning of "fraud" instead of using the word "misrepresentation," which may more appropriately describe the deceitful misconduct that took place. Whether there is both undue influence and fraud in a given situation depends on whether the facts support both conclusions.

Another distinction between undue influence and fraud is the manner in which these actions often take place. Undue influence usually is a process that involves a course of conduct over a period of time, and which involves numerous interactions between the alleged perpetrator and the alleged victim. Over the course of time, the perpetrator gradually obtains control and begins to subjugate the victim's free will to the perpetrator's will. The commission of fraud often occurs over a short period and may involve as few as one or a limited number of interactions between the alleged perpetrator and the alleged victim. A common factor in both undue influence and fraud situations is that vulnerable adults may be more susceptible to victimization.

An additional distinction between proving undue influence as opposed to fraud is the role of a presumption. In most states, there is a presumption

---

[6]   Herster v. Herster, 122 Pa. 239 (1889).

[7]   *In re* Ricks, 160 Cal. 467, 117 P 139 (1911).

[8]   Shirley v. Ezell, 130 Ala. 352, 30 So. 456 (1913).

[9]   *In re* Hollis' Will, 234 Iowa 761, 12 N.W.2d 163 (1949).

of undue influence that may apply, although the elements of the presumption may vary.[10] If the claim is based solely on fraud, there is less case law to support a presumption of fraud, although if there are facts that support a "badge of fraud," these often will support at least an inference of an intent to defraud.[11] While badges of fraud typically involve an action to defraud a creditor, the existence of one or more of these factors may create such an inference in a case involving property transfers pursuant to a last will, trust, beneficiary designation, or exercise of a power of attorney. Badges of fraud include a close relationship between the parties to the alleged fraudulent transaction, inadequacy of consideration, and the receipt or retention of the property after the transaction by the transferor or transferee.[12] "Badges of fraud are not conclusive, but are more or less strong or weak, according to their nature and the number occurring in the same case, and may be overcome by evidence establishing the bona fides of the transaction. However, a concurrence of several badges will always make a strong case."[13] Furthermore, in a "fraud" case, as opposed to an "undue influence" case, with elements of misrepresentation, the burden of proof may require "clear and convincing" evidence.

In some states, courts have determined that there was a presumption of fraud or *prima facie* evidence of fraud. In one case, the Virginia Supreme Court determined that where a scrivener having a position of trust and confidence made a will benefiting the scrivener's wife, there was a presumption of fraud, which shifted the burden of producing evidence to rebut the presumption to the proponent.[14] The court also noted that the presumption of fraud was supported by suspicious circumstances, including the elimination of a prior beneficiary, the scrivener's failure to send a draft of the will to the testator in advance, not reading the will to the testator, and not observing the testator reading the will. In reversing the dismissal of the fraud claim and remanding the case to the trial court, the Virginia Supreme Court also upheld the trial court's determination that there was insufficient evidence to support a presumption of undue influence. At least in Virginia, it appears

---

[10] The presumption of undue influence is discussed in greater depth in chapters 6 and 7.

[11] New Englander Capital Corp. v. Zises, 60 Misc 3d 659, 665, 79 N.Y.S.3d 502, 506, 507 (2018).

[12] *Id.* at 507.

[13] Bentley v. Caille, 289 Mich. 74, 78, 286 N.W. 163, 164 (1939) (citations omitted).

[14] Carter v. Williams, 246 Va. 53, 58, 431 S.E.2d 297, 300 (1993).

that there may be a presumption of fraud similar to a presumption of undue influence in terms of shifting the burden of producing evidence. In an unpublished Michigan case[15] involving a disputed conveyance of jointly held real property to a trust, the court cited an earlier case[16] that found that the establishment of the key elements of fraud will be *prima facie*[17] evidence of fraud.[18] This conclusion appears to be comparable to a presumption of fraud.

One further distinction between a claim for undue influence and a claim based on fraud relates to the applicable statute of limitation. Fraud claims can be asserted during a period after discovery of the alleged fraud notwithstanding the prior running of the statute of limitations because the statute may be tolled prior to discovery. The tolling of the statute of limitations under a fraud claim offers the challenger a possible alternative remedy if the limitations period for an undue influence claim has expired. Similarly, a fraud claim keeps open for the proponent the risk of a challenge based on fraud if there are facts that support such a claim.

While acts of undue influence may be (but aren't required to be) intentional, fraud is essentially an intentional tort.[19] Therefore, to support a claim of fraud, one must generally establish intent.[20] However, fraud may also be established where a party acts in culpable ignorance as to the truth or falsity of an assertion.[21] In addition to proving the existence of a misrepresentation of a material fact, generally, reliance also must be established.[22] While the burden of proof that's required for a contestant to establish the elements of undue influence is generally by a preponderance of the evidence,[23] the burden required to establish the elements of fraud in the procurement of a

---

[15] *Beuschel,* 2014 WL 6679306 at 5.

[16] Mallery v. Van Hoeven, 322 Mich. 561, 52 N.W.2d 341 (1952).

[17] Wex Legal Dictionary/Encyclopedia. *Prima facie* may be used as an adjective to establish a fact or raise a presumption unless disproved or rebutted.

[18] *Beuschel,* 2014 WL 6679306 at 5.

[19] City of Atascadero v. Merrill Lynch, Pierce, Fenner & Smith, 68 Cal. App. 4th 445, 482, 80 Cal. Rptr. 2d 329 (1998).

[20] *Id. See also* Michigan Model Civil Jury Instructions (M. Civ. J.I.) 170.46 and 179.12.

[21] Perlman v. Time, Inc., 64 Ill. App. 3d 190, 380 N.E.2d 1040, 1045, 20 Ill. Dec. 831, 836 (1st Dist. 1978).

[22] Gerill v. Jack L. Hargrove Builders, 128 Ill.2d 179, 538 N.E.2d 530, 536; 131 Ill. Dec. 155, 161 (1989).

[23] *See* Illinois Pattern Jury Instructions - Civil 200.02A *Notes on Use* and 21.01. *See also* M. Civ. J.I. 179.44 and 179.10.

will or trust in some states may require clear and convincing evidence.[24] In Michigan, the burden of proof generally required in fraud cases is clear and convincing evidence, but in cases involving the use of fraud to procure a will or trust, the preponderance of evidence standard applies.[25]

Because of the insidious nature of undue influence, a clear and convincing standard would be an insurmountable burden. Undue influence is a process whereby a settlor's intent is corrupted and the will of another supplants that of the settlor:

> Undue influence is not a one-time act; it involves a pattern of manipulative behaviors to get a victim to do what the exploiter wants, even when the victim's actions appear to be voluntary or are contrary to his or her previous beliefs, wishes, and actions.[26]

Nonetheless, depending on the facts and circumstances, fraud may remain a viable means of invalidating an instrument. An example of fraud that has occurred in reported cases is the proposal by the alleged perpetrator that he or she should be named as the "representative devisee" under the alleged victim's will or trust.[27] The same type of fraud could arise if the perpetrator becomes a "joint tenant" under a joint account based on a representation to the alleged victim that he or she would divide the joint account among the intended beneficiaries but fails to do so. In both situations, the alleged perpetrator misrepresents that such a beneficiary designation or joint ownership will facilitate the future distribution of the property to the intended beneficiaries. After the alleged victim's death, the alleged perpetrator has full control of the property and is under no legal compulsion to carry out the intended devises. Another example is providing a will or trust to a testator or settlor who is not able to read the instrument or who does not in fact read the instrument. In these circumstances, there can be a question of whether the alleged victim knew and agreed with the dispositive

---

[24] *See* Illinois Pattern Jury Instructions - Civil 800.02B to 800.03. Further, M. Civ. J.I. 179.12 recognizes that when a challenge to a trust is premised upon fraud in the procurement, a separate jury instruction (different from that related to undue influence) is required.

[25] Compare M. Civ. J.I. 150.51 and 179.20 to M. Civ. J.I. 128.01 and 128.02.

[26] Bonnie Brandle, Candice J. Heisler, & Lori A. Stiegel, *The Parallels Between Undue Influence, Domestic Violence, Stalking, and Sexual Assault*, 17 J. Elder Abuse Negl. 38 (2005).

[27] Gordon v. Burris, 153 Mo. 223, 54 S.W. 546 (1899); Davis v. Calvert, 5 G. & J. 269 (Md. 1833).

provisions or understood the purpose of the dispositive provisions, particularly if they benefit the alleged perpetrator or the perpetrator's family or principal, above and beyond what the victim intended.

DURESS

As noted earlier, duress is sometimes asserted by a challenger as an alternative basis to an undue influence claim. Generally, duress exists when the alleged perpetrator, through certain generally defined unlawful acts, forces the alleged victim to perform an act under circumstances that deprive the victim of the exercise of free will. "While the equitable principles of duress and undue influence are frequently pled together, they are not the same, and a party may have legitimate strategic reasons based on facts or law to plead and prove one but not the other. To claim duress a person must be so oppressed from the *wrongful* conduct of another as to deprive him of free will."[28] "[T]o succeed with respect to a claim for duress, [the challengers] must establish that they were illegally compelled or coerced to act by fear of serious injury to their persons, reputations or fortunes."[29] "The question as to what constitutes duress is a matter of law, but whether duress exists in a particular case is a question of fact. The term 'duress' as it is used by the law, means such violence or threats made by the party or some person acting for or through him, or by his advice or counsel, as are calculated to produce, on a person of ordinary intelligence a just fear of injury to person."[30] "The test is not the nature of the threats, but rather . . . whether or not the [victim] really had a choice, whether the victim had the freedom of exercising [her] will."[31] "The threat must be of such character as to destroy the free agency of the party to whom it is directed. It must overcome his will and cause him to do that which he would otherwise not do, and which he was not legally bound to do."[32] The threat must be imminent and the victim must not be able to protect himself.[33] The "[f]ear of financial ruin is insufficient to establish economic duress; it must be established that the person applying coercion acted unlawfully."[34]

---

[28] *McKenna*, 500 S.W.3d at 856 (citations omitted).

[29] Farm Credit Servs, PCA v. Weldon, 232 Mich. App. 662, 681–682, 591 N.W.2d 438, 447 (1998), *cert. denied*, 529 U.S. 1021 (2000).

[30] Estate of Adams, 547 S.W.3d 545, 551 (Ky. Ct. App. 2018).

[31] Kremer v. Kremer, 912 N.W.2d 617, 628 (Minn. App. 2006).

[32] Bailey v. Arlington Bank and Trust, 693 S.W.2d 787, 788 (Tex. Ct. App. – Fort Worth 1985).

[33] *Id.* at 788.

[34] *Farm Credit Servs*, 232 Mich. App. at 682.

There are only a few reported cases in which the legal term "duress" has independently supported a challenge to an estate planning instrument or action. In an early case, a court examined a transfer of real property to an irrevocable trust made by an older man who was infatuated with a younger woman. The transfer provided only a lifetime annuity to the older man and the remainder to family members. The transfer to the trust was made at the request of the older man's son, who threatened to have the father placed under guardianship if the transfer to the trust was not made. The court voided the transfer as having been made under duress.[35] Another duress case involved the threat of criminal prosecution to persuade the threatened party to sign an agreement that was favorable to the party making the threat.[36] A further example of duress in a situation involving estate planning was a threat to call off a wedding shortly before it occurred, unless a prenuptial agreement that limited spousal rights upon the party's death was signed.[37] In a similar fact pattern, the court determined that a prenuptial agreement that limited inheritance rights, signed by one party having been counseled by an inexperienced attorney hired by the other party under a short timeframe before the wedding, should be set aside on the basis of duress.[38]

Duress, not to be confused with coercive persuasion in an undue influence situation, usually requires an illegal act, such as a threat of death, bodily injury, or damage to reputation or fortune. Accordingly, the indicia of duress generally include direct evidence of the underlying threat to the alleged victim or family member of the alleged victim, resulting in the granting of a benefit to the alleged perpetrator. Although other suspicious circumstances, such as those described in preceding chapters, may be simultaneously at work, the existence of an illegally compelled or coerced act as a result of a threat or fear of serious bodily injury or death, or of serious damage to the victim's reputation or fortune, is an essential element for a challenge to invalidate an instrument or action taken on the basis of duress as legally defined.

Notwithstanding the technical meaning of "duress," reported undue influence or fraud cases involving estate planning instruments and actions frequently use the term "duress" as a substitute for the terms "coercion" or "coercive persuasion." These cases often are describing excessive pressure or threats to influence a person to take or decline to take action, although

---

[35] Hogan v. Leeper, 37 Okla. 655, 133 P 190 (1913).
[36] *McKenna*, 500 S.W.3d at 135.
[37] *Kremer*, 912 N.W.2d at 628.
[38] Estate of Hollett, 150 N.H. 39, 45, 834 A.2d 378 (2003).

they lack the threat of serious injury to their person, reputation, or fortune. As noted earlier, cases have found duress when there is a threat to
commence a criminal prosecution unless the demanded action occurs.
This situation appears to fall within the traditional legal meaning of duress.
Whether the threat of guardianship as an inducement to establish and fund
a trust amounts to duress will depend upon the facts, because it does not
appear to fall within the traditional legal meaning of duress. The same can
be said for the refusal at the eleventh hour to go through with a wedding
ceremony unless one party signs a prenuptial agreement substantially disin-
heriting the other party in the case of death.

As with undue influence, and sometimes with fraud, duress likely will
occur when the alleged victim is in a vulnerable state and the threat is
immediate and drastic, so that the victim succumbs to the threat of serious
injury or death or the loss of reputation or fortune. However, unlike undue
influence or fraud, the victim may have none of the vulnerabilities commonly associated with an alleged victim in those situations and may have
full testamentary, mental, and physical capacity. Examples of duress include
the threat of death or serious bodily injury to the victim or a family member, or blackmail or extortion, such as a threat of exposing information that
could seriously damage the alleged victim's reputation or business. These
facts alone, without the existence of other common vulnerabilities, may be
sufficient for a challenger to argue successfully that an instrument or action
and the resulting benefit to the alleged perpetrator should be invalidated
on the basis of duress.

There are a limited number of circumstances, described earlier, in
which legally defined duress will support a challenger's efforts to void an
instrument or action taken by the testator, settlor, transferor, or donor. Acts
of coercion and threats are more likely to be indicators of undue influence,
unless there is a serious threat to the person, reputation, or fortune.[39] Unlike
undue influence, there is no presumption of duress. In cases where excessive
coercion is applied to the alleged victim, courts may refer to such conduct
as duress in concluding that the alleged victim has been unduly influenced.

The variation in court opinions on the meaning of the terms "fraud"
and "duress," when coupled with the term "undue influence," may be indicative of a court's reliance upon multiple grounds when it determines that
a challenged instrument or act did not reflect the alleged victim's free will.
Nevertheless, undue influence, fraud, and duress also are separate causes
of action for challenging suspicious instruments or transactions.

---

[39] M. Civ. J.I. 142.40.

CHAPTER 6

The Presumption of Undue Influence[1]

As indicated in chapter 4, the existence of elements that constitute the presumption of undue influence can be sufficient indicia that undue influence has occurred. When all the elements of this presumption are met, a *prima facie* case of undue influence sufficient to withstand a dispositive motion generally is established. So, what is the presumption? In the most general terms, it is an evidentiary construct used by courts in recognition of the psychological process that can result from the abuse of a fiduciary or confidential relationship. There are other presumptions that generally are recognized to exist in estate planning arena. The four prominent presumptions are:

a. **Presumption of due execution**: A person is presumed to have duly executed estate planning documents; hence, the burden of proving irregularities in the execution of such documents initially falls upon the challenger to an instrument.

b. **Presumption of sufficient capacity**: A person is presumed to have sufficient capacity to execute an estate planning document, unless they have previously been legally determined to lack capacity, thereby placing the initial burden of proving lack of capacity upon the challenger of an instrument.

c. **Presumption of validity**: Importantly, in the absence of a finding that the presumption of undue influence exists, duly executed instruments generally are presumed to be valid. It is this very

---

[1] Adapted in part from an article previously published by BNA: Bloomberg BNA, Sandra D. Glazier, Esq., Thomas M. Dixon, Esq., & Thomas F. Sweeney, Esq., *What Every Estate Planner Should Know About Undue Influence: Recognizing It, Insulating/ Planning Against It . . . And Litigating It*, TAX MANAGEMENT MEMORANDUM (2015).

presumption of validity that elevates the significance and importance of the presumption of undue influence.

d. **Presumption of undue influence**: This is the focus of this chapter.

WHAT IS THE PRESUMPTION OF UNDUE INFLUENCE AND WHY IS IT IMPORTANT?

In the absence of a finding that a "presumption of undue influence" applies, duly executed instruments generally are presumed to be valid.[2] Because of the very nature of undue influence cases, and in order to combat the secrecy generally associated with acts of undue influence, most states have imposed a construct to create a "presumption of undue influence" when certain circumstances are met. As such, the purpose of this presumption is to address the inherent disadvantage a contestant would otherwise suffer due to the very nature of how undue influence generally occurs. The mechanism of the presumption varies from state to state, but being able to satisfy the requirements for imposition of the presumption may have a significant impact on the outcome of the case. As previously stated, a finding that the presumption has been established can negate the grant of a dispositive motion against the challenge, thereby ensuring that the contestant will have his or her day in court. It may even provide an adequate basis, if not sufficiently rebutted, to prove that undue influence occurred, without further factual support. In Michigan, *In re Erickson Estate*[3] established that the presumption arises when the challenger can show all of the following:

1. A confidential or fiduciary relationship exists between the grantor and a fiduciary.
2. The fiduciary or an interest is represented by the fiduciary benefits from a transaction.
3. The fiduciary had an opportunity to influence the grantor's decision in that transaction.[4]

To give rise to the presumption, the pertinent question generally will be whether a confidential or fiduciary relationship existed at the time the challenged documents were created.[5]

---

[2] *In re* Cosgrove's Estate, 290 Mich. 258, 262, 287 N.W. 456, 457, 458, 125 A.L.R. 410 (1939).

[3] *In re* Erickson Estate, 508 N.W.2d 181, 202 Mich. App. 329 (1993).

[4] *Id.* at 331.

[5] *In re* John Stirling White Trust, 2018 WL 4576631 (2018) (citing Bill and Dena Brown Trust, 312 Mich. App. 684, 702; 880 N.W.2d 269 (2015)).

In Michigan, the effect of the presumption is not to shift the burden of persuasion (commonly known as the "burden of proof"), but rather, to shift the burden of production from the person claiming undue influence to the proponent of the instrument.[6] The [challenger] may satisfy the burden of persuasion with the presumption of undue influence, which remains as substantive evidence, and the [challenger] will always satisfy the burden of persuasion, when the [proponent] fails to offer sufficient evidence to rebut the presumption.[7]

One court concludes that "[p]resumptions in the law are almost invariably crystallized inferences of fact. Experience has taught that if certain evidentiary facts be established, there is such a strong practical likelihood that another stated fact will be true that that fact may be presumed."[8]

In other states, establishing the presumption of undue influence serves to shift the burden of proof to the proponent. As of July 14, 2014, Florida (by way of example) amended section 733.107 of the Florida statutes by enacting the following:

> (2) In any transaction or event to which the presumption of undue influence applies, the presumption implements public policy against abuse of fiduciary or confidential relationships and is therefore a presumption shifting the burden of proof under ss. 90.301-90.304.[9]

In California, following earlier appellate decisions that the establishment of the presumption shifted the burden of proof to the proponent,[10] the California legislature amended its Probate Code in 1995 to establish a series of complex rules, *inter alia*, governing the application of the presumption and when it shifts the burden of proof to the proponent in a variety of factual situations.[11] Like California,[12] Florida[13] and other states (such as

---

[6] Kar v. Hogan, 399 Mich. 529, 537, 251 N.W.2d 77, 79 (1976). But see *In re* Estate of Mortimore, unpublished opinion of the Michigan Court of Appeals issued May 17, 2011 (Docket No. 297280), 2011 WL 1879737, 2011 Mich. App. LEXIS 905 (2011).

[7] *Kar*, 399 Mich. at 541, 542.

[8] *Id* at 540. *See also* MICH. R. EVID. (MRE) 301; Widmayer v. Leonard, 422 Mich. 280 (1985).

[9] Florida Statute §733.107.

[10] Estate of Auen, 30 Cal. App. 4th 300, 313 (1994) (cited by California Supreme Court in support of Rice v. Clark, 28 Cal. 4th 89 (2002)).

[11] See CAL. PROB. CODE § 21380 *et seq.*

[12] *Estate of Auen*, 30 Cal. App. 4th at 309.

[13] Langford v. McCormick, 552 So. 2d 964, 967 (Fla. 1st DCA 1989), *review denied*, 562 So. 2d 346 (Fla. 1990); Jordan v. Noll, 423 So. 2d 368, 369 (Fla. 1st DCA 1983),

Michigan), impose the presumption largely as a result of the circumstances surrounding a confidential or fiduciary relationship. But unlike Michigan, in Florida, once the presumption of undue influence has been established, the proponent cannot shift the burden of proof back to the contestant. Instead, the proponent is required to prove that the will *was not* the product of undue influence by a preponderance of the evidence.[14]

The additional circumstances required in order to impose a presumption of undue influence, as stated earlier, can vary. By way of example, a Georgia court recognized that:

> [a] presumption of undue influence arises when it is shown that the will was made at the request of a person who receives a substantial benefit, who is not a natural object of the maker's estate, and who held a confidential relationship with the testator. [Cit.] However, "[a] person standing in confidential relation to another is not prohibited from exercising any influence whatever to obtain a benefit to himself. The influence must be what the law regards as undue influence. Such influence that . . . would give dominion over the will to such an extent as to destroy free agency, or constrain one to do against his will what he is unable to refuse."[15]

Although a survey of the various presumption statutes and standards applicable in each state is beyond the scope of this book, the existence of such distinctions is noted so that the reader can be advised of the importance of determining what the appropriate standard entails, as well as its potential impact.

RELATIONSHIPS THAT SATISFY THE RELATIONSHIP ELEMENTS OF THE PRESUMPTION

Most (if not all) presumptions contain some reference to a confidential or fiduciary relationship. So, what satisfies these relationship requirements? The existence of a confidential or fiduciary relationship is sometimes a question of fact.[16] The term is very broad, embracing both

---

review denied, 430 So. 2d 451 (Fla. 1983); Jacobs v. Vaillancourt, 634 So. 2d 667, 671 (1994).

[14] *See* Diaz v. Ashworth, 963 So. 2d 731 (Fla. 3d DCA 2007), FLA. STAT. ANN. § 733.107.

[15] *See* Holland v. Holland, 277 Ga. 792, 793, 596 S.E. 123, 125 (2004).

[16] Taylor v. Klahm, 40 Mich. App. 255, 264–265, 198 N.W.2d 715, 720–721 (1972).

technical fiduciary relations and informal relations that exist whenever one man trusts in and relies upon another.[17] A confidential relationship can be found to exist when a person enfeebled by poor health relies on another to conduct banking or other financial transactions.[18] Courts have held that "a confidential relationship is not confined to any specific association of persons but arises any time there appears on the one side an overmastering influence or, on the other, weakness, dependence, or trust, justifiably reposed."[19] Further, courts have recognized that:

> [w]henever there is a relationship between two people in which one person is in a position to exercise dominant influence upon the other because of the latter's dependency upon the former, arising either from weakness of the mind or body, or through trust, the law does not hesitate to characterize such a relationship as fiduciary in character. *Foster v. Ross*, 804 So.2d 1018, 1022–23 (Miss. 2002) (citing *Madden v. Rhodes*, 626 So.2d at 617 (Miss. 1993)). A moral, personal, or domestic relationship, which would impose the duties of a fiduciary also will be considered confidential under the appropriate circumstances. *Mullins v. Ratcliff*, 515 So.2d 1183, 1191 (Miss. 1987).[20]

A fiduciary is a person who stands in a position of confidence and trust vis-à-vis another person.[21] A fiduciary relationship also has been defined as a "relationship in which one person is under a duty to act for the benefit of the other on matters within the scope of the relationship."[22] A fiduciary relationship also has been recognized to arise "from the reposing of faith, confidence, and trust and the reliance of one upon the judgment and advice of another."[23] Such a relationship may be found to exist "when

---

[17] Van't Hof v. Jemison, 291 Mich. 385, 393–394, 289 N.W. 186, 189 (1939) (citing BLACK'S LAW DICTIONARY, *Fiduciary or Confidential Relations*, 775 (3d ed. 1933)).

[18] *In re* Swantek Estate, 172 Mich. App. 509, 514, 432 N.W.2d 307, 310 (1988).

[19] *In re* Matter of Estate of Johnson, 237 So. 3d 698 (2017) (citing Norris v. Norris, 498 So. 2d 809, 812 (Miss. 1986)).

[20] *Id.*

[21] *In re* Estate of Wood, unpublished opinion of the Michigan Court of Appeals issued January 3, 2008 (Docket No. 268024), 2008 WL 53149 4, 2008 Mich. App. LEXIS 12 (2008).

[22] *In re* Estate of Karmey, 468 Mich. 68, 75, 658 N.W.2d 796, 799 (2003) (citing BLACK'S LAW DICTIONARY (7th ed. 1999)).

[23] *In re* Monier Khalil Living Trust, ___ Mich. App. ___ , ___ N.W.2d ___, 2019 WL 2111650 (2019) (citing Vicencio v. Ramirez, 211 Mich. App. 501, 508, 536 N.W.2d 280 (1995)).

confidence is reposed on one side and there is a resulting superiority and influence on the other, and the relation and duties involved need not be legal, but may be moral, social, domestic, or merely personal."[24,25]

Michigan courts have held that there are four typical ways in which a fiduciary relationship can arise:

a. One person places trust in the faithful integrity of another, who as a result gains superiority or influence over the first.
b. One person assumes control over and responsibility for another.
c. One person has a duty to act for or give advice to another person on matters falling within the scope of the relationship.
d. There is a specific relationship that has traditionally been recognized as involving fiduciary duties, as with a lawyer and a client or a stockbroker and a customer.[26]

There are a number of relationships that are fiduciary as a matter of law, such as principal/agent, guardian/ward, trustee/beneficiary, lawyer/client, physician/patient, clergy/penitent, accountant/client, and

---

[24] State v. Campbell, 756 N.W.2d 263, 270 (Minn. App. 2008) (citing Toombs v. Daniels, 361 N.W.2d 801, 809 (Minn. 1985)).

[25] It is even possible that the establishment of a joint or multi-party account may create fiduciary obligations. In *Campbell, id.*, the court held that:

> . . . fiduciary obligations may be, but are not necessarily a part of, joint account arrangements. We recognize that the joint account is a starting point for analysis; it establishes a financial relationship. When each party is able to make unlimited withdrawals, there are clearly opportunities for abuse. To enter into the relationship, some level of trust exists between or among the parties to the account. The relationship and the trust may be nominal or far reaching. The important point is that in addition to the joint account, other factors must be weighed in determining whether a fiduciary relationship exists. These factors include the following: (1) the legal, familial, or personal relationship between the parties; (2) the capacity or sophistication of the parties; (3) who contributed the funds to joint accounts and in what ratio; and (4) the parties' understanding of their respective roles and responsibilities within the relationship. We do not suggest that this is an exhaustive list.

Id. at 272. It is noteworthy that on appeal, evidence of the joint nature of banking accounts, that the contributions were solely made by the decedent, and that the co-owner utilized funds for his own personal benefit was found to provide sufficient evidence of a breach of a fiduciary relationship, which supported a conviction for financial exploitation of a vulnerable adult under MINN. STATE § 609.2335 (1). State v. Campbell, 2012 WL 6554410 (Minn. 2012).

[26] *In re* Estate of Karmey, 468 Mich. at 75.

stockbroker/investor.[27] Courts have recognized that a fiduciary relationship exists as a matter of law from the grant of a power of attorney.[28] When a person becomes another's agent because he is imbued with express *or* implied authority to represent or act on behalf of the other, a fiduciary relationship has been found to exist.[29] In Michigan, unless there is a dispute whether the named relationship exists, it will be deemed a fiduciary relationship as a matter of law.[30]

There are other relationships that might satisfy the requirement of a confidential or fiduciary relationship (in addition to those relationships listed earlier) for purposes of imposing the presumption of undue influence.[31] It has been observed that "[a]ny type of relationship between two human beings in which the parties do not keep each other at arm's length may be deemed confidential if one of the parties shows any type of trust or confidence in the other."[32,33]

SPOUSAL RELATIONSHIPS AND THE PRESUMPTION

It has been said that trust is an essential component of a good marital relationship. That may well be the reason that many states recognize a spousal privilege in acknowledgment that an open and honest dialogue is an extension of communications exchanged between a husband and wife and confidence reposed. A natural extension of this may be the requirement

---

[27] *Id.* at 74 n. 2, 3.

[28] *In re* Susser Estate, 254 Mich. App. 232, 236, 657 N.W.2d 147, 150 (2002). *See also Campbell*, 756 N.W.2d at 271 (citing MINN. STAT. § 523.21 (2006) and Northfield Care Ctr. v. Anderson, 707 N.W.2d 731, 737 (Minn. App. 2006)).

[29] *In re* Monier Khalil Living Trust, ___ Mich. App. ___ , ___ N.W.2d ___, 2019 WL 2111650 (2019) (citing Law Offices of Jeffrey Sherbow, PC v. Fieger & Fieger, PC, 326 Mich. App. 684, 930 N.W.2d 416 (2019), slip op. at 6, 7).

[30] *In re* Susser Estate, 254 Mich. App. at 236.

[31] Gregory W. MacKenzie, Bennett Blum, M.D., and Rex Swanda, Ph.D., *Representing Estate and Trust Beneficiaries and Fiduciaries* § 7:5 ALI-ABA Course of Study Materials, July 2011, at 9.

[32] *Id.* § 7:5 at 9.

[33] Interestingly, the Texas appellate court recently held that the signing of a durable power of attorney on the same day as a will raised a presumption of undue influence that precluded summary disposition. *In re* Estate of Danford, 550 S.W.3d 275, at *19 (Tex. Ct. App. – Houston 2018). But in Michigan, a different result occurred. *See Brown*, 312 Mich. App. at 880.

for litigants alleging undue influence by a spouse to demonstrate how the spouse abused the relationship to attain the interest received, or may even result in the imposition of a higher standard or the finding of a relationship beyond merely that of husband and wife before the presumption will arise as between them in undue influence cases. That being said, it's not impossible for undue influence to be found to exist between spouses, although generally it must be based on a relationship *in addition* to that of husband and wife.[34]

In one case, the court said:

> We do not know of any rule of law or morals which makes it unlawful or improper for a wife to use her wifely influence for her own benefit or for that of others, unless she acts fraudulently, or extorts benefits from her husband when he is not in a condition to exercise his faculties as a free agent.[35]

It may, however, be important to note that in the previously referenced case, the court went on to find that the husband ". . . was entirely able to control his own actions, and was not weak enough to be a mere instrument in any one's hands. There can be no fatally undue influence without a person incapable of protecting himself, as well as a wrong-doer to be resisted. Neither is found here."[36]

It appears that undue influence cases involving spouses, one of whom is deceased, most often appear in the context of blended families, where the ultimate beneficiaries of one spouse's largess may be other than those who would have been the natural objects of the other spouse's estate.[37] Consequently, nationwide, there are numerous situations where undue influence by a spouse has been found to occur.[38]

---

[34] *In re* Will of Jones, 362 N.C. 569, 578–580 (2008).

[35] Latham v. Udell, 38 Mich. 238, 241–242 (1878). *Also Kar,* 399 Mich. at 555–556 (Levin, J., dissenting) and Nederlander v. Nederlander, 205 Mich. App. 123, 127, 517 N.W.2d 768, 771 (1993), *lv. denied,* 442 Mich. 854 (1993).

[36] *Latham,* 38 Mich. at 242.

[37] *See Mortimore,* at 12–15. *See also Karmey,* at 75.

[38] *See In re* Everett's Will, 105 Vt. 291, 166 A. 827,836 (Vt. 1933), in which the Vermont court, addressing the situation where the alleged perpetrator was the decedent's spouse, recognized the varied nature of undue influence when it found in pertinent part that:

> Undue influence in this connection means whatever destroys free agency and constrains the person whose act is under review to do that which is contrary to his own untrammeled desire. It may be caused by physical force, by duress,

THE EFFECT OF THE PRESUMPTION

Once established, the effect of the presumption generally is to cast an obligation on the proponent of an instrument to come forward with sufficient evidence opposing the presumption. The Michigan Supreme Court explained:

> Almost all presumptions are made up of permissible inferences. Thus, while the presumption may be overcome by evidence introduced, *the inference itself remains* and may provide evidence sufficient to persuade the trier of fact even though the rebutting evidence is introduced. *But always it is the inference and not the presumption that must be weighed against the rebutting evidence.*[39]

---

by threats, or by importunity. It may arise from persistent and unrelaxed efforts in the establishment or maintenance of conditions intolerable to the particular individual. It may result from conduct designed to create an irresistible ascendency by imperceptible means. It may be exerted by deceptive devices without actual fraud. Any species of coercion, whether physical, mental, or moral, which subverts the sound judgment and genuine desire of the individual, is enough to constitute undue influence. Its extent or degree is inconsequential as long as it is sufficient to substitute the dominating purpose of another for the free expression of the wishes of the person signing the instrument. The nature of undue influence is such that it often works in veiled and secret ways; hence it is impossible to lay down any hard and fast rule by which its exercise must or may be manifested. Direct evidence of it is seldom available. Nor is this necessary, since it may be shown by circumstances which have a legitimate tendency to prove that it was used. The nature of the testamentary disposition, as we have seen, whether natural or unnatural, may be considered in connection with other evidence under the issue of undue influence. Opportunity must necessarily be shown, but opportunity alone does not justify the inference of undue influence. Furthermore, influence by whatever means exerted, and however urgent and persistent, will not suffice to avoid a will unless carried to the point of destroying the free agency of the testator. Neither suggestion, solicitation, advice, nor importunity, unless carried to the extent indicated, will avoid a will. This is especially true when, as here, the person charged with undue influence is the spouse of the decedent. Their relation is such that a greater latitude in the influence either may exert over the other without its becoming undue in the eyes of the law is recognized. But even here, if the influence is such as to destroy the free agency of the one executing the instrument by supplanting his or her will by that of the other, it will vitiate the act. [Internal citations omitted.]

[39] *Widmayer*, 422 Mich. 280, 289; 373 N.W.2d 538, 542 (1985) (emphasis added).

The effect of the presumption is that it, at a minimum, generally shifts the burden of production from the person claiming undue influence to the person denying undue influence.[40] As indicated previously, in some states, the presumption actually shifts the burden of proof itself.

Importantly, even in those states where only the burden of production is shifted, once the presumption has been met, summary disposition in favor of the proponent of an instrument may be precluded, because "[t]he plaintiff may satisfy the burden of persuasion with the presumption of undue influence, which remains as substantive evidence, and the plaintiff will always satisfy the burden of persuasion when the defendant fails to offer sufficient evidence to rebut the presumption."[41] If no such presumption has been established, then it must be determined, aside from the presumption, whether the party asserting undue influence has established such.[42]

However, the existence of a relationship of trust is not a necessary element of undue influence, but its existence is relevant in determining whether a presumption of undue influence arises.[43]

From an estate planning perspective, it may be prudent to remain cognizant of the elements of the presumption of undue influence in varying jurisdictions, as a court may well determine that the presumption is procedural in nature and, therefore, the elements of the state where the documents are being litigated may be applied even if the drafted documents indicate that a different jurisdiction's laws will govern the instrument and its interpretation.

---

[40] *Kar*, 399 Mich. at 541, 542.
[41] *Kar*, 399 Mich.
[42] *In re* Estate of Mikeska, 140 Mich. App. 116, 121, 362 N.W.2d 906, 909 (1985).
[43] *See id.* at 121.

CHAPTER **7**

Rebutting the Presumption[1]

Just as the elements required to impose the presumption of undue influence vary from state to state, the same is also true with regard to the requirements for rebutting the presumption.

In many states (Michigan included), the presumption is evidentiary in nature (as opposed to statutory). In such states, the question often arises as to when "sufficient" evidence has been presented to convert the presumption into a mere "inference."

Broadly viewed, to rebut the presumption, the proponent will need to introduce credible evidence that the instrument represents the intent of the testator/grantor, and that such intent was not supplanted with the intent of another. Evidence to consider when attempting to rebut the presumption may include:

- Independent and competent counsel
- A full geriatric psychiatric assessment
- A MME on the date of execution by a long-term treating physician
- Evidence of a change in the relationship
- Expressions of intent made to credible and disinterested third parties (preferably before or contemporaneous with the execution)
- Expressions of the rationale (by the testator/grantor) as to the basis for the disposition or changed position, in front of independent professional witnesses

---

[1] Adapted in part from an article previously published by BNA: Bloomberg BNA, Sandra D. Glazier, Esq., Thomas M. Dixon, Esq., & Thomas F. Sweeney, Esq., *What Every Estate Planner Should Know About Undue Influence: Recognizing It, Insulating/ Planning Against It . . . And Litigating It,* Tax MANAGEMENT MEMORANDUM (2015).

In some states, where the presumption performs an evidentiary purpose, the quantum of evidence necessary to rebut the presumption may vary depending upon the circumstances that gave rise to the imposition of the presumption.

When the jurisdiction merely indicates that "substantial" evidence must be presented in order to rebut the presumption, what does that mean? To survive a dispositive motion, one needs to establish that there is a genuine issue of material fact; this would require "some" evidence. "Substantial" is greater than "some."

In Arkansas, the appellate court made this finding:

> [W]hen the burden shifts from the contestants of the testamentary document to the proponents of it, such as where there is a presumption of undue influence, the proponent can show by clear preponderance of the evidence that she took no advantage of her influence and that the testamentary gift was a result of the testator's own volition. However, where a beneficiary of a testamentary instrument actually drafts or procures it or there is a confidential relationship so dominating or so overpowering as to overcome the testatrix's free will, the proponent of the instrument must prove beyond a reasonable doubt that the decedent had both the mental capacity and freedom of will to make the will legally valid.[2]

In New Jersey, the appellate court held that:

> [o]rdinarily, the burden of proving undue influence falls on the will contestant. Nevertheless, we have long held that if the will benefits one who stood in a confidential relationship to the testator and if there are additional "suspicious" circumstances, the burden shifts to the party who stood in that relationship to the testator. Suspicious circumstances, for purposes of this burden shifting, need only be slight. When there is a confidential relationship coupled with suspicious circumstances, undue influence is presumed and the burden of proof shifts to the will proponent to overcome the presumption. Although that burden of proof is usually discharged in accordance with the preponderance of the evidence standard, if the presumption arises from "a professional conflict of interest on the part of an

---

[2] Lenderman v. Martin, 1999 WL 407519 (Ark. Ct. App. 1999) (internal citations omitted).

attorney, coupled with confidential relationships between a testator and the beneficiary as well as the attorney," the presumption must instead be rebutted by clear and convincing evidence.[3]

In Pennsylvania, once the presumption of undue influence has been established, it appears that the proponent can prove the validity of the challenged disposition by clear and convincing evidence that it was not the result of undue influence.[4]

In Tennessee, in order to rebut the presumption, the proponent needs to establish the fairness of the transaction by clear and convincing evidence. One way of showing that, where demonstrating fairness would be otherwise difficult, is by showing that the testator had the benefit of independent advice.[5]

However, Nebraska appears to indicate that, in that state, the presumption of undue influence should not be treated as a true evidentiary presumption. In *In re Estate of Clinger*,[6] the court held that the presumption of undue influence, under prior case law in Nebraska, was not a true presumption within the meaning of evidentiary rule 301, but rather was intended to provide only a permissible or probable inference. Consequently, the Nebraska court specifically discourages referring to the presumption of undue influence as a presumption. This may largely be because, in Nebraska, the presumption is not by itself considered evidence of undue influence. If there is nothing other than the presumption, the case will not be permitted to be presented to a jury. As such, once the presumption is rebutted, it disappears. Therefore, the court held that a contestant could not prevail if the evidence in support of the presumption and to rebut it result in a "tie," because the contestant always bears the burden of persuasion.

The Nebraska approach, however, is contrary to Michigan's evidentiary approach to the presumption. Pursuant to *Kar v. Hogan*,[7] if the trier of fact finds that the evidence by the proponent in rebuttal to the presumption is

---

[3] *In re* Estate of Stockdale, 196 N.J. 275, 953 A.2d 454 (2008).

[4] *In re* Estate of Pedrick, 505 Pa. 530, 482 A.2d 215 (1984); Estate of Reichel, 484 Pa. 610, 400 A.2d 1268 (1979); *In re* Clark's Estate, 461 Pa. 52, 334 A.2d 628 (1975); *In re* Quein's Estate, 361 Pa. 133, 62 A.2d 909 (1949); Burns v. Kabboul, 407 Pa. Super. 289, 595 A.2d 1153 (1991); *In re* Estate of Simpson, 407 Pa. Super. 1, 595 A.2d 94 (1991); *In re* Mampe, 2007 Pa. Super. 269, 932 A.2d 954 (2007); *In re* Estate of Stout, 2000 Pa. Super. 37, 746 A.2d 645 (2000).

[5] Matter of Estate of Depriest, 733 S.W.2d 74 (Tenn. Ct. App. 1986); Richmond v. Christian, 555 S.W.2d 105 (Tenn. 1977).

[6] *In re* Estate of Clinger, 292 Neb. 237 (2015).

[7] *Kar*, 399 Mich.

equal to that provided by the presumption, then the proponent has failed to discharge his duty of producing sufficient rebuttal evidence, and the "mandatory inference" remains unscathed. This does not mean, in Michigan, that the ultimate burden of proof has shifted from the contestant to the proponent, but rather, that the contestant may satisfy the burden of persuasion with the use of the presumption, because it remains as substantive evidence, and that the contestant will always satisfy the burden of persuasion when the proponent fails to offer sufficient rebuttal evidence.

Recently, the Michigan Court of Appeals analyzed the effect of that "mandatory" presumption, essentially holding that a preponderance of evidence was required to rebut the presumption of undue influence:

> The trial court recognized that there was evidence presented that would support a conclusion that [the decedent] was unduly influenced. At the same time, the trial court recognized that there was evidence presented that would result in a conclusion that [the decedent] was not unduly influenced. In the end, the trial court ruled that "it was just a decision that the Court had to come down on." The trial court's statements recognize that [the proponent] presented evidence to rebut the presumption of undue influence but when weighed against opposing evidence in favor of the presumption, the trial court essentially found the evidence equally convincing. As such [the proponent] did not overcome her duty to rebut the presumption. Therefore, the mandatory presumption of undue influence remained unscathed and we conclude that appellants established that [the proponent] unduly influenced [the decedent].[8]

Therefore, in Michigan, once the presumption of undue influence is established, it may create a "mandatory presumption" that the instrument, instruments and/or transactions in question are the product of undue influence (and hence void) which the proponent of the instrument or transaction must then rebut by (perhaps, at least) a preponderance of the evidence.[9]

---

[8] *In re* Estate of Mortimore, unpublished opinion of the Michigan Court of Appeals issued May 17, 2011 (Docket No. 297280), 2011 WL 1879737, 6, 2011 Mich. App. LEXIS 905, 14 (2011); *lv. denied,* Hanneman v. Fiser (*In re* Estate of Mortimore), 491 Mich. 925, 813 N.W.2d 288 (mem), 289 (Mich. 2012).

[9] *See Young, J., dissenting, In re* Estate of Mortimore, 2011 WL 1879737, at 929, *also citing Kar,* 399 Mich., at 542. Importantly, the comments by Justice Young in his

In *In re Estate of Reid,*[10] the Mississippi Supreme Court found that once the presumption was established the proponent needed to rebut the presumption with clear and convincing evidence of the (a) good faith of the beneficiary/ proponent, (b) the grantor's full knowledge and deliberation on the consequences of the action, and (c) the grantor's independent consent and action. In *In re Estate of Burren,*[11] the Illinois appellate court found that:

> [t]o overcome a presumption of undue influence in a will contest, a fiduciary who benefits from a will must present clear and convincing evidence that in the will, the testator freely expressed his own wishes and not the wishes of the fiduciary. Courts have considered such factors as whether the fiduciary "made a full and frank disclosure of all relevant information; * * * [whether] adequate consideration was given; *and [whether the testator] had independent advice before completing the transaction.*"[12]

In *Matter of Estate of Seegers,*[13] the Oklahoma appellate court held that:

> When the legal presumption of undue influence has arisen, the burden of proof is upon the party seeking to take the benefit of the new disposition to rebut the presumption by showing that the confidential relationship had been severed or that *the party making the disposition had competent and independent legal advice in the preparation of the will.*[14]

Because the existence of competent independent counsel can clearly present a strong defense to a claim of undue influence (and perhaps to the level of evidence required to rebut the presumption), while addressed in this chapter, an analysis of what constitutes independent advice of counsel is discussed further in chapter 1.

In Illinois, where no jury instruction on the presumption of undue influence is given to the jury, once the presumption has been rebutted,

---

dissenting opinion were with reference to controlling law as set forth in existing appellate decisions and not expressed with respect to contrary holdings expressed by the majority of the court in *Mortimore.*

[10] *In re* Estate of Reid, 825 So. 2d 1 (2002).

[11] *In re* Estate of Burren, 2013 IL App. (1st) 120996, 374 Ill. Dec. 85, 994 N.E.2d 1022 (App. Ct. 1st Dist. 2013), *appeal denied,* 377 Ill. Dec. 764, 2 N.E. 1045 (Ill 2013).

[12] *Id.* (internal citations omitted; emphasis added).

[13] Matter of Estate of Seegers, 733 P.2 418, 1986 Okla. Civ. App. 21 (1986).

[14] *Id.* at 423 (emphasis added; internal citations omitted).

it is a question of law for the court to decide as to whether sufficient evidence has been presented to rebut the presumption.[15] As a consequence, the court acts as the "gatekeeper."[16]

LAWYERS AS BENEFICIARIES

When a lawyer is a beneficiary of the client's estate, perhaps the ethical considerations mandate imposition of a higher standard for rebuttal of the presumption. In *In re Mardigian Estate*,[17] the Michigan Supreme Court recognized the important ethical considerations when an attorney is to receive a bequest:

> [a] lawyer should not suggest to his client that a gift be made to himself or for his benefit. If a lawyer accepts a gift from his client, he is peculiarly susceptible to the charge that he unduly influenced or overreached the client. If a client voluntarily offers to make a gift to his lawyer, the lawyer may accept the gift, *but before doing so, he should urge that his client secure disinterested advice from an independent, competent person who is cognizant of all the circumstances. Other than in exceptional circumstances, a lawyer should insist that an instrument in which his client desires to name him beneficially be prepared by another lawyer selected by the client.* [Ethical Consideration 5–5, American Bar Association, ABA Model Code of Professional Responsibility, <https://www.americanbar.org/content/dam/aba/migrated/2011_build/professional_responsibility/mod_code_prof_resp.authcheckdam.pdf> (accessed June 13, 2018)] [https://perma.cc/8YQY-TQ5R].[18]

The case of *In re Grow's Estate*,[19] recently cited by the Michigan Supreme Court in *In re Mardigian Estate*,[20] reflects the importance in undue influence

---

[15] *See* Illinois § 200.00 jury instructions comments on c. *Effect of Presumption*, 4. *See also* note on use, Illinois jury instruction § 200.03.

[16] Michigan recently eliminated the instruction on the presumption in those instances where the presumption has been rebutted. Nonetheless, *In re* Gerald 1. Pollack Trust, 309 Mich. App. 125, 867 N.W.2d 884 (2015), appears to support the argument regarding the enhanced role of the judge as gatekeeper when addressing issues related to the presumption of undue influence in Michigan.

[17] *In re* Mardigian Estate, 502 Mich. 154, 917 N.W.2d 325 (2018).

[18] *Id*, 154 (emphasis added).

[19] *In re* Grow's Estate, 299 Mich. 133, 140, 299 N.W. 836, 839 (1941).

[20] *Mardigian*, at 186.

cases of independent counsel in rebutting the presumption. But what constitutes sufficiently independent counsel, as opposed to a mere scrivener, may merit further analysis. The provision of professional legal advice and services, as contrasted to serving as a mere scrivener, requires the "interpretation and application of legal principles to guide future conduct or to assess past conduct."[21] A "scrivener" is merely someone who transcribes or memorializes what others tell him or her.[22] An attorney who prepares a will, "without adequately counseling the testator is a mere scrivener and not an independent legal adviser."[23] It is against this backdrop that the analysis contained in a New Jersey case, as to the quantum of evidence required to rebut the presumption, may become important.

In *Haynes v. First Nat. State Bank of New Jersey*,[24] the court held that the quantum of evidence required to rebut the presumption of undue influence once the presumption was found to exist (when no independent counsel was utilized to provide advice to the testator) is a higher clear and convincing standard. In that case, while the decedent had her estate plan drafted by an attorney (someone other than the beneficiary), that attorney was procured by and had represented the decedent's daughter, upon whom the decedent had been dependent because of debilitating afflictions and her advanced years. Of importance was the court's acknowledgment that while the presumption of undue influence may generally be rebutted by a preponderance of the evidence, there are other cases where:

> . . . the presumption of undue influence is so heavily weighted with policy that the courts have demanded a sterner measure of proof than that usually obtaining upon civil issues. That is the situation, for instance, where an attorney benefits by the will of his client and especially where he draws it himself.
>
> It has been often recognized that a conflict on the part of an attorney in a testimonial situation is fraught with a high potential for undue influence, generating a strong presumption that there was such improper influence and warranting a greater quantum of proof to dispel the presumption. Thus, where the attorney who drew the will was the sole beneficiary, the Court required

---

[21] Alomari v. Ohio Dep't of Pub Safety, 626 F Appx 558, 570 (6th Cir. 2015).

[22] *See* People v. Lee, No. 306192, 2012 WL 6097316, at *2 (Mich. App., Dec 6, 2012) (one who transcribes results generated by a machine is a *scrivener*).

[23] State v. Beaudry, 53 Wis. 2d 148; 191 N.W.2d 842 (1971).

[24] Haynes v. First Nat. State Bank of New Jersey, 87 N.J. 163, 432 A.2d 890, 23 A.L.R.4th 347 (1981).

"substantial and trustworthy evidence of explanatory facts" and "candid and full disclosure" to dispel the presumption of undue influence. *And, where an attorney-beneficiary, who had a preexisting attorney-client relationship with the testatrix, introduced the testatrix to the lawyer who actually drafted the challenged will, this Court has required evidence that was "convincing or impeccable."*[25]

The *Haynes* court went on to indicate that when the testator is advised by a truly independent attorney, the standard would then be the lower (preponderance) standard.

The *Haynes* court engaged in an extensive analysis of the policy reasons (citing numerous cases) why the imposition of a more rigorous clear and convincing standard should be applied when the testator does not independently choose the attorney to draw up his estate planning documents, as well as when the testator's attorney has placed himself in a conflict of interest or a conflict of professional loyalty between the testator and the beneficiary.

In some states, a bequest to an attorney (or member of the attorney's family) who is unrelated to the testator may not receive a bequest unless the testator received the independent advice of counsel.[26] Even a contract providing benefits to an attorney (who has otherwise provided legal services) may be invalid when an explanation of every provision was provided but "unselfish and competent advice" was not provided or obtained.[27]

When the presumption of undue influence is imposed against an attorney, the quantum of evidence required to rebut the presumption may also be higher than in other instances.

In *In re Mardigian*, citing *Donovan v. Bromley*, the court recognized that:

> . . . this court has long applied a different framework when an attorney drafts a testamentary instrument for her own benefit. In those cases, we recognized as early as 1897 that the attorney's palpable self-interest "arous[es] suspicion and raises a presumption more or less strong that undue influence has been exerted . . ."[28]

It may be important to remember that an attorney-client relationship arises whenever a layperson consults a lawyer in his or her professional

---

[25] *Id.* at 178, 179 (internal citations omitted; emphasis added).

[26] *See* K.S.A 59–605 (b).

[27] *See* Israel v. Sommer, 292 Mass 113, 124, 197 N.E. 442, 448 (1935).

[28] *In re* Mardigian Estate, 502 Mich. at 183 (citing Donovan v. Bromley, 113 Mich. 53, 54, 71 N.W. 523 (1897)).

capacity, with the intent to seek professional legal advice, and the attorney accepts the responsibility of acting on that person's behalf in some professional capacity.[29] No formal signing of papers or payment of retainer is required to create an attorney-client relationship, although, if either of these is done, an attorney-client relationship clearly exists.[30] The Michigan Court of Appeals has agreed with the authorities cited in 7 Am Jur 2d *Attorneys at Law* §118, 187, 188 (1997) that:

> [T]he relation of attorney and client is not dependent on the payment of a fee, nor is a formal contract necessary to create this relationship. The contract may be implied from conduct of the parties. The employment is sufficiently established when it is shown that the advice and assistance of the attorney are sought and received in matters pertinent to his profession.[31]

"The rendering of legal advice and legal services by the attorney and the client's reliance on that advice or those services is the benchmark of an attorney-client relationship."[32] Therefore, when the grantor's attorney is a beneficiary, even if another attorney is recruited to draft the pertinent document, the presumption of undue influence may still apply. Cases relating to the importance of competent independent counsel (and what that means) are therefore included to illustrate the importance of such counsel as a means of rebutting the presumption.

Despite the fact that California also requires "procurement" as an element of the presumption of undue influence, in *In Estate of Auen*[33] because "the relationship between attorney and client is a fiduciary relation of the very highest character . . . [t]ransactions between attorneys and their clients are subject to the strictest scrutiny."[34] In *Auen,* the court found that "when an attorney is acting as an attorney, any benefit other than compensation

---

[29] Dalrymple v. National Bank & Trust, 615 F. Supp 979 (WD Mich 1985).

[30] *See* Zych v. Jones, 84 Ill App. 3d 647, 406 N.E.2d 70 (1980).

[31] Leith Danou, Danou-Gappy Group v. Cummings, 2006 Mich. App. LEXIS 135, 8–9 (Mich Ct. App. Jan. 17, 2006), citing Macomb County Taxpayers Ass'n v. L'Anse Creuse Public Schools, 455 Mich. 1, 11, 564 N.W.2d 457, 462(1997). *See also* 7 Am Jur 2d *Attorneys at Law* §136, 189 (1997).

[32] *Macomb County Taxpayers,* 455 Mich. at 11.

[33] *In* Estate of Auen, 30 Cal. App. 4th 300, 35 Cal. Rptr. 2d 557, 562, 1994 Cal. App. LEXIS 1189 (Cal. App. 1994).

[34] *Id.* at 562 (internal citations omitted).

for legal services performed would be 'undue.'"[35] In *Auen*, the attorney beneficiary was not the scrivener, but the attorney-beneficiary handled various legal matters for the decedent. She held powers of attorney on the decedent's bank accounts and referred to herself orally and in writing as the decedent's attorney. The decedent also regularly referred to the attorney-beneficiary as her attorney (despite also having developed a personal relationship with the decedent). The attorney-beneficiary also did errands for the decedent, helped the decedent with shopping, made social visits, and included the decedent in family gatherings. The will was drafted by a personal friend of the attorney-beneficiary who rented office space from and shared secretarial services with the attorney-beneficiary. The attorney-beneficiary's secretary and the scrivener attorney were witnesses to the will. As a consequence of these key facts, the court held that the scrivener was not "an independent advisor" and that the attorney-beneficiary was unable to rebut the presumption of undue influence.

In adopting the rationale of *Auen*,[36] the W. Virginia Supreme Court of Appeals in *Lawyer Disciplinary Bd. v. Ball* went on to find that:

> [A] question of undue influence often arises when a person in a position of trust and confidence becomes the object of the other party's generosity. Such scrutiny is especially important when attorney-beneficiaries are involved, since the intensely personal nature of the attorney-client relationship, coupled with the specialized training and knowledge that attorneys have, places attorneys in positions that are uniquely suited to exercising a powerful influence over their clients' decision.[37]

The issue of whether a "suite-mate" satisfies the requirements of "independent counsel" when an unrelated attorney becomes a beneficiary under an estate planning instrument was reviewed in *Atty. Greiv. Comm'n v. Saridakis*.[38] In *Saridakis*, upon realizing that his client (who was also a close personal friend) wished to leave him a bequest, the attorney recommended that the client seek out independent counsel. The client indicated that he didn't know another attorney and asked the attorney-beneficiary to locate another attorney in order to carry out her desired disposition. The

---

[35] *Id.* at 562, 563.

[36] *Id.*

[37] Lawyer Disciplinary Bd. v. Ball, 219 W. Va 296, 304, 633 S.E.2d 241 (2006).

[38] Atty. Greiv. Comm'n v. Saridakis, 402 Md. 413, 936 A.2d 886 (2007).

testatrix also informed her godson of her intentions to leave a bequest to her attorney, which the godson viewed as natural and reasonable given his awareness of the close relationship that the testatrix had with her attorney. A competent estate planning attorney rented space in the same office suite and shared a receptionist and a conference room with the attorney-beneficiary. They did not share clients and each maintained distinct law practices. The court held that when a bequest to an attorney-beneficiary is involved, "[t]he independent counsel required by the Rule must be truly independent."[39] It found that an attorney who shares space with the attorney did not qualify as independent counsel to the donor client, where (as here) they shared an office suite, conference room, and receptionist.

In *In re Moses' Will*,[40] the Mississippi Supreme Court held that in order to rebut a presumption of undue influence applicable to a bequest to an attorney beneficiary, it must be found that the decedent had the benefit of "independent advice and counsel of one entirely devoted to her interest."[41] The attorney beneficiary ("Holland") contended that the decedent indeed had the benefit of such advice. Here, the drafting attorney was "a reputable and respected member of the bar who had no prior connection with Holland and no knowledge of [decedent's] relationship with him." The decedent personally contacted the drafting attorney, made an appointment, and met with the drafting attorney alone. The drafting attorney inquired into the decedent's property interests and marital background and determined that the decedent was not married. He also asked whether decedent had any children and determined that she had none. He advised the decedent that her provision of more accurate descriptions of certain real estate and personal property interests would be beneficial, and she supplied the same. The drafting attorney provided no further advice of counsel. The drafting attorney prepared the will and mailed it to the decedent. The decedent alerted the drafting attorney to a mistake in the will and the drafting attorney corrected the same and mailed the decedent a revised draft. The drafting attorney never inquired why the decedent was excluding blood relatives or why she was preferring Holland as a beneficiary, nor was there any discussion about Holland's possible attorney-client relationship with the decedent. The drafting attorney testified that he wrote the will according to the decedent's instructions and that the drafting attorney had no interest in how the decedent disposed of her property. The will was executed in the

---

[39] *Id.* at 426.

[40] *In re* Moses' Will, 227 So. 2d 829 (1969).

[41] *Id.* at 833.

presence of two witnesses, one of whom had previously worked for Holland and his associate. The court found that:

> [i]t is clear from his own testimony that, in writing the will, the attorney-draftsman, did no more than write down, according to the forms of law, what [decedent] told him. There was no meaningful independent advice or counsel touching upon the area in question and it is manifest that the role of the attorney in writing the will, as it relates to the present issue, was little more than that of scrivener. The chancellor was justified in holding that this did not meet the burden nor overcome the presumption.[42]

In *State v. Beaudry,*[43] the courts were again faced with assessing what constituted "independent counsel" for purposes of a bequest by a client to his attorney. The court addressed:

> . . . the problem in which a lawyer finds himself when asked to draw a will for a friend or a relative who wishes to make a bequest to him or to a member of his family. We adopted the view that when a testator wishes to make his attorney or a member of his immediate family a beneficiary in his will, ordinary prudence requires that the will be drawn by some other lawyer of the testator's own choosing so that any suspicion of undue influence by the lawyer beneficiary is avoided.[44]

In *Beaudry,* just as in *Saridakis,* the court recognized the need for independent counsel:

> Beaudry's professional obligations were not discharged by the way he secured the drafting of this will even if he were not a beneficiary. It was Mr. Beaudry's duty to provide an attorney, not a scrivener. *In the Estate of O'Loughlin* (1971), 50 Wis. 2d 143, 183 N. W. 2d 133, we said that *one who drafts a will without adequately counseling the testator is a mere scrivener and not an independent legal adviser. Other courts have noted the requirement of independent legal advice may not be met if the scrivener is in fact a close associate of the attorney beneficiary. See In re Will of Moses* (Miss. 1969), 227 So. 2d 829; Annot. (1968), Wills: Undue Influence in Gift to Testator's Attorney, 19 A. L. R. 3d

---

[42] *Id.* at 834.
[43] State v. Beaudry, 53 Wis. 2d 148, 191 N.W.2d 842 (1971).
[44] *Id.* at 150, 151.

575, 598. In *Reilly v. McAuliffe* (1954), 331 Mass. 144, 117 N. E. 2d 811, it was said *advice which is incompetent, perfunctory or given without adequate knowledge of the testator's situation is not sufficient. When the attorney selected by the proposed attorney beneficiary is a close friend, the rule requires that attorney to meet all the tests for an independent legal attorney selected solely and exclusively by the testator himself.* See *In re Lobb's Will* (1944), 173 Or. 414, 145 Pac. 2d 808.[45]

While the attorney grievance and disciplinary actions cited here do not per se form the foundation of a cause of action to set aside the instruments in question, they are nonetheless demonstrative of the level of "independence of counsel" required when an attorney-beneficiary relies on the mere fact that they were not the actual author of an instrument in dispute pursuant to which the presumption has been established and they (or members of their family) receive a significant gift or bequest.

THE EFFECT OF THE PRESUMPTION ONCE REBUTTED

Once rebutted, what is the effect of the presumption? The effect will also vary depending upon the state. Because Nebraska has indicated that the presumption of undue influence has no evidentiary bearing, even if not rebutted, it appears insufficient for the rendition of a verdict in favor of the contestant. Something more is almost always required. But in other jurisdictions, where the presumption of undue influence itself carries evidentiary weight, once rebutted, minimally it appears to still carry at least a permissive inference if not a presumption of fact.[46] The "presumption of fact" approach would seem to support Georgia's approach, where the Georgia appellate court held that "[i] n the face of a rebuttable presumption of undue influence, '[b]ecause that presumption does not vanish in the face of evidence contrary to the presumed fact, it alone is sufficient to support the jury's finding as to undue influence.'"[47]

The three most common approaches to an evidentiary presumption are known as the *Thayer* (or *bursting bubble*) approach, the *Morgan* approach, and the "*prima facie* presumption."

---

[45] *Id.* at 154 (emphasis added). *See also* Israel v. Sommer, 292 Mass. 113, 123, 197 N.E. 442, 447 (1935).

[46] *See* Ernest F. Roberts, *An Introduction to the Study of Presumptions,* 4 VILL. L. REV. 1 11–13 (1958).

[47] Bean v. Wilson, 283 Ga. 511, 661 S.E.2d 518 (2008).

Illinois applies the Thayer/bursting bubble approach. Commentary on the Illinois jury instructions provide a concise analysis of this approach in addressing its procedural impact:

> For most presumptions, including this one, Illinois has adopted the Thayer-Wigmore "bursting bubble" theory. Under this view, the plaintiff must first produce sufficient evidence to make a submissible case on each of the elements necessary to give rise to the presumption. (These elements are sometimes called the "basic facts.") Having done so, the burden of going forward with the evidence (but not the burden of persuasion) shifts to the defendant. The defendant can attack either the basic facts, the presumed fact, or both.
>
> If the defendant attacks only the basic facts (for example, claiming that there was no attorney-client relationship at the time of the transaction in question), then the case is submitted to the jury with this instruction. If the jury finds the basic facts in plaintiff's favor, then the presumption requires the jury to find in favor of the plaintiff.
>
> If the defendant attacks the presumed fact (that is, produces evidence that he did not exert undue influence over the decedent), then the court must determine whether the presumption remains. Whether the presumption has been overcome is always a question for the court. If the court determines that the defendant has produced sufficient evidence to overcome the presumption, then the "bubble bursts" and the presumption disappears from the case. The plaintiff must then rely on specific evidence of actual undue influence or some other theory of invalidity. The jury is given the usual issues and burden of proof instructions, but the presumption is gone and the jury is told nothing about the presumption.
>
> If the defendant's evidence is insufficient to rebut the presumption, then the presumption remains operative. If the defendant has not attacked the basic facts or if the evidence of If If *(sic)* the defendant's evidence is insufficient to rebut the presumption, then the presumption remains operative. If the defendant has not attacked the basic facts or if the evidence of the basic facts is so favorable to the plaintiff that it satisfies the *Pedrick* standard, then the court will direct a verdict for the plaintiff. Otherwise, the case will be submitted to the jury under this instruction for the jury to determine the basic facts.[48]

Important to this approach appears to be the court's role as "gate-keeper" in determining whether the presumption has been "burst."

---

[48] Illinois Jury Instructions – Will Contest § 200.00 at 13 (internal citations omitted).

Under the Morgan approach:

> A presumption is an assumption of fact resulting from a rule of
> law which requires such fact to be assumed from another fact of law
> which requires such fact to be assumed from another fact or group
> of facts found or otherwise establed in the action.
>   . . . except for presumptions which are conclusive or irrefutable
> under the rules of law from which they arise, (a) if the facts from
> which the presumption is derived have any probative value as evi-
> dence of the existence of the presumed fact, the presumption con-
> tinues to exist and the burden of establising the non-existence of
> the presumed fact is upon the party against whom the presumption
> operates, (b) if the facts from which the presumption arises have no
> probative value as evidence of the presumed fact, the presumption
> does not exist when evidence is introduced which would support a
> finding of the non-existence of the presumed fact, and the fact which
> would otherwise be presumed shall be determined from the evi-
> dence exactly as if no presumption was or had ever been involved.[49]

Under the "*prima facie* presumption," a compromised approach is
utilized. Application of the "*prima facie* presumption" results in the presumption, once rebutted, nonetheless providing an inference.[50] As a consequence, even once rebutted, the presumption would provide the contestant
with the benefit of an inference on the premise that a presumption is essentially an assumption of fact resulting from a rule of law, which requires such
fact to be assumed from another fact or group of facts found or otherwise.[51]

In Michigan, once established, a presumption shifts the burden of
going forward with evidence.[52] Therefore, the party in whose favor the presumption operates is entitled to a directed verdict if the adversary produces
insufficient evidence to rebut the presumption.[53] But if the presumption is
rebutted, "the matter will go to the jury with an appropriate instruction to
the effect that the presumption has been rebutted, but, if the presumption
was logically supported by the underlying facts, the jury is free to weigh the
facts and make an inference if it feels that is appropriate."[54]

---

[49] Roberts, *supra* note 46, at 33.

[50] *Id.* at 35.

[51] *Id.* at 35.

[52] Michael D. Wade, Hon. Dennis C. Kolenda, MICHIGAN COURTROOM EVIDENCE
ANNOTATED FOURTH EDITION, 2009 Supp § 301.1, 60.

[53] *See id.*

[54] *Id., Outcome of a Presumption*, 59.

In essence, the presumption, once rebutted, remains an inference. An inference is:

> [A] conclusion that may be drawn from facts admitted in evidence as to a matter material to the case. An inference exists as a matter of common experience and logic, and while it may be recognized or even specifically authorized as a matter of law, its function is limited to permitting the trier of fact to find the facts sought to be established. An inference is the basic ingredient of all circumstantial evidence. Sometimes statutes use the term "inference" when either prima facie evidence or presumptive evidence is intended.[55]

In *Widmayer v. Leonard*,[56] the Michigan Supreme Court specifically referred to and recognized that the implication and use of presumptions was a particularly confusing area of the law. The court indicated that through its opinion it was going to attempt to clarify it. The court reflected that the "burden of proof" in any case is actually made up to two distinct burdens: (1) the burden of producing or going forward with evidence, and (2) the burden of persuasion. According to *Widmayer*, the burden assigned to a party against whom a presumption is asserted has the burden of going forward with evidence but does not have the burden of persuasion, as the burden of persuasion remained with the plaintiff (or in our cases, the contestant). *Widmayer* nonetheless continued to recognize the "inference" that may remain following the rebuttal of the presumption. As a result, the court indicated that

> [a]lmost all presumptions are made up of permissible inferences. Thus, while the presumption may be overcome by evidence introduced, the inference itself remains and may provide evidence sufficient to persuade the trier of fact even though the rebutting evidence is introduced. But always it is the inference and not the presumption that must be weighed against the rebutting evidence.[57]

Whether an inference remains, the presumption bursts entirely, or the presumption remains throughout (as in the case of certain statutorily imposed presumptions), prudence dictates that a contestant should be prepared to present evidence beyond that needed to establish the presumption.

---

[55] Lawrence A. Dubin, Glen Weissenberger, & A.J. Stephani, Michigan Evidence Courtroom Manual, ch. 301, 41 (2014).

[56] Widmayer v. Leonard, 422 Mich. 280, 289 (1985).

[57] *Id.*

CHAPTER 8

No-Contest Clauses and the Importance of Probable Cause[1]

Because undue influence often is veiled in secrecy, the potential impact of a no contest clause can be severe. Often the proponent of the instrument had or has control of the environment. They know and may have control over all of the pertinent facts and evidence. The challenger to the instrument may now be on the outside. If the challenger has been isolated from the individual, the challenger may lack knowledge of what has transpired.[2] While the challenger may have more than just a feeling that something is wrong and that the instrument does not reflect the individual's prior expressions of intent, proving that their gut feeling is right may be difficult and costly. If the proponent is now the fiduciary of the estate governed by the instrument, the proponent may control the purse strings and have the ability to utilize the assets of the estate to fund the defense. Importantly, the challenger may face the potential consequences of a "no contest" or *in terrorem* clause. Because of the potentially chilling effect of a "no contest"

---

[1] Adapted from an article previously published by Thomas F. Sweeney, Esq., Thomas F. Dixon, Esq., & Thomas E.F. Fabbri, Esq., *Probable Cause Exception to Enforcement of Will and Trust In Terrorem Clauses: Determining the Factors in Applying the Exception and Considering Opportunities for an Early Determination of Whether the Exception Has Been Satisfied*, 33 MICH. PROB. & ESTATE J. 2 (2013), and from Bloomberg BNA, Sandra D. Glazier, Esq., Thomas M. Dixon, Esq., & Thomas F. Sweeney, Esq., *What Every Estate Planner Should Know About Undue Influence: Recognizing It, Insulating/Planning Against It . . . And Litigating It*, TAX MANAGEMENT MEMORANDUM (2015).

[2] McPeak v. McPeak, 233 Mich. App. 483, 496, 593 N.W.2d 180, 187 (1999), *lv. denied*, 461 Mich. 926, 605 N.W.2d 318 (Table) (1999).

clause, it is important to understand what may constitute "probable cause" in order to provide an exception to application of a "no contest" provision.

While some states, such as Michigan, permit the challenger to proceed without loss of benefit if probable cause to the challenge exists, this "safe haven" does not exist in every state. In a state where this probable cause "safe haven" does not exist, it might be possible for the parties to find themselves in a "winner take all" scenario.[3] This could occur because the contestant challenged an instrument that was subject to a no-contest clause and did not prevail. The same result could also occur if a person proffers an instrument for administration when he knew or had reason to know that the propounded instrument was not valid, and such conduct is found to itself amount to a challenge, which triggers the *in terrorem* clause (in a previously executed version of the instrument, which ultimately is determined to be valid).[4] In a state where the probable cause "safe haven" exists, the attorney representing a contestant needs to know whether a beneficiary petition seeking a determination of probable cause, in and of itself, constitutes a challenge that could trigger the *in terrorem* clause.[5] Perhaps, in such cases, the threat of forfeiture under an *in terrorem* clause may be avoided when an independent (non-beneficiary) fiduciary brings the challenge.

---

[3] *See* EGW v. First Federal Savings Bank of Sheridan, 413 P.3d 106, 2018 WY 25 (WY S. Ct. 2018). In EGW, the Wyoming Supreme Court affirmed that because the grantors had contested the validity grantor's revocable trust premised upon a claim of undue influence, the no-contest clause not only barred the son from receiving any benefits under the trust but also his issue. The pertinent language in the contest provided that if his son, grandchildren, sister or his sister's children challenged his trust directly or on behalf of his son or grandchildren, any interest in the trust of "any descendant of mine" shall immediately terminate. The case cites to other jurisdictions that recognize the validity of no-contest clauses enforced against beneficiaries who did not participate in the challenge. *See,* Tunstall v. Wells, 144 Cal. App. 4th 554, 565, 50 Cal. Rptr. 3d 468, 475 (2006); *In re* Houston's Estate, 371 Pa. 396, 89 A.2d 525, 526 (1952); *and,* Perry v. Rogers, 52 Tex. Civ. App. 594, 114 S.W. 897 (1908).

[4] See *In re* Estate of Kirkholder, 171 A.D. 153, 154 (N.Y. App. Div. Jan. 22, 1916); *In re* Estate of Bergland, 180 Cal. 629, 634, 635–636 (1919); *In re* Estate of Gonzalez, 102 Cal. App. 4th 1296, 1306, 1308 (2002); *See also* Claudia G. Catalano, J.D., Annotation, *What Constitutes Contest or Attempt to Defeat Will Within Provision Thereof Forfeiting Share of Contesting Beneficiary,* 3 A.L.R.5th 590 (1992).

[5] *See In re* Miller Osborne Perry Trust, 299 Mich. App. 525, 831 N.W.2d 251 (2013), *lv. denied,* 495 Mich. 892, 839 N.W.2d 195 (2013); *In re* Robert E. Whitton Revocable Trust, unpublished Mich. App. 2018 WL 3788381 (Aug 9, 2018).

NO-CONTEST CLAUSES GENERALLY

No-contest clauses have a checkered history, in part, because they can affect a forfeiture of an estate interest and, in part, because their enforceability has varied among those states whose courts or legislatures have considered them. Where no-contest clauses are allowed by law, it is to permit the post-death enforcement of an estate plan by punishing an unsuccessful challenger of that estate plan, and in some cases, the administration of that plan. Some states, by legislation or court ruling, have created an exception to the enforcement of no-contest clauses where there is sufficient evidence to create probable cause for the challenge, whether or not the challenge is successful. When no-contest clauses are recognized, they tend to be narrowly interpreted and applied. Often, when they are sought to be applied, the courts tend to apply a balancing test between an individual's right to have an estate plan implemented after death and protecting against wrongful creation of an estate plan based on one or more of several factors, including undue influence, duress, misrepresentation, and fraud. While the existence of a no-contest clause by itself is not an indicia of undue influence where such clauses are legal, it is possible that the inclusion of such a clause may, itself, be an additional indicia of undue influence if substantial other indicia of undue influence also are present, such as a long-standing intention to provide for family members without a no-contest clause.

WHAT IS THE "PROBABLE CAUSE" EXCEPTION?

Although the scope of a no-contest clause may be broader than attempting to dissuade a challenge to a document, most are intended to punish a challenger to the dispositive terms of the document. This leads, in those states where there is a probable clause exception, to an inquiry regarding the meaning of the term "probable cause." There is general acceptance that meeting the "probable cause" test does not require the challenger to prevail in the challenge itself. However, it may require the challenger to demonstrate a reasonable belief, at the time the challenge is officially asserted, that there were substantial facts and circumstances in existence to support an allegation of lack of capacity or undue influence. A reasonable belief is that of a hypothetical, reasonable person, exercising ordinary prudence in evaluating the facts and circumstances then present. This is sometimes described as a requirement that the challenger act in good faith. While the opinion of legal counsel, sought in good faith and after disclosure of the facts and circumstances, can be supportive, the existence of such an opinion will not necessarily avoid a forfeiture. Some states require that the facts and circumstances indicate a substantial likelihood of success, while others require that the facts and circumstances indicate that there is a reasonable likelihood of success.[6]

In a case of first impression, *Schiffer v. Brenton*,[7] the Michigan Supreme Court held that *in terrorem* (also referred to as "penalty" or "no-contest") clauses in wills were valid and enforceable, irrespective of the good faith or bad faith of the contest. The *Schiffer* court reasoned that

> . . . such provisions serve a wise purpose; they discourage a child from precipitating expensive litigation against the estate, and encourage and reward other children in their effort to sustain their parent's disposition of his property if such contest is precipitated; they discourage family strife, they discourage litigation, and the law abhors litigation.[8]

Michigan law under *Schiffer*, as it developed over time, was uniformly codified with respect to wills and trusts with the adoption of the Estate and Protected Individuals Code ("EPIC") on April 1, 2000, for wills, and the Michigan Trust Code ("MTC") on April 1, 2010, for trusts. Michigan now has a common statutory provision authorizing the use of *in terrorem* clauses in wills and trusts and an exception to their enforcement, if there is proba-ble cause to contest a will or trust containing an *in terrorem* clause.

A penalty clause typically reduces or eliminates a devise to a devisee who challenges the validity of part or the entire instrument, whether it be a will, a codicil to a will, a trust, or an amendment to a trust. The clause may also include a similar penalty if a devisee challenges the administration of a will or trust. However, while recognizing the validity of *in terrorem* clauses, Michigan provides that a penalty clause shall not be given effect if probable cause exists for instituting a proceeding to contest an instrument.

Michigan essentially establishes a balancing test between, on the one hand, respecting a testator's or settlor's right to provide for the disposition

---

[6] See discussion regarding meaning of "probable cause": as an exception to enforcement of no-contest clauses. Thomas F. Sweeney, Esq., Thomas M. Dixon, Esq., & Thomas E.F. Fabbri, Esq., *Probable Cause Exceptions to Enforcement of Will and Trust In Terrorem Clauses: Determining the Factors in Applying the Exception and Consider-ing Opportunities for an Early Determination of Whether the Exception Has Been Satisfied*, 33 MICH. PROB. & EST. PLAN. J., Winter, 2013, at 2.

[7] Schiffer v. Brenton, 247 Mich. 512, 520, 226 N.W. 253, 255 (1929).

[8] *Id.*

of his or her assets after death to such persons and subject to such conditions desired by the decedent (commonly referred to as donative intent), and on the other hand, protecting against a misfeasance or malfeasance that corrupted the real intent of the testator or settlor. The Reporter's Comment describes the drafting rational as follows:

> A court should understand that the rule recognizes the testator's legitimate desire and expectation that the testamentary plan will be implemented without spiteful disruption and spurious claims. At the same time, the exception is to permit challenge and questioning when there is a reasonable basis for concern. Courts should police the rule and its exception carefully and thoughtfully, or the balancing that was sought will disappear.
>
> Penalty provisions should not result in a court's unwittingly assisting misfeasance or malfeasance. In order to provide courts with the ability to balance these conflicting interests, a probable cause exception exists to the rule that otherwise validates *in terrorem* clauses.[9]

There are two important legal questions raised with respect to determining whether probable cause exists in a given situation and the manner in which a court deals with this question: (1) What factors should be considered in determining whether probable cause exists? (2) At what stage in a proceeding may a court determine whether probable cause exists?

Both of these questions are addressed in the next section.

WHAT FACTORS SHOULD BE CONSIDERED IN DETERMINING WHETHER PROBABLE CAUSE EXISTS?

The first question about the factors to be considered in determining whether probable cause exists was intentionally not answered by the drafters of Michigan Compiled Laws (MCL) 700.3905 and 700.7113 in order to permit the development of case law to provide guidance based on the facts in a particular case. But what is important is that the probable cause exemption not swallow the rule.[10]

---

[9] *See* MICHIGAN COMPILED LAWS (MCL), REPORTER'S COMMENTS 700.2518, 700.3905, and 700.7113.

[10] This is indicated from the Reporter's Comment under MCL 700.3905 (and quoted in the Reporter's Comment to MCL 700.7113), which states that:

The Uniform Probate Code (UPC) also does not seek to define the probable cause exception.[11]

Reviewing other areas of the law that address the concept of probable cause may assist in determining the factors to apply a probable cause exception in will and trust contests involving an *in terrorem* clause.

In the criminal law setting, probable cause signifies evidence sufficient to cause a person of ordinary prudence and caution to conscientiously entertain a reasonable belief in the defendant's guilt.[12] These factors can be summarized as sufficient information available to such person to cause a prudent person to conscientiously believe a person is guilty of a crime. This exception requires significantly less than the standard of evidence to convict the accused.

A cause of action for malicious criminal prosecution arises when one person causes another to be arrested for a crime for which the arrestee is ultimately found not guilty or against whom the criminal case is dismissed. In such cases, a plaintiff must demonstrate that the civil defendant acted with an ulterior purpose otherwise improper in the normal conduct of the proceeding. The defense to a malicious prosecution claim depends on the civil defendant having probable cause to file the criminal complaint.[13] Michigan's civil jury instructions regarding malicious prosecution cases make the following provision:

> Defendant had probable cause if, based on the facts and circumstances known to [him / her] at the time [he / she] [initiated / continued] the criminal proceeding, [he / she] reasonably believed that plaintiff was guilty of a crime. Probable cause may be based on information received from others, but only if the information is of such a reliable kind and from such reliable sources that a reasonable person would believe the information is true.[14]

Courts must be vigilant in policing the concept of probable cause and require that there be some substantial basis in fact for a contest or other challenge. If any flimsy excuse is sufficient, the exception swallows the rule.

[11] 333 UNIFIED PROBATE CODE §§ 2–517 and 3.905.

[12] People v. Green, 255 Mich. App. 426, 661 N.W.2d 616 (2003). *See also* People v. Salimone, 265 Mich. 486, 490, 251 N.W. 594, 595 (1933), where probable cause was defined as "a reasonable ground of suspicion, supported by circumstances sufficiently strong in themselves to warrant a cautious man in the belief that a person accused was guilty of the offense with which he is charged."

[13] Pilette Indus v. Alexander, 17 Mich. App. 226, 169 N.W.2d 149 (1969). See RESTATEMENT (SECOND) TORTS §§ 653–672.

[14] M. CIV. J.I. 117.04.

This jury instruction focuses on what a hypothetical person would reasonably believe based on the facts and circumstances known to the person, including such information from other reliable sources that appears to be reliable.

The Restatement (Second) of Property recognizes *in terrorem* clauses "unless there was probable cause for making the contest or attack"[15] of a will or trust. In doing so, it provides that:

> [T]he term "probable cause" means the existence, at the time of the initiation of the proceeding, of evidence which would lead a reasonable person, properly informed and advised, to conclude that there is a substantial likelihood that the contest or attack will be successful. The evidence needed to establish probable cause should be less where there is a strong public policy supporting the legal ground of the contest or attack. . . . A factor that bears on the existence of probable cause is that the beneficiary relied upon the advice of disinterested counsel sought in good faith after a full disclosure of the facts.[16]

It is important to note that the Restatement (Second) of Property definition does not require that one possess all of the evidence needed for a successful prosecution of the contest of the will or trust. It merely requires a substantial likelihood of success based on what is known at the commencement of the proceeding. However, the Restatement (Second) of Property includes an additional consideration involving the inquiry: whether the person commencing the proceeding was advised by disinterested and reasonably informed counsel. It suggests that where there is a strong public policy, the evidence to support probable cause may be less.

The Restatement (Third) of Property continues to recognize the validity of *in terrorem* clauses "unless probable cause existed for instituting the proceeding."[17] In doing so, it provides in part as follows:

> Probable cause exists when, at the time of instituting a proceeding, there was evidence that would lead a reasonable person,

---

[15] RESTATEMENT (SECOND) OF PROP.: WILLS AND OTHER DONATIVE TRANSFERS § 9.1.

[16] RESTATEMENT (SECOND) OF PROP.: WILLS AND OTHER DONATIVE TRANSFERS § 9.1, cmt. j.

[17] RESTATEMENT (THIRD) OF PROP.: WILLS AND OTHER DONATIVE TRANSFERS § 8.5.

properly informed and advised, to conclude that there was a sub-stantial likelihood that the challenge would be successful. A fac-tor that bears on the existence of probable cause is whether the beneficiary relied upon the advice of an independent legal coun-sel sought in good faith after full disclosure of the facts. The mere fact that the person mounting the challenge was represented by counsel is not controlling, however, since the institution of a legal proceeding challenging a donative transfer normally involves representation by legal counsel.[18]

This later version of the Restatement essentially reaffirms the prior version of the Restatement, except to indicate that the existence of disin-terested and reasonably informed counsel is not necessarily satisfied solely because the petitioner has retained an attorney to make the contest.

In *Nacovsky v. Hall (In re Griffin Trust)*,[19] Michigan essentially applied the Restatement (Third) concept of probable cause to a trust contest (before Michigan had a statute on point). In doing so, the appellate court found:

Probable cause exists when, at the time of instituting the pro-ceeding, there was evidence that would lead a reasonable person, properly informed and advised, to conclude that there was a sub-stantial likelihood that the challenge would be successful.[20]

In *In re Estate of George Eugene Stan*,[21] Michigan again addressed the application of probable cause, citing *In re Griffin Trust* and its citation of Restatement (Third) § 8.5, comment c. In *In re Estate of George Eugene Stan*, one daughter's petition for formal administration of a pourover will that named her the personal representative was objected to by a second daugh-ter. The decedent's trust contained an *in terrorem* clause providing for for-feiture if a beneficiary or heir unsuccessfully contested the admission of the will to probate or any provision of the will or trust. The second daugh-ter alleged wrongdoing by the first daughter regarding probate property

---

[18] RESTATEMENT (THIRD) OF PROP.: WILLS AND OTHER DONATIVE TRANSFERS § 8.5, comment c.

[19] Nacovsky v. Hall (*In re* Griffin Trust, 281 Mich. App. 532, 760 N.W.2d 318 (2008) (reversed on other grounds)).

[20] *Id.* at 540.

[21] *In re* Estate of George Eugene Stan, 301 Mich. App. 435, 839 N.W.2d 498 (2013), *lv. denied*, 495 Mich. 922, 843 N.W.2d 170 (2014).

before she was appointed personal representative. The court applied MCL 700.2518 and MCL 700.3905 because the will expressly incorporated the trust's *in terrorem* clause, apparently by referring to the will and by having a pour-over device to the trust. The second daughter's objection to the appointment of her sister was a contest of the will. The court concluded that the assertion of ". . . any ground which would justify the removal of a personal representative under MCL 700.3611(2) is equally sufficient to support an interested person's objection to the initial appointment of a personal representative under MCL 700.3203(2)."[22] Because the first sister took possession of the probate property and may have failed to account for that property prior to her appointment, those facts were sufficient to satisfy the probable cause standard, avoid a forfeiture, and affirm the lower court's refusal to enforce the clause, albeit for different reasons. The court also ruled that because there was no proceeding that contested the trust, there was no contest with respect to the trust under MCL 700.7113.

Appellate courts in several other states have considered the factors for applying the exception of probable cause in a will or trust dispute involving an *in terrorem* clause.

The Iowa Supreme Court, in *Geisinger v. Geisinger*,[23] relied upon the Restatement of Law, Torts § 675 when addressing the validity of an *in terrorem* clause in a case involving a dispute over the construction of a will and codicils. In *Geisinger,* the court held that a person has probable cause for initiating civil proceedings against another if he (a) reasonably believes in the existence of facts upon which his claim is based, and that under such facts the claim may be valid at common law or under an existing statute, or (b) believes that the claim may be valid in reliance upon the advice of counsel he receives and acts upon.

A Kansas appellate court, in *In re Estate of Wells*,[24] relied in part upon the rule of the Restatement of Property § 429 (1944), which held that a contestant acts with probable cause when there is a substantial belief that a will is invalid, but ultimately the court settled upon the definition contained *In re Estate of Campbell*,[25] which adopted the definition of probable cause contained in comment j of the Restatement (Second) § 9.1.[26]

---

[22] *Id.* at 117.

[23] Geisinger v. Geisinger, 241 Iowa 283, 41 N.W.2d 86 (1950).

[24] *In re* Estate of Wells, 26 Kan. App. 2d 282, 983 P.2d 279 (Kan. Ct. App. 1999) (citing *In re* Estate of Foster, 190 Kan. 498, 500, 376 P.2d 784, 786, 98 A.L.R.2d 795 (1962)).

[25] *In re* Estate of Campbell, 19 Kan. App. 2d 795, 801, 876 P.2d 212, 216 (1994).

[26] *Id.*

Arizona statutory law precludes enforcement of a penalty clause when probable cause to contest a will exists.[27] In *Rodriguez v. Gavette (In re Estate of Shumway)*,[28] the Arizona Supreme Court adopted the Restatement of Property exception of "probable cause":

> We believe the RESTATEMENT's standard for probable cause properly balances the conflicting policy interests and therefore adopt it over the other potential standards, including that framed by the court of appeals and those presented by the parties, which included the colorable claim and Rule 11 standards. We include the good faith element rejected by the court of appeals. While we agree that good faith is not the sole test, we believe subjective belief in the basis of the challenge is part of the required belief in the substantial likelihood of success. We will apply the RESTATEMENT's test flexibly, especially when strong policy supports grounds for challenge - as in the case of suspected undue influence, the principal ground for contest in the present case. The RESTATEMENT's standard of a "reasonable person, properly informed and advised" who concludes there is a substantial likelihood of success in the contest is, of course, a question initially for the trial court. In addressing that question, the trial judge should, as the RESTATEMENT requires, refer to the evidence known at the time the contest was initiated.[29]

In *Winningham v. Winningham*,[30] with regard to the issue of probable cause, the Supreme Court of Tennessee held that:

> . . . a contest will not work a forfeiture where there is, in addition to good faith, probable cause, and reasonable grounds for instituting the suit. In *Woolard v. Ferrell*, 26 Tenn. App. 197 (Tenn. App. 1942), the Court of Appeals applied reasoning from malicious prosecution law to analyze the issue of probable cause to contest a will with a forfeiture clause. That court quoted from a treatise on malicious prosecution, stating, the law as to reasonable or probable cause is defined to be such a state of facts in the mind of the prosecutor as would lead a person of ordinary caution and prudence to believe, or entertain an honest or strong suspicion,

---

[27] Ariz. Rev. Stat. § 14–2517.

[28] Rodriguez v. Gavette (*In re* Estate of Shumway), 198 Ariz. 323, 327, 9 P.3d 1062, 1066, 330 Ariz. Adv. Rep. 20 (Ariz. 2000).

[29] *Id.*

[30] Winningham v. Winningham, 966 S.W.2d 48 (Tenn. 1998).

that the person is guilty. It does not depend on the actual state of the case in point of fact, but upon the honest and reasonable belief of the party commencing the prosecution . . . . The question of probable cause applies to the nature of the suit, and the point of inquiry is whether the defendant had probable cause to maintain the particular suit upon the existing facts known to him.

* * *

More recently, this Court has defined the existence of probable cause in the context of a malicious prosecution suit as being independent of the subjective mental state of the prosecutor, requiring "only the existence of such facts and circumstances sufficient to excite in a reasonable mind the belief that the accused is guilty of the crime charged." *Roberts v. Federal Express Corp.*, 842 S.W.2d 246, 248 (Tenn. 1992).[31]

As noted in *Winningham*, even though this requirement for exemption from forfeiture is usually discussed in the language of "probable cause" with reliance on malicious prosecution decisions, "reasonable ground" or "reasonable justification" is the more appropriate characterization of the factor to be applied. While the advice of counsel may constitute probable cause in cases of malicious prosecution, it will not defeat a forfeiture unless the suit to contest the will was reasonably justified under all of the circumstances.
The *Winningham* court also noted that:

While the advice of counsel may constitute probable cause in cases of malicious prosecution, it will not defeat a forfeiture unless the suit to contest the will was reasonably justified under all of the circumstances. As stated in *In Re Friend's Estate*, 209 Pa. 442 (1903), ". . . if the mere advice of counsel can be regarded as probable cause for instituting proceedings to contest a will, there would be none without cause, and in every instance such a [forfeiture] clause as the testatrix inserted in hers would be nugatory."[32]

The essential point in *Winningham* is that the petitioner must show that under all the circumstances, the contest was reasonably justified. This includes a showing that a reasonably prudent person would have believed

---

[31] *Id.* at 52.

[32] *Id.* at 52.

or entertained an honest or strong suspicion that there was probable cause to contest the instrument, and that the advice of informed counsel is not by itself sufficient, but is a factor to be considered, along with other factors.

The various sources of law discussed here provide several common factors for determining the exception of "probable cause" with respect to a will or trust contest when there is an *in terrorem* clause. While some of these sources emphasize one factor over another, this variation may reflect, in part, the application of the balancing of the conflicting interests at play in contests involving *in terrorem* clauses. These common factors include:

a. **Time of determination**: The facts and circumstances considered by the court in determining probable cause generally are those in existence at the time a proceeding to determine probable cause is commenced. The later discovery of facts and circumstances not known to the petitioner at the time the proceeding is commenced generally are not considered material to the question of probable cause. The issue of "time of determination" may be analogous to the operative time for a determination of whether a claim or defense is frivolous. In such instances, such determinations are premised on the circumstances at the time the claim or defense was asserted.[33]

b. **Source of information**: The facts and circumstances must be known to the petitioner and may include information received from others, but only if the information is reliable in kind and from a reliable source.

c. **Belief of a reasonable person**: The belief of the petitioner should satisfy a "reasonable person" standard. In other words, a hypothetical, reasonable person, exercising ordinary prudence, after considering the available facts and circumstances, including those obtained from reliable sources, and being reasonably informed and advised, must believe there is a requisite likelihood that the contest will be successful. As in the defense of a malicious prosecution claim, showing that a reasonable person would believe there is probable cause to contest a will or trust is not the same as proving the validity of the contest itself by a preponderance of the evidence.

d. **Opinion of independent or disinterested counsel**: The opinion of legal counsel, sought in good faith after a disclosure of the facts and circumstances, can be supportive of a finding of probable cause. However, an affirmative counsel's opinion will not by itself necessarily avoid a forfeiture if the facts and circumstances then known are

---

[33] Jerico Const v. Quadrants, 257 Mich. App. 22, 36, 666 N.W.2d 310 (2003).

insufficient to show the requisite likelihood of success. Although an opinion of counsel does not appear to be a mandatory requirement, an opinion from an independent or disinterested counsel based on the available facts and circumstances and an informed legal analysis will carry more weight than no opinion or an opinion that lacks these components.

e. **Requisite likelihood of success**: Some sources of law state that the facts and circumstances should indicate that there is a *substantial* likelihood of success, while others indicate there should be a *reasonable* likelihood of success. This difference may be explained by focusing on the word "substantial," which, depending on the context, can be considered either a qualitative term or a quantitative term. Regardless of the adjective used, what is clear is that the term does not refer to a preponderance of the evidence, which has a quantitative meaning. Rather, the term appears to refer to a qualitative factor. Is there sufficient substance to establish a reasonable likelihood that the contest may succeed? That determination is not dependent on the contest actually succeeding in an evidentiary hearing. Rather, the term is intended to exclude contests that are based on a "flimsy excuse" or that have no or minimal substance from continuing.

f. **Good faith requirement**: Some sources of law state a requirement that the petitioner's belief must have been reached in good faith, while others do not make this a specific requirement. A good faith requirement would appear to be satisfied if the petitioner's belief is that of a reasonable person, properly informed and advised, rather than simply a subjective belief, not shared by a hypothetical reasonable person.

g. **Flexible application of exception based on public policy**: Some sources of law state that the exception should be flexibly applied, including using a lower standard of evidence, when a public policy (such as protecting against forgery or undue influence) would support the grounds for the contest. Courts uniformly recognize that there is a public policy against giving validity to wills or trusts resulting from forgery, undue influence, lack of testamentary capacity, duress, or fraud. Accordingly, the same flexibility should be available to the court in considering any petition based upon one of the aforementioned public policy grounds. More importantly, the flexibility granted to a court should reflect the court's focus on the facts and circumstances produced to support the substance of the allegation of probable cause, and not on the particular legal basis underlying the assertion of probable cause.

The previously referenced factors, while primary, are not necessarily exclusive factors for courts to consider in applying the probable cause exception in a particular case. This is because "courts must be vigilant in policing the concept of probable cause and require that there be some substantial basis in fact for a contest or other challenge. If any flimsy excuse is sufficient, the exception swallows the rule."[34]

Strategically, one may wish to consider when might be the best time to seek a probable cause determination. First, one should review the pertinent statute of limitation with regard to bringing a contest. When it comes to will or codicil contests, the statute of limitations often is determined based on when the instrument is presented to the court.[35] Because trusts (and trust amendments) may not otherwise be subject to court supervision, the time to contest a trust or trust amendment may be governed by a different set of principles, such as the death of the grantor, when the trust became irrevocable, or a period premised upon when information is provided by the trustee.[36] In Michigan, a trust contest with regard to a revocable grantor trust must be brought within the earlier of two years after the settlor's death or six months after the date the trustee has provided information to the petitioner regarding the trust and the petitioner's interest under the trust.[37]

AT WHAT STAGE IN A PROCEEDING MAY A COURT DETERMINE WHETHER PROBABLE CAUSE EXISTS?

Discussing the factors for a finding of probable cause may lead to the important question of how soon after the commencement of the contest should a court consider the issue of probable cause?

In the criminal law context, probable cause is determined at the preliminary examination, conducted at the initial stages of the criminal proceeding. In *People v. Greene*,[38] the court stated:

> [A]t the preliminary examination, the prosecution need not prove beyond a reasonable doubt that the defendant committed

---

[34] MCL, REPORTER'S COMMENTS 700.3905 and 700.7113.

[35] *See* MCL 700.3401 *et seq.*

[36] *See, e.g.*, MCL 700.7604(1), 700.7814(2)(c).

[37] *Id.*

[38] People v. Greene, 255 Mich. App. 426, 443–444, 661 N.W.2d 616 (2003).

the crime charged. The threshold for the evidence necessary to bind over a defendant for trial is much lower than the evidence needed to convict a defendant of the crime at trial.

* * *

If the evidence introduced at the preliminary examination conflicts or raises a reasonable doubt about the defendant's guilt, the magistrate must let the fact finder at trial resolve those questions of fact.

* * *

Circumstantial evidence and reasonable inferences arising from the evidence are sufficient to support the bind-over of the defendant if such evidence establishes probable cause.[39]

The principle under criminal law described here suggests that, in cases in which there is a contest involving a will or trust that contains an *in terrorem* clause, resolution of the probable cause issue need not wait until the trial. In fact, there may be advantages to having this issue resolved sooner rather than later in many cases.

In cases where there are sufficient undisputed relevant facts and circumstances regarding probable cause, the determination of whether probable cause exists is a question of law to be decided by the court. In such cases, advancement of the resolution of this issue may have merit, rather than having the resolution wait until the case is tried. A determination of the existence of probable cause does not mean that the petitioner has won the contest, only that the *in terrorem* clause will not result in a forfeiture if the petitioner loses. Depending on the jurisdiction (and whether a presumption of undue influence has been established), the petitioner generally will still have the burden of proof regarding the contest.

If the petitioner provides no relevant facts and circumstances (or the presumption of undue influence cannot be established), the court may determine that there is no basis for advancing the probable cause exception, as a matter of law, which may result in the end of the proceeding.

If there are insufficient undisputed facts and circumstances to allow the court to determine the existence of probable cause as a matter of law,

---

[39] *Id.* at 626, 627.

the petitioner will know that forfeiture may occur, unless the petitioner is able to prevail in an evidentiary hearing on the mixed questions of fact and law regarding the issue of probable cause. Even though this would be an evidentiary hearing, the exception to be met by the petitioner is one of probable cause and not a preponderance of the evidence. In these cases, an early decision on probable cause may be a more efficient use of the time of both the court and counsel in determining this preliminary question in cases involving *in terrorem* clauses. An early determination by the court as a matter of law or in an evidentiary hearing may also facilitate an earlier resolution of these cases, although that can never be guaranteed.

To date, no state has required that the challenger establish probable cause by a preponderance of the evidence standard. A reasonable reconciliation of these different standards suggests that it may be the quality of the evidence regarding the circumstances under which an instrument was created as opposed to the amount of evidence presented that may influence a determination of whether probable cause exists. Establishing that a presumption of undue influence exists may itself be sufficient to establish probable cause for a contest under many circumstances. This may be because the existence of a "presumption of undue influence" generally precludes dismissal of a will or trust challenge on a summary basis when the challenge is one premised upon the exertion of undue influence. Nonetheless, rather than simply relying upon the "presumption of undue influence," it may be advisable to attempt to put forth additional facts and circumstances to enhance the probability that probable cause will be established.

CHAPTER 9

A Litigation Perspective[1]

By their very nature, undue influence cases tend to be complex, fact-intensive, and challenging. For the proponent of an instrument, often a straightforward, simple, believable, and thematic approach is the most effective method to present proofs. For the challenger, however, the presentation of proofs (especially in the absence of the presumption or following the rebuttal of the presumption) can be much more difficult. The challenger must often piece together suspicious circumstances and apply them to the known facts in order to portray a mosaic explanation of the "back story" to the creation of the challenged instrument. Unlike the influence portrayed in the movie *Misery*, in most cases, the action tends to be much more subtle than "hobbling," and we seldom have the benefit of the "director's lens" with which to view the conduct (although "smoking guns" might be found during the course of discovery).

These cases require not only a knowledge of the law, but also a working knowledge of the facts, an understanding of the potential interplay and impact of dependency and vulnerabilities, including cognitive difficulties, and a great deal of strategy. Moreover, the use of experts in a variety of different fields can play a significant role in the preparation and analysis, pre-trial motion, discovery, and trial stages of a case. In these cases, an understanding of the complexities of family dynamics, cognitive and other medical and mental health issues and records, as well as the legal issues presented may necessitate outside assistance and a holistic approach to the case.

---

[1] Portions of this chapter were adapted from two articles published by BNA: Sandra D. Glazier, Esq., *Capacity and Ethical Considerations When Representing Vulnerable Adults*, 43 TAX MANAGE. ESTATES GIFTS TRUSTS J. (2018); and Bloomberg BNA, Sandra D. Glazier, Esq., Thomas M. Dixon, Esq., & Thomas F. Sweeney, Esq., *What Every Estate Planner Should Know About Undue Influence: Recognizing It, Insulating/Planning Against It . . . And Litigating It*, TAX MANAGEMENT MEMORANDUM (2015).

In many other respects, litigating undue influence cases involve the same kind of planning, strategies, and litigation skills and techniques required in other forms of civil litigation. Hence, the focus here is on selected topics and other considerations that distinguish undue influence cases from most other forms of litigation.

IT'S NOT ONLY ABOUT THE MONEY

Like any commercial dispute, allocation (or reallocation) of money generally is the core issue in undue influence challenges. What distinguishes these cases is that they are rarely *only* about the money. By their very nature, will and trust challenges generally involve long-standing and often complicated family relationships that bring with them all the emotions and motivations associated with those long-standing relationships. For example, such motivations can commonly include sibling rivalry, jealousy, competition for the perceived affection of a deceased relative, vindictiveness, anger, and, of course, on occasion, outright hatred. The list goes on. These motivations sometimes are not obvious because people often are guarded, deliberately or otherwise, against showing their true feelings and intentions. Such concerns are augmented by the fact that the aging baby boomer generation often leaves children and spouses (thus, potential beneficiaries) from multiple marriages, which often results in more complex relationships. Whether representing the proponent or the challenger, it is important for litigators to assess the motivations of clients and opposing parties (and sometimes, scores of influential relatives) to weigh the impact such motivations can have on important considerations such as case strategy, the testimony of witnesses, and settlement negotiations.[2] In particular, these volatilities often make settlement more complicated than mere rational assessment of financial risk. It is folly for counsel to ignore such profound influences in a case. It is also important in properly counseling clients through the course of the litigation to openly discuss these issues, which in turn may improve client satisfaction with the outcome of the litigation. As a litigator, recognition and management of these considerations can be every bit as important as the skill of establishing an effective record during depositions or in cross-examination at trial.

---

[2] These non-financial motivations have been recognized by clinicians who have expertise in assessing vulnerability to undue influence. Sanford I. Finkel, M.D., *Ten Pitfalls in Litigating a Contested Will*, 16 AMERICAN ASSOCIATION FOR JUSTICE, 5–6 (Winter 2009).

As referenced earlier, due to their very nature, undue influence cases are almost always based on circumstantial evidence. More often than not, the challenger had limited access or contact with the decedent and, therefore, likely was not a witness to many of the alleged events giving rise to the contest. Isolation can even be present when the decedent had contact with third parties who have little or no past knowledge of the functioning and intentions of the decedent or the nature of the relationship between the decedent and the alleged perpetrator. The key point is that challengers rarely have direct proof of the elements of the claim and, therefore, the discovery, assessment, and presentation of circumstantial proofs becomes essential.

LEVELING THE PLAYING FIELD

As discussed in chapters 4 and 6, the law has recognized the difficulty of alleging and proving circumstantial cases caused by isolation and secrecy. To level the playing field, the law allows a challenger to establish a "presumption of undue influence" based on a relatively modest burden of proof of (1) the existence of a confidential or fiduciary relationship, (2) the fiduciary benefited, and (3) the fiduciary had an opportunity to influence the grantor. From a litigation perspective, a key benefit of establishing the presumption (in jurisdictions such as Michigan) is that the challenger may be immune from a dispositive motion and thus is guaranteed the opportunity to present the case to a fact finder. (As stated earlier, other benefits of establishing the presumption of undue influence may include a probable cause determination to void the operation of an *in terrorem* clause and ultimate victory if the proponent is unable to produce substantial evidence rebutting the presumption.) When applicable, an early determination that the presumption does or does not exist may create offensive or defensive advantages. As one might glean from the distinction between Michigan and Florida or California law relating to the evidentiary and persuasive weight of the presumption, as a litigator, it is important to understand the elements necessary to establish and rebut the presumption. This knowledge can assist not only in litigating such issues but also proves helpful in the estate planning stage.

The law additionally levels the playing field in these circumstantial cases by relaxing discovery and evidentiary (relevancy) standards relating to admission of evidence at trial.[3] Importantly, counsel both for proponents

---

[3] In general, all evidence, both direct and circumstantial, that bears upon the question of undue influence should be admitted. All evidence that tends to prove or disprove that an instrument was procured by undue influence should be admitted.

and for challengers must bear in mind the strategic considerations of the court's role as "gatekeeper" for both the scope of discovery, as well as admission of proofs at trial. Judges who take a narrow view of the scope of relevancy and, therefore, discovery and admissibility, may make a successful challenge exceedingly more difficult or outright impossible. For these reasons, disputes regarding the scope of discovery and admissibility of evidence are both common and critical to the outcome of undue influence cases.

CASE PERSPECTIVE: LONGITUDINAL VS. ACUTE

Because undue influence challenges often are based on circumstantial evidence, the opposing parties often present their cases from two entirely different perspectives.

A challenger likely will view the case longitudinally and thereby present a collection of circumstantial facts over time. A challenger tends to establish such things as the vulnerabilities of the decedent, the changes in estate planning intentions of the decedent, evolving isolation of the decedent, secretive actions of a proponent, growing dependency, and any number of the "red flag" indicia of undue influence. The challenger will need to determine whether a chronological, thematic, or combined approach best portrays the longitudinal story to be presented.

It is against this backdrop that other elements that tend to demonstrate the existence of influence that is "undue" will be superimposed. Absent a finding of the presumption of undue influence, the challenger often bears a heavy burden to establish that the grantor's estate planning desires were actually supplanted by the will of another. Therefore, it is important that the challenger develop a rational and credible theme,

---

In re Loree's Estate, 158 Mich. 372, 379, 122 N.W. 623, 624 (1909). Evidence of undue influence after the date on which the testator made his or her will is relevant and admissible as tending to show a continuance of undue influence. Walts v. Walts, 127 Mich. 607, 610, 86 N.W. 1030, 1031 (1901); Leffingwell v. Bettinghouse, 151 Mich. 513, 518, 115 N.W. 731, 733 (1908). *See also In re* Vhay's Estate, 225 Mich. 107, 108, 195 N.W. 674 (1923). The remoteness in time of the evidence only affects the weight such evidence should be given, not whether such evidence is admissible. Balk's Estate, 289 Mich. 703, 706, 287 N.W. 351, 352, 353, 124 A.L.R. 431 (1939); *see also* McPeak v. McPeak, 233 Mich. App. 483, 496, 593 N.W.2d 180, 187 (1999). There should be no arbitrary time limit placed upon what might prove relevant, and all material evidence should be produced. *In re* Loree's Estate, *id.* at 376, 377.

which demonstrates how and why the grantor's will was supplanted for that of another.

In contrast, proponents of an instrument may likely emphasize an "acute view" that's focused on discreet moments of time. For example, the proponent's proofs may feature the execution of amendments to an estate plan when third parties are available to allegedly corroborate testamentary capacity based on statements made by and in the presence of the decedent and his or her apparent knowing and voluntary execution of the instrument. These discreet events, if viewed in isolation and stripped of any proofs relating to pre-execution and post-execution, make challenges extraordinarily difficult. Because it generally is presumed that documents are valid, absent a showing of fraud, duress, or undue influence, in the absence of an established presumption, the proponent's story generally is an easier one to present. This may be further buttressed, in part, because the trier of fact is not charged with changing the outcome simply because a different disposition may be deemed more appropriate or reasonable.[4]

Nonetheless, whether one represents the proponent or the challenger, it may still be important to establish the nature of the relationship and why the decedent desired the provisions of the instrument.

---

[4] MICHIGAN MODEL CIVIL JURY INSTRUCTIONS (M. CIV. J.I.) 170.04, 179.07. The comments to M. CIV. J.I. 170.04 are instructive. They provide that:

> This instruction contains cautions as to the rights of a person in the making of his will. These cautions are believed necessary to prevent the often mistaken belief of most jurors that the decedent cannot disinherit heirs and other relatives by his or her will and to prevent the jurors from improperly trying to substitute their judgment for the judgment of the maker of the will. See *In re* Allen's Estate, 230 Mich. 584 (1925).
>
> The testator has a right to dispose of his property as he sees fit. *In re* Kramer's Estate, 324 Mich. 626 (1949). The law does not require property to be disposed among the testator's heirs. *In re* Fay's Estate, 197 Mich. 675 (1917). It concerns no one what a person's reasons were in his distribution by will. Brown v. Blesch, 270 Mich. 576 (1935). The jury has no right to substitute its judgment for the judgment of the testator. *In re* Hannan's Estate, 315 Mich. 102 (1946). The jury has no right to consider that the testator did an apparent injustice in his will. *In re* Livingston's Estate, 295 Mich. 637 (1940). While the testator's blood relations are the natural objects of his bounty, such bounty is not limited by blood relationship, and his blood relations have no natural or inherent right to his property. Spratt v. Spratt, 76 Mich. 384 (1889).

THE ROLE AND IMPORTANCE OF
THE DRAFTING ATTORNEY IN THE
EVENT OF LITIGATION

There is a natural tendency for a drafting lawyer of challenged estate planning documents to assert the attorney-client privilege. The importance of the scrivener's files and testimony cannot be overstated, and scriveners should anticipate that their actions (and inactions) will be subject to thorough discovery. Such evidence may be pivotal to either making or rebuffing a challenge.

As with any case when the validity of the estate planning documents are contested, in undue influence cases, often there is the possibility or even the likelihood that the scrivener will be asked (or compelled) to testify at trial.[5] Model Rules of Professional Conduct preclude the scrivener

---

[5] While the use of expert witnesses in undue influence cases can be impactful, it is important to remember that the testimony of the scrivener attorney and witnesses to the execution of pertinent dispositive instruments are also extremely important. Whether the scrivener attorney will be treated as an expert or a lay witness may be subject to debate. One should, however, remember that MICH. R. EVID. (MRE) 701 permits lay witness opinion testimony when that testimony is rationally based on the perceptions of the witness and is helpful to a clear understanding of the witness's testimony or the determination of a fact in issue. As a consequence, the impressions and opinion of the scrivener attorney and witnesses present at the time of execution, supported by sufficiently detailed factual observations, can prove extremely important. While not every jurisdiction permits testimony on the ultimate issue to be determined by the fact finder, MRE 704 does. As a result, the testimony of the scrivener attorney and witnesses to execution on observations and resulting opinions as to the decedent's capacity at the time of execution and the voluntariness of the decedent's actions in the formulation of the plan will be important to the defense of the instruments. Michigan case law bears this out. In *In re* Bednarz Trust, 2009 Mich. App. LEXIS 1349 (Mich Ct. App. June 16, 2009), the court recognized the importance of the attorney's testimony regarding his observations and findings at the time the challenged documents were executed. The proponents of the instruments also offered the testimony of a doctor, who explained that some vascular dementia patients experience varying lucidity, comprehension, and communication capabilities from day to day and hour to hour. The contestants argued that testimony from the decedent's psychiatrist, who opined that the decedent was legally incapacitated, outweighed the attorney's testimony because she was a medical professional, based upon her observations two weeks before the instruments were executed. However, the Court of Appeals recognized that "[t]he opinion of a physician as to mental

from serving as a trial advocate when that lawyer also is likely to be a necessary witness in a contested proceeding.[6] As a result, scriveners should avoid taking on the role of the trial advocate in such circumstances. The more challenging tactical question is whether a law partner of the scrivener should serve as the trial advocate. The Model Rules of Professional Conduct (MRPC) allow such representation unless the role results in a conflict of interest under Rule 1.7 or 1.9.[7] Certainly, in cases where the actions (or inactions) of the scrivener are directly implicated in the alleged undue influence, the trial advocate may be placed in the untenable position of defending, directly or indirectly, the conduct of his or her own partner. In some cases, there may be malpractice implications involving the scrivener which would make the advocacy role of the partner even more tenuous or even outright prohibited where the advocate's own interest (by virtue of his partner's and his law firm's potential exposure) could materially limit the representation of the client.[8] In practice, the considerations as to whether a scrivener or a lawyer in the scrivener's firm should serve as the trial advocate in undue influences cases vary dramatically depending upon the facts and circumstances of the case in question. Each case must be considered on its own merits so that the trial advocacy is conducted in a manner that promotes the client's best interests.

---

competency, aside from the question of insanity, is entitled to no greater consideration than that of a layman having equal facilities for observation" (citing Bradford v. Vinton, 59 Mich. 139, 154; 26 N.W. 401 (1886)).

[6] MODEL RULES OF PROF'L CONDUCT (MRPC) r. 3.7: "(a) A lawyer shall not act as advocate at a trial in which the lawyer is likely to be a necessary witness unless: (1) the testimony relates to an uncontested issue; (2) the testimony relates to the nature and value of legal services rendered in the case; or (3) disqualification of the lawyer would work substantial hardship on the client. (b) A lawyer may act as advocate in a trial in which another lawyer in the lawyer's firm is likely to be called as a witness unless precluded from doing so by Rule 1.7 or Rule 1.9."

[7] *Id.*

[8] MRPC r. 1.7: "(a) Except as provided in paragraph (b), a lawyer shall not represent a client if the representation involves a concurrent conflict of interest. A concurrent conflict of interest exists if: (1) the representation of one client will be directly adverse to another client; or (2) there is a significant risk that the representation of one or more clients will be materially limited by the lawyer's responsibilities to another client, a former client or a third person or by a personal interest of the lawyer."

THE IMPORTANCE OF A DETAILED CHRONOLOGY AND DEVELOPMENT OF A DISCOVERY PLAN

As indicated, undue influence cases lend themselves to a longitudinal view of the evidence before, during, and after execution of the instrument. Consequently, from the outset of representation, the development of a detailed chronology can be crucial. In preparing the chronology, it may be helpful to use consistent references and terminology (to the extent possible). Doing so will facilitate the use of word search capabilities should the chronology become lengthy. The use of a chronology that identifies sources and individuals involved in a noted transaction may assist in identifying witnesses and preparing for depositions and trial testimony. Additionally, because undue influence cases tend to be extremely fact-sensitive, careful identification of citations to the source of the information contained in the chronology (such as identification of Bates-stamped document pages) can prove invaluable. Counsel should consider developing a chronology that is overinclusive, because in circumstantial cases, seemingly innocuous evidence may take on greater importance as additional facts are discovered.

In cases involving a considerable volume of documents, conversion of PDF documents into an optical character recognition (OCR) or other text searchable format also can be extremely helpful. Further, the use of document management systems that enhance the ability to easily search depositions, documents, and other materials can prove extremely beneficial during discovery and at trial.

Court-imposed timelines and other factors might constrain the time available for discovery. Therefore, it is important to develop a discovery plan early and to revisit it throughout preparation of the case, as factual patterns, theories, themes, or initial assumptions are affected.

Using Experts and Understanding the Medical Evidence

As with any case, counsel should consider using experts in an undue influence case when such persons can, by virtue of knowledge, skill, experience, training, or education, assist the trier of fact in understanding scientific, technical, or other specialized evidence.[2] Also, like any other types of cases, the extent and types of experts needed will vary from case to case. The considerations are many, and they usually will include whether the case is a bench or jury trial and, if a bench trial, the judge's level of knowledge and past experience in presiding over undue influences cases.

When litigating challenges that can justify the expense, counsel for both sides should consider retaining a seasoned forensic expert, such as a geriatric psychiatrist or psychologist. The primary role of such an expert is to opine, from a comprehensive perspective, on a person's vulnerability to undue influence and to assess the risk factors supporting that opinion.[3]

Because capacity and vulnerability often are issues that are found in will and trust contests, the use of a qualified expert can assist in putting the individual's vulnerabilities into context. It is rare that an estate planning attorney who

---

[1] Adapted from an article previously published by BNA: Bloomberg BNA, Sandra D. Glazier, Esq., Thomas M. Dixon, Esq., & Thomas F. Sweeney, Esq., *What Every Estate Planner Should Know About Undue Influence: Recognizing It, Insulating/Planning Against It . . . And Litigating It*, TAX MANAGEMENT MEMORANDUM (2015).

[2] *See* MICH. R. EVID. (MRE) 702.

[3] In some jurisdictions, the expert may be permitted to opine on the ultimate issue of whether undue influence was exerted. *See* MRE 704. *See also* Daniel A. Plotkin, James E. Spar, & Howard L. Horwitz, *Assessing Undue Influence*, 44 J. AM. ACAD. PSYCHIATRY LAW (September 2016), http://jaapl.org/content/44/3/344.

assisted in preparing and witnessing such documents will testify that they felt the individual lacked the requisite capacity to engage in the transaction or that the transaction was the product of undue influence. Statistically, 84 percent of probate judges surveyed reported that testimony from an expert mental health professional was "somewhat or extremely influential" in undue influence cases.[4] The use of a competent expert can assist in defending or challenging the instrument by putting facts into context. The law generally provides that requisite capacities are task-specific, as opposed to being determined by global mental status or psychiatric diagnosis.[5] In fact, undue influence can be found to exist when the victim has no mental disorder or mental "defect" but is passive or otherwise vulnerable to manipulation (as evidenced by the experience of cult members who do not suffer from cognition deficits).[6]

Often, the opinion of a mental health professional retained to assess and evaluate whether a transaction is the product of undue influence will include:

- A personal history, preferably corroborated by third parties or other resources
- Information regarding the nature and history of relationships with family members and significant others
- Questions about the individual's mental and emotional status, as well as their susceptibility and vulnerability to undue influence (recognizing that a finding of cognitive impairment is not necessarily required, but when it exists, it may make the individual more vulnerable to manipulation)
- Addressing issues of dependency (recognizing that the more dependent—emotionally, physically, or both—an individual is, the greater may be their vulnerability to undue influence)
- The potential amplification of the impact of cognitive impairments and dependency when the victim perceives the influencer to be in a position of authority
- An assessment of "legal risk factors" and a review of financial records, as well as the extent to which the purported influencer was aware of the victim's vulnerabilities[7]

---

[4] Plotkin, *Assessing Undue Influence, supra* note 2, at 344–351 (citing James E. Spar, M.D., Marc Hankin, J.D., & Ann B. Stodden, *Assessing Mental Capacity and Susceptibility to Undue Influence,* 12 BEHAV. SCI. LAW 391–403 (1995)).

[5] Plotkin, *Assessing Undue Influence, supra* note 2, at 345.

[6] *Id.*

[7] Plotkin, *Assessing Undue Influence, supra* note 2, at 347–349.

Apart from offering such opinions, a qualified expert can play an expansive role in the litigation, and early retention of such an expert is often critical for one or more of the following reasons:

1. If the alleged victim is still living, counsel for both sides should consider whether an "independent" medical exam could be helpful to the client's case. These examinations principally are focused on the individual's testamentary capacity and, if competent, the person's vulnerability to undue influence. These assessments usually include a psychosocial profile and assessments of both physical and emotional dependency.

2. The expert can provide counsel with an early and accurate assessment of the case. Qualified experts likely will see things that will not yet be obvious to counsel. Such expertise is particularly helpful when the person who allegedly was influenced possibly suffered from mental health disorders such as depression, anxiety disorder, delirium, or other cognitive impairment due to psychiatric or other significant medical issues.

3. The expert can help develop a more targeted discovery plan, particularly because of their knowledge of the patterns associated with such cases.

4. The expert can assist in preparing for depositions of treating physicians and other health care professionals, particularly because treating health care providers often are less focused on mental health issues and more focused on immediate medical issues and the necessity to keep the patient alive and stable. A fuller understanding of the medical conditions and their possible impact on vulnerability may help counsel elicit useful testimony from treating physicians both as fact and as expert witnesses.

5. The expert can be helpful in preliminary motion practice such as motions regarding the scope of discovery, motions seeking to establish the presumption, and early motions for summary disposition. The expert's involvement with motion practice may include reports of a medical evaluation or a preliminary report regarding vulnerability to undue influence based on the evidence available at that time.

6. An expert can help wade through large volumes of medical records, testimony, and other discovery information to help better synthesize evidence for the effective presentation of proofs at trial.

Because contests often are initiated post-death, it is common that the retained forensic expert will not have the opportunity to conduct his or her own examination of the decedent. However, regardless of whether an examination is conducted, qualified forensic experts can perform valuable post-death assessments based on medical records, witness testimony, and other discovery sources.[8] While such "records-only" evaluations lack some of the advantages of a hands-on assessment, they usually are based on broader sources of information over a greater period of time and, therefore, may well offer a more comprehensive perspective of the decedent. It is for this very reason that treating physicians are not necessarily in a better position to testify to issues of capacity and vulnerability. Moreover, treating physicians and other health care professionals often lack qualifications to fully assess the mental status of a patient and often are focused on other aspects of a patient's care at the time of treatment.

In addition to the forensic expert, counsel should consider additional testifying experts, including:

- Physicians with appropriate specialties who can interpret the medical record and explain medical conditions and how they may affect competency or vulnerability and dependency
- Non-physician health care professionals in specialties that relate to important issues such as cognitive functioning (e.g., speech and language pathologists)
- An expert in pharmacology, to understand and explain the potential impact of medications and polypharmacy
- Standard-of-care experts, where concern might exist that a lawyer's or health care provider's action or inaction made the decedent more vulnerable to undue influence
- A legal expert on issues relating to the independence of counsel
- Financial or forensic accounting experts, who may be helpful when identifying and tracking financial transactions is required

In addition to testimonial experts, in cases involving substantial volumes of medical records, a nurse or other medical professional may prove invaluable as a medical records consultant. Among other things, the consultant can organize and interpret medical records, help prepare a comprehensive

---

[8] Carmelle Peisah, Sanford I. Finkel, Kenneth Shulman, Pamela S. Melding, Jay S. Luxenberg, Jeremia Heinik, Robin J. Jacoby, Barry Reisberg, Gabriela Stoppe, A. Barker, Helen Cristina Torrano Firmino, & Hayley I. Bennett, *The Wills of Older People: Risk Factors for Undue Influence, for* International Psychogeriatic Association Task Force on Wills and Undue Influence, 21 Int. Psychogeriatr., 7–15, 13 (2009).

and accurate medical record chronology, and assist counsel in preparing for depositions and trial testimony of medical-related witnesses.

It also can be helpful to research possible experts, in addition to those named by the opposing party. Having an understanding of the expert's philosophic bent and prior opinions and writings may prove invaluable in the selection of an expert, as well as in the cross-examination of the opposing party's expert.

UNDERSTANDING THE MEDICAL EVIDENCE

Because the "capacity" to make a will or trust often represents a low level of understanding such that it can exist despite significant cognitive or other impairments, understanding the interaction and inter-relationship of such conditions in the context of the overall relationship of the parties and the potential interplay of vulnerabilities may be key to the successful challenge or defense of a proposed instrument.

Where significant health conditions exist, it may prove beneficial to retain the services of appropriate health care providers who can provide a better understanding of the medical issues and any impact they may have on the individual's vulnerabilities. Understanding the "medicine" can truly assist in how one approaches discovery and the presentation of proofs at trial. It may also help in the selection of experts who may present testimony or demonstrative evidence at the time of trial.

THE ROLE OF "INFORMED CONSENT" IN CONTEST CASES

Litigation over lack of testamentary capacity or undue influence frequently involves medical evidence and the testimony of treating health care professionals. Health care professionals are required by law to obtain "informed consent" from patients before they conduct certain medical procedures. Although debatable, the concepts of informed consent and testamentary capacity are similar (but not necessarily identical). Consequently, the facts and circumstances that relate to how health care personnel handled informed consent with the subject person can become important as both substantive evidence and in knowing how it will likely influence the testimony of health care professionals.

Informed consent generally is defined as the ability to understand (1) the condition that needs treatment, (2) the treatment options (including no treatment), and (3) the possible benefits and drawbacks for each treatment option in order to be in a position to make an informed choice. The treating physician must determine, after examination of the patient, whether the patient is able to "participate in medical treatment, or as applicable, mental health treatment decisions."[9] A recent article that was intended to provide a practical framework to guide psychiatrists through solving problems of capacity and informed consent reflected that the assessment of informed consent might occur along a "sliding scale," known as "Drane's sliding scale." This psychiatric article reflected that:

> Drane's "sliding scale" model modulates the threshold to determine the patient's decisional capacity based on risk-to-benefit ratio of the decision, to help with the analysis. For example, the greater the risk associated with the patient's treatment refusal, the lower the threshold for deeming the patient as not having decisional capacity.[10]

Health care professionals should and generally do look to the patient for informed consent unless the patient formally delegates the decision-making to someone else, or when the patient is otherwise incapable of providing informed consent due to severe medical problems, dementia, or other forms of cognitive impairment. In litigating undue influence cases, whether as proponent or challenger, counsel should expect that the testimony of health care professionals will be affected by the manner in which informed consent was handled (and documented) at the time of treatment. So, for example, where there is no clear indication in the medical record that informed consent was obtained from another individual, attorneys should well expect that the health care provider responsible for informed consent will testify that the patient was capable of giving informed consent and in fact did so. In reality, we know that often it is questionable whether a patient is genuinely capable of giving informed consent, and that health care providers also may understandably rely on the informal consent of a caring spouse or other family member. Regardless of the reality of the situation at the time of treatment, the health care professional may be reluctant to acknowledge that it was even questionable whether the patient was capable of giving informed consent. In contrast, where a health

---

[9] *See* MICHIGAN COMPILED LAWS 700.5508 (1).

[10] Yelizaveta Sher, M.D. & Sermsak Lolak, M.D., *Ethical Issues: The Patient's Capacity to Make Medical Decisions*, 31 PSYCHIATR. TIMES 1 (2014).

care professional required informed consent from a legal representative of the patient, this fact can be extremely important to demonstrating lack of testamentary capacity or diminished capacity and vulnerability. Further, although health care professionals may testify that they believe the patient validly gave informed consent, if pressed, the providers may often concede that there was no specific assessment performed for informed consent, and that the professional is not really trained to perform such an assessment. In addition, when pressed, health care professionals may acknowledge that although the patient was able to give informed consent, they ultimately looked to family members or others to make medical decisions. As a challenger, such testimony can neutralize the testimony of biased health care providers that they obtained informed consent.

ALERT AND ORIENTED X3 AND THE CAPACITY INQUIRY[11]

In cases that involve questions of testamentary capacity or diminished capacity due to medical and/or mental health issues, there is understandably much attention paid to whether health care professionals assessed the orientation of the vulnerable adult, particularly during time periods when key estate planning related events took place. Although the topic of orientation could itself be the subject of a lengthy and detailed article, suffice it to say that a health care provider's assessment of "alert and oriented x3" should rarely be the final word as it relates to an assessment of testamentary capacity or diminished capacity. Generally speaking, the term "alert" in the medical context means simply that the patient is awake (not asleep and not unconscious). Also, an assessment of "oriented x3" is subject to much variation in terms of both interpretation and the method of assessment used by the health care professional. Moreover, keep in mind that a four-year-old child is generally capable of being "alert and oriented x3." Further, just because an individual is only "alert and oriented x2" does not necessarily mean they lack capacity, but it may be demonstrative of vulnerability.

---

[11] A&Ox3 is a clinical term of art for alert and oriented to person, place, and time. Segen's Medical Dictionary (2012), https://medical-dictionary.thefreedictionary.com/alert+and+oriented+x+3. If a person is noted to be A&O at a level less than 3, that generally indicates that they were unable to identify the place or the time, or perhaps both, if they are only noted to be A&O x1.

CHAPTER 11

The Attorney-Client Privilege[1]

Given the potential importance of the drafting attorney's testimony when an estate planning transaction is challenged, an understanding of ethical responsibilities relating to the privilege can be extremely helpful. One generally would start the analysis with a review of the applicable state's Rules of Professional Conduct. These rules basically identify that the privilege is an edifice relating to communications intended to be confidential between a "client"[2] and an attorney with regard to rendering legal advice.[3,4]

---

[1] Adapted from an article previously published by BNA: Bloomberg BNA and Sandra D. Glazier, Esq, *Testimony from Beyond the Grave: The Gravamen of the Attorney-Client Privilege in Will and Trust Contests* 57 Tax Management Memorandum 494 (2016).

[2] The use of quotation marks is to place emphasis on the importance of the term "client." Often, cases regarding the application of the privilege involve an analysis of whether the communication is with the person who is the "client," as well as whether the communication relates to the rendition of legal advice.

[3] The scope of an attorney's moral or professional obligation to maintain the "confidences" of a client may be broader than those provided under the evidentiary confines of the attorney-client privilege. *See* Craig L. Unrath & Melissa N. Schoenbein, *Privileges*, ch. 7 in *Illinois Civil Trial Evidence*, Illinois Institute for Continuing Legal Education 7–20 (2015), which in pertinent part reflects:

> 3. [7.9] Confidentiality. In addition to the attorney-client privilege, attorneys are also bound under rules of confidentiality, which encompass the attorney-client evidentiary privilege as well as the attorney's fiduciary duty to the client. Profit Management Development, Inc. v. Jacobson, Brandvik & Anderson, Ltd., 309 Ill. App. 3d 289, 721 N.E.2d 826, 835, 242 Ill. Dec. 547 (2nd Dist. 1999). A lawyer's ethical obligation to guard the confidences and secrets of his or her client is broader than the attorney-client privilege. *In re* January 1976 Grand Jury, 534 F.2d 719, 728 (7th Cir. 1976). Unlike the evidentiary privilege, the ethical precept exists "without regard to the nature or source of information or the fact that others share the knowledge." 534 F.2d at 728 n.8, quoting ABA Model Code of Professional Responsibility, EC 4–4 (1974).

[4] In Illinois, the privilege appears to have been extended to persons outside the auspices of the lawyer's offices when they are integrally involved in the estate planning

THE PRIVILEGE FROM AN EVIDENTIARY PERSPECTIVE

Understanding the privilege's *evidentiary* implications may be far more complex. In analyzing the potential evidentiary implications of the privilege, one may start with a review of Uniform Rules of Evidence 501, but such a review generally is not enough.

> Uniform Rule[s] of Evidence 501 clearly espouses an exception to the privilege as to a communication relevant to an issue between parties who claim through the same deceased client, regardless of whether the claims are by testate or intestate succession or by transaction *inter vivos*.[5]

In addition to the Uniform Rules of Evidence, Rule 502(d) of the Uniform Laws Annotated (2000) provides, in pertinent part, that when there is a dispute between parties claiming a right to the former property of a testator, "[t]here is no privilege under this rule: . . . [a]s to a communication relevant to an issue between the parties who claim through the same deceased client, regardless of whether the claims are by testate or intestate succession or by transaction *inter vivos*."[6]

While there are a number of states that have adopted something analogous to Uniform Rules of Evidence 501 or Rule 502 (d) of the Uniform Laws Annotated,[7] these "uniform" rules have not been universally adopted, leaving many litigants (and estate planning attorneys) largely reliant upon the complexities of the common law.[8] By way of example,

---

efforts (as agents for the client), including accountants and other financial advisors. *See* Adler v. Greenfield, 2013 Ill. App. (1st Dist.) 121066 (2013), *and* Brunton v. Kruger, 380 Ill. Dec. 366, 8 N.E.3d 536 (Ill. App. 4th Dist. 2014).

[5] Unif. R. Evid. 501(d)(2).

[6] Morgan v. Pendelton, 2000 WL 486934, 27 Conn. L. Rptr. 39 (Conn. Super. Ct. April 13, 2000).

[7] By way of example, and without limitation, Alaska, Arkansas, Delaware, Maine, Nebraska, New Hampshire, North Dakota, Oklahoma, Oregon, Vermont, and Wisconsin, per Morgan v. Pendelton, *id.*

[8] While New York has N.Y. C.P.L.R. 4503(b) (McKinney 2016) and New Jersey has N.J. R. Evid. 504(2), which address the waiver or absence of a privilege in actions involving the probate and the validity or construction of wills, trusts, and other relevant instruments, these rules or exceptions relating to the privilege may not be

and without limitation, Michigan Rules of Evidence 501 merely provides that the "Privilege is governed by the common law, except as modified by statute or court rule."[9,10] Federal Rules of Evidence 501 essentially refers a litigant back to the pertinent state's evidentiary rules for issues generally relating to matters (such as will and trust contest proceedings) that otherwise would fall within the purview of the state court system.[11] As a consequence, an understanding of the common law in the applicable jurisdiction (and in the state where the confidential communication occurred) may be extremely important.

WHY IT'S IMPORTANT TO DETERMINE WHETHER A COMMUNICATION IS PRIVILEGED IN THE CONTEXT OF WILL AND TRUST CONTESTS

As discussed in chapter 4, most states recognize the need for liberal discovery, especially when litigation about the validity of a testamentary instrument emanates from a claim of undue influence.[12] In Michigan, the

---

applied if the pertinent instrument is subjected to administration and contest in another jurisdiction.

[9] MICH. R. EVID. (MRE) 501.

[10] While § 501 of each state's evidentiary rules may vary, it appears many haven't adopted the exception found in UNIF. R. EVID. 501(d)(2).

[11] FED R. EVID. (FRE) 501.

[12] In general, all evidence, both direct and circumstantial, that bears upon the question of undue influence should be admitted. All evidence that tends to prove or disprove that an instrument was procured by undue influence should be admitted. *In re* Loree's Estate, 158 Mich. at 379. Evidence of undue influence after the date on which the testator made his or her will is relevant and admissible as tending to show a continuance of undue influence. Walts v. Walts, 127 Mich. 607, 610, 86 N.W. 1030, 1031 (1901); Leffingwell v. Bettinghouse, 151 Mich. 513, 518, 115 N.W. 731, 733 (1908). *See also In re* Vhay's Estate, 225 Mich. 107, 108, 195 N.W. 674 (1923). The remoteness in time of the evidence only affects the weight that such evidence should be given, not whether such evidence is admissible. Balk's Estate, 289 Mich. 703, 706, 287 N.W. 351, 352, 353, 124 A.L.R. 431 (1939); *see also* McPeak v. McPeak, 233 Mich. App. 483, 496, 593 N.W.2d 180, 187 (1999). There should be no arbitrary time limit placed upon what might prove relevant, and all material evidence should be produced. *In re* Loree's Estate, 158 Mich. at 376, 377.

scope of discovery generally is governed by Michigan Court Rules (MCR) 2.302 (B) (1), which as of January 1, 2020, provides that:

> Parties may obtain discovery regarding any *non-privileged* matter that is relevant to any parties' claims or defenses and proportional to the needs of the case, taking into account pertinent factors, including whether the burden or expense of the proposed discovery outweighs its likely benefit, the complexity of the case, the importance of the issues at stake in the action, the amount in controversy, and the parties' resources and access to relevant information. Information within the scope of discovery need not be admissible into evidence to be discoverable.[13]

Consequently, "one should view the attorney-client privilege as itself an exception to the general proposition that permits liberal discovery of relevant evidence."[14]

Of key significance to many will and trust contests are the testimony and file contents of the estate planning attorney. Therefore, it may be of great importance whether the attorney will be subjected to discovery or be compelled to testify. The implications of the privilege and the resulting "competence" of the attorney to testify may ultimately depend upon the answers to the following questions:

1. Was the communication privileged when it was made?
2. Do any exceptions to the privilege exist?
3. If privileged and no exception exists, has the privilege been explicitly or implicitly waived?

WHAT IS A PRIVILEGED COMMUNICATION?

Because the assertion of the privilege tends to be an impediment to the search for truth, the privilege is generally narrowly construed.[15] Many confuse the privilege with the attorney work-product doctrine.[16] The result of an

---

[13] MICH. CT. R. (MCR) 2.302(B) (1) (emphasis added). This is not dissimilar to FED. R. CIV. P. 26.

[14] EDNA SELAN EPSTEIN, 1 THE ATTORNEY-CLIENT PRIVILEGE AND THE WORK PRODUCT DOCTRINE 11,12 (5th ed. 2012).

[15] *See* United States v. Goldberger & Dubin, PC, 935 F.2d 501, 504 (2nd Cir. 1991).

[16] Generally, the work-product doctrine relates to written or oral materials prepared by or for an attorney in the course of legal representation. It is important to note

attempt to discover "privileged" information as opposed to information falling within the confines of "attorney work-product" can vary greatly.[17] However, a review of the work-product doctrine is beyond the scope of this book.

To be privileged, at its inception, the communication must be communicated in confidence for the purpose of obtaining legal advice.[18,19,20]

---

that, unlike the "privilege," this doctrine may be pierced, in the context of litigation, upon a showing of "substantial need" and "undue hardship." *See* FED. R. CIV. P. 26(b)(3) and MCR 2.302(3)(a). Even though both FED. R. CIV. P. 26(b)(3) and MCR 2.302(3)(a) provide for discovery of work-product upon such showings, each continues to provide protection for mental impressions, conclusions, and opinions of legal theories of an attorney or other representative of a party "concerning the litigation."

[17] It may also be important to note that in many jurisdictions, the "work-product doctrine" may be limited to materials prepared "in anticipation of litigation." *See* FED. R. CIV. P. 26 (b)(3) and MCR 2.302(3)(a). Whether materials that were not prepared "in anticipation of litigation" will otherwise be deemed discoverable is beyond the scope of this book.

[18] *See* United States v. Osborn, 561 F.2d 1334 (9th Cir. 1977).

[19] In the ever-changing world of electronic storage and communication, whether a communication has a reasonable expectation of confidentiality also continues to change. Clients may choose to digitally upload all or a portion of their estate planning documents to websites for safekeeping. As a consequence, with the proliferation of sites intended to assist clients in the storage of important communications and documents, the potential for waiver of the privilege (if not preclusion of its application) may be enhanced. Therefore, use of sites like the Michigan Peace of Mind Registry for Advanced Directives may result in a waiver of the privilege, at least as to the contents of the documents recorded with the registry. Transmission of documents and email communications to or from a client's work email may result in the absence of a reasonable expectation of confidentiality or privacy, especially if the employer or business has provided notice that such communications may be monitored or otherwise will not enjoy rights of privacy. Some corporate environs provide notice to users when they log on to the system that the company has reserved the right to review their communications. In such an environment, it may be unreasonable to assume that the privilege will attach to communications emanating from or read on that machine or system.

[20] *See also* Nacos v. Nacos, 124 A.D. 3d 462, 1 N.Y.S.3d 90 (1st Dep't, 2015), where communications with family members who were also lawyers were not found to be subject to the privilege because there was no showing that the communications were related to a consultation with such family members for the purpose of obtaining their legal advice. Moreover, the agency doctrine did not provide privilege protection because the party was perfectly capable of speaking directly to her attorney for legal services without the assistance of family members (who were lawyers).

In the context of estate planning, the privilege generally will apply to communications between "a client and her attorney regarding the preparation of a will."[21] Although not recommended, it's not uncommon (especially in will or trust contests cases) for a family member to communicate with the attorney or to otherwise be present during a portion of the time when an aged or infirm family member consults with the attorney in regard to the creation of dispositive instruments. "Such a presence will constitute a failure to protect the 'confidence' of the communication and make it discoverable."[22,23] While some might consider this a "waiver" of the privilege, the presence of a family member (who is not an actual party to the representation) may, in fact, preclude the privilege from ever applying to that particular communication. Further, because that family member is not the "client" in regard to the estate planning advice or services sought, that contact and communication itself will not be covered by the privilege.

However, let us assume that the pertinent communications indeed take place in private; what then? In *Zook v. Pesce*,[24] the Maryland court reviewed the privilege in the context of testamentary dispositions:

> The attorney-client privilege is "a rule of evidence that prevents the disclosure of a confidential communication made by a client to his attorney for the purpose of obtaining legal advice." "The privilege is based upon the public policy that 'an individual in a free society should be encouraged to consult with his attorney whose function is to counsel and advise him and he should be free from apprehension of compelled disclosures by his legal advisor." It has been recognized as "the oldest of the privileges for confidential communications known to the common law." Indeed, for over 150 years, this Court has recognized that "[n]o rule is better

---

[21] Brown v. Edwards, 640 N.E.2d 401, 404 (Ind. App. 1st Dist. 1994) (citing Briggs v. Clinton County Bank & Trust Co., 452 N.E.2d 989, 1012 (Ind. App. 2nd Dist. 1983)).

[22] EPSTEIN, *supra* note 14, at 66. *See also* Snedeker v. Snedeker, 2011 U.S. Dist. Lexus 89408 (S.D. Ind. 2011).

[23] An exception to this statement may be when the attorney is jointly engaged by a husband and wife for estate planning purposes, at least as it relates to protecting the confidence of both spouses from others, unless such person is claiming under one of them.

[24] Zook v. Pesce, 438 Md. 232, 91 A.3d 1114 (Md. 2014).

established than 'that communications which a client makes to his legal adviser for the purpose of professional advice or aid shall not be disclosed, unless by the consent of the client for whose protection the rule was established." This privilege is reflected in the Maryland Code, as well.

The privilege survives even after the client's death. Invoking the purpose of fostering free communication between attorney and client, the Supreme Court has explained:

> Knowing that communications will remain confidential even after death encourages the client to communicate fully and frankly with counsel. While the fear of disclosure, and the consequent withholding of information from counsel, may be reduced if disclosure is limited to posthumous disclosure in a criminal context, it seems unreasonable to assume that it vanishes altogether. Clients may be concerned about reputation, civil liability, or possible harm to friends or family. Posthumous disclosure of such communications may be as feared as disclosure during the client's lifetime.
>
> Thus, even though the client may be deceased, the communication remains privileged.
>
> Nevertheless, the privilege is not absolute. Only those communications "pertaining to legal assistance" and "made with the intention of confidentiality" are covered by the privilege. Additionally, this Court has explained that the privilege does not "extend to communications made for the purpose of getting advice for the commission of a fraud' or a crime."[25]

Therefore, if the attorney is not *consulted* for legal advice, but rather merely acts as a scrivener, the communications between the client and the attorney may not be considered to be subject to the privilege.[26]

Assuming the communication takes place in private and with the intent of obtaining legal advice, is that the end of the inquiry? The short answer is no. It is equally important to understand that not everything contained within a communication is privileged. This is a list of examples of items that might be communicated between a client and the attorney for

---

[25] *Id.* at 241–242 (internal citations omitted).
[26] *See* Novak v. Reeson, 110 Neb. 229, 193 N.W. 348 (Neb. 1923). *See also* Lamb v. Lamb, 124 Ill. App. 3d 68, 74, 64 N.E.2d 873 (Ill. App. 4th Dist. 1984).

purposes of obtaining advice, and which might not fall under the umbrella of the privilege:

1. The name of the client[27]
2. Facts contained in a confidential communication[28]
3. Facts observed by the attorney and not directly conveyed by the client[29]
4. The client's appearance and handwriting[30]
5. The subject matter of the communication[31]
6. Attorney notes[32]
7. Drafts of documents (even if prepared by the attorney) intended for (eventual) public disclosure[33,34]
8. The existence and contents of a written instrument executed by the client that has been actually delivered to a third party[35,36]

---

[27] Shatkin Investment Corp. v. Connelly, 128 Ill. App. 3d 518, 470 N.E.2d 1230, 1235, 83 Ill. Dec. 810 (2nd Dist. 1984) (quoting Annotation, 16 A.L.R.3d 1047, 1050 (1967)). An exception arises when divulging the identity of an attorney's client would result in substantial prejudice to the client. People v. Williams, 97 Ill.2d 252, 454 N.E.2d 220, 241, 73 Ill. Dec. 360 (1983). ILL. CIV. TRIAL EVID. ch. 7, *Privileges*, at 7–17.
[28] Philadelphia v. Westinghouse Elec. Corp, 205 F. Supp. 830, 831 (E.D. Pa. 1962).
[29] EPSTEIN, *supra* note 14, at 68.
[30] *In re* Grand Jury Proceedings, 791 F.2d 663, 665 (8th Cir. 1986).
[31] J.P. Foley v. Vanderbuilt, 65 F.R.D. 523, 526 (S.D.N.Y. 1974).
[32] But these may be subject to the work-product doctrine. *See* EPSTEIN, *supra* note 14, at 132.
[33] EPSTEIN, *supra* note 14, at 132.
[34] For New York practitioners, one may wish to see Vincent C. Alexander, *Supplementary Practice Commentaries, C4503:2(b) Living Client's Will* (2016), which cites what is characterized as a "surprising ruling" in *Estate of Freilich*, 179 Misc. 2d 884, 686 N.Y.S.2d 294 (Surr. Ct. Bronx Co., 1999), where the court held that the privilege did not protect disclosure of the contents of a still-living individual's will or trust, even though prepared by an attorney, despite its general private nature, where such disclosure was "necessary" in certain litigation.
[35] Schattman v. American Credit Indem. Co, 34 A.D. 392, 397–398; 54 N.Y.S. 225 (N.Y. 1898). In this case, the court held that "[a]ny statement or communication by the client to the attorney, or any advice given by the attorney as to the construction, meaning or effect of the instrument, would be incompetent; but a mere statement of the fact that a paper writing was executed and delivered in the presence of the attorney, and the statement of the contents of that instrument was acquired by the attorney by reading, would not involve a communication from the client to his attorney. Thus, the independent fact of the execution of the written instrument, its delivery by one party to the other, or the contents of the instrument, where the knowledge of the contents had been acquired by the attorney in some other way than through a communication from his client, would not be within the prohibition of the statute."
[36] In Baxter v. Baxter, 92 Misc. 567, 156 N.Y. 521, *aff'd*, 173 A.D. 998, 159 N.Y.S. 1009 (N.Y. 1915), the court held that because the contents and intent of a deed had

9. Documents transmitted to the attorney that, in the hands of the client, wouldn't be subject to the privilege[37,38]
10. Observations and communications made by or to an attorney (or his agents) in their capacity as witnesses[39]
11. Communications made by a party other than the client to the attorney[40]
12. Invoices for services rendered[41]
13. Communications made in the presence of others[42]

IMPORTANCE OF ATTORNEY TESTIMONY

The potential importance of the scrivener attorney's testimony (and contemporaneous notes) cannot be overstated, nor should it be underestimated. In some states, the "dead man statute" may preclude other witnesses from offering competent testimony because they might benefit

---

been delivered by the client to his wife, even though the deed was never recorded and only a mutilated copy of the deed existed, weren't privileged once disclosure of the deed and its contents were imparted by the client to his wife. As a result, the attorney was permitted to testify as to the contents of the deed *and* communications associated with its preparation.

[37] EPSTEIN, *supra* note 14, at 342, 343. *See also* United States of America v. Osborn, 561 F.2d 1334 (9th Cir. 1977).

[38] In *Osborn*, 561 F.2d. at 1337, 1338, the court adopted the analysis of the Supreme Court from the case of Fisher v. United States, 425 U.S. 391, 96 S. Ct. 1569, 48 L. Ed.2d 39 (1976). Fisher, *id.* espoused that preexisting documents "transferred by the client to the attorney, are protected by the attorney-client privilege only if such documents (1) could not have been obtained from the client by court process when the documents were still in the client's possession because of some privilege of the client, and (2) had been transferred to the attorney by the client for the purpose of obtaining legal advice."

[39] *In re* Ford Estate, 206 Mich. App. 705, 708, 522 N.W.2d 729 (Mich. App. 1994).

[40] *See* Caro v. Meerbergen, 51 Conn. L. Rptr. 650, 2011 WL 1565976 (March 29, 2011) (citing *In re* Sean H., 24 Conn. App. 135, 142, 143, *cert. denied*, 218 Conn. 904 (Conn. 1991)).

[41] While some states have held that invoices are, under the right set of circumstances, protected under the privilege, it appears that many states take a more limited and fact-dependent approach to the issue. *See* Mary Gillick, *Attorney-Client Privilege and Invoices*, 154 TRUSTS & ESTATES 40–44 (2015). *See also* Eizenga v. Unity Christian Sch. of Fulton, 54 N.E.3d 907, 2016 Ill. App. (3d) 150519, 2016 WL 2610736 (Ill. App. 3d, May 6, 2016).

[42] Eicholtz v. Grunerwald, 331 Mich. 666, 21 N.W.2d 914 (Mich. 1946).

under the instrument. An analysis of the implications of "dead man" statutes also is beyond the scope of this book. It is, however, important to understand that because of such statutes, as well as because of circumstances attendant to matters like competency and undue influence, the ability to "waive" the privilege may be of the utmost importance in preserving the testator's true intent and in the determination of the validity of an instrument.

In cases where the validity of an instrument is challenged for a purported lack of capacity or because it is alleged to be the product of undue influence, the testimony of the scrivener attorney can be of significant importance. The steps the attorney took, communications had with the testator, and the attorney's observations and impressions generally will be important aspects of the proponent's case. Things the attorney may have failed to do may become important aspects of the challenger's case. Under certain circumstances, the testimony of the scrivener attorney may prove to be as important (if not more important) than the testimony of treating professionals or other medical experts.[43]

---

[43] While the use of expert witnesses in undue influence cases can be impactful, it is important to remember that the testimony of the scrivener attorney and witnesses to the execution of pertinent dispositive instruments also are extremely important. Whether the scrivener attorney will be treated as an expert in the field of estate planning or merely a lay fact witness may be subject to debate. One should, however, remember that MRE 701 permits lay witness opinion testimony when that testimony is rationally based on the perceptions of the witness and is helpful to a clear understanding of witness testimony or the determination of a fact in issue. As a consequence, the impressions and opinion of the scrivener attorney and witnesses present at the time of execution, supported by sufficiently detailed factual observations, can prove extremely important. While not every jurisdiction permits testimony on the ultimate issue to be determined by the fact finder, MRE 704 does. As a result, the testimony of the scrivener attorney and witnesses to execution on observations and resulting opinions as to the decedent's capacity at the time of execution and the voluntariness of the decedent's actions in the formulation of the plan will be important to the defense of the instruments. Michigan case law bears this out. In *In re* Bednarz Trust, 2009 Mich. App. LEXIS 1349 (Mich. Ct. App. June 16, 2009), the court recognized the importance of the attorney's testimony regarding his observations and findings at the time the challenged documents were executed. The proponents of the instruments also offered the testimony of a doctor, who explained that some vascular dementia patients experience varying lucidity, comprehension, and communication capabilities from day to day and hour to hour. The contestants argued that

When the privilege is found to be inapplicable (or is waived), declarations of the testator either to support or rebut a presumption of undue influence leading up to, at the time of, and after the creation and execution of the testamentary instrument through the time of death may, in many states, be deemed admissible.[44,45] Nevertheless, it is important that an analysis not end with the generalized statements regarding the potential inapplicability of the privilege in post-death litigation between persons claiming through the testator.

What if the attorney is considered a partisan witness? While *Booher v. Brown*[46] historically had been an oft-cited case with regard to "implied waiver" of the privilege, it was later largely overturned.[47] It is, however, noteworthy that when overturned, courts were careful to reflect that one of the reasons cited in *Booher* for preserving the privilege remained viable, and that is when the attorney is called upon to act as a partisan witness to establish collateral claims against the estate.[48]

---

testimony from the decedent's psychiatrist, who opined that the decedent was legally incapacitated, outweighed the attorney's testimony because she was a medical professional who based her opinion upon her observations two weeks before the instruments were executed. However, the Court of Appeals recognized that "[t]he opinion of a physician as to mental competency, aside from the question of insanity, is entitled to no greater consideration than that of a layman having equal facilities for observation" (citing Bradford v. Vinton, 59 Mich. 139, 154, 26 N.W. 401 (Mich. 1886)).

[44] *See* Saliba v. Saliba, 202 Ga. 791,799, 44 S.E.2d 744,751 (Ga. 1947).

[45] Use of the phrase "testamentary instrument" should, however, not be narrowly construed. Recently, in *Eizenga*, 54 N.E.3d, the Illinois court held that "[i]n fact, a closer examination of the exception leads us to the conclusion that it is the rationale behind it that is of paramount importance, rather than the question of whether the situation involves a will contest." *Eizenga, id.* at ¶ 25c. In *Eizenga, id.*, the implied waiver concept was deemed to include a myriad of communications between the grantor and his attorney, as well as memorandum, notes, records, and timesheets maintained by the attorney, where beneficiaries of prior iterations of the trust alleged that the attorney was the perpetrator of undue influence in the modification of beneficiary provisions contained within grantor's revocable *inter vivos* trust.

[46] Booher v. Brown, 173 Or. 464, 145 P.2d 71 (Or. 1944).

[47] In *Booher, id.*, the attorney was "partisan" because he also represented a party who was asserting a breach of contract to make a will claim against the estate.

[48] *See* Tanner v. Farmer, 243 Or. 431, 435, 414 P.2d 340 (Or. 1966). BURR W. JONES, 5 COMMENTARIES ON THE LAW OF EVIDENCE IN CIVIL CASES 4108 (2d ed. 1926).

IMPLIED WAIVER OF THE PRIVILEGE

Common law generally recognizes that confidential communications between a client and his attorney are privileged from inquiry in the absence of a waiver by the client.[49] Clearly, if the client provides an "expressed" waiver of the privilege, disclosure of confidential communications by the attorney may occur.[50]

It is commonly recognized that the personal representative or executor (collectively, "executor") essentially stands in the shoes of the decedent and consequently may expressly waive the privilege.[51] In *In re Estate of Colby*,[52] a New York court reflected that "[t]he other jurisdictions which have considered the issue, however, are unanimous in holding that a Testator's successor in interest may waive the privilege."[53] The premise for this proposition is that because "the client could have waived the privilege to protect himself or to promote his interest, it is reasonable to conclude that, after his death, his personal representative stands in his shoes for the same purposes."[54]

In *Mayorga v. Tate*,[55] another New York court further analyzed why an executor should be permitted to waive the privilege. In *Mayorga*, the court espoused:

> [T]he basic thesis that it makes no sense to prohibit an executor from waiving the attorney-client privilege of his or her Testator, where such prohibition operates to the detriment of the Testator's estate, and to the benefit of an alleged tortfeasor against whom

---

[49] *See* Stevens v. Thurston, 112 N.H. 118, 289 A.2d 398, 399 (N.H. 1972).

[50] *See* EPSTEIN, *supra* note 14, at 390. Moreover, the waiver need not even be knowingly or voluntarily made. *Id* at 391.

[51] *See Stevens*, 112 N.H. at 118.

[52] *In re* Estate of Colby, 187 Misc. 2d 957, 23 N.Y.S.2d 631, 633 (N.Y. slip op. 21174 2001).

[53] Citing 67 A.L.R.2d 1268; Cain v. Killian, 156 Neb. 132, 54 N.W.2d 368 (Neb. 1952); OHIO REV. CODE § 2317.02[A].

[54] *In re* Estate of Colby, 187 Misc. 2d at 634.

[55] Mayorga v. Tate, 302 A.D.2d 11, 18–19, 752 N.Y.S. 353 (N.Y. slip op. 09415 2002), *relying in pertinent parts on* JOHN HENRY WIGMORE, 8 EVIDENCE AT TRIALS IN COMMON LAW § 2329 at 639 (McNaugton rev. 1961) *and* Spectrum Sys. Intl. Corp. v. Chemical Bank, 78 N.Y.2d 371, 377, 575 N.Y.S.2d 809, 581 N.E.2d 1055 (N.Y. App. Div. 1991).

the estate possesses a cause of action. "That an executor * * * may exercise authority over all the interests of the estate left by the [Testator], and yet may not incidentally have the right, in the interest of that estate, to waive the [attorney client] privilege * * * would seem too inconsistent to be maintained under any system of law." New York should not, in our view, adhere to the proposition condemned by *Wigmore* as "too inconsistent to be maintained." We therefore conclude that, under the terms of CPLR 4503, just as under the common law, an executor may waive the attorney-client privilege of his or her Testator.[56]

While implied waiver theories (discussed next) may be limited in application (depending upon jurisdiction, facts, and circumstances), the importance of the executor's ability to waive the privilege may be that it can be extended to additional situations where the executor believes it to be in the best interest of the estate or helpful in defense of claims made (whether through, under or) against the testator or by his estate.[57,58] However, the executor may not be able to waive the privilege if waiver will result in dissipation or diminution of the estate.[59] In some states, the latitude given to the executor with regard to waiver of the privilege may also be limited if

---

[56] *Mayorga,* 302 A.D.2d at 18, 19 (internal citations omitted).

[57] *See* Caro v. Meerbergen, 51 Conn. L. Rptr. 650, 2011 WL 1564976 (Conn. March 29, 2011), distinguishing Gould, Larson, Bennett, Wells, and McDonnell, PC v. Panico, 273 Conn. 315, 869 A.2d 653 (Conn. 2005), where the litigants sought to impose the waiver as to unexecuted documents from the situation where the executor explicitly waived because he believed it to be in the estate's best interest to do so.

[58] A consideration beyond the scope of this book but which should not be overlooked might include whether an intentional waiver is contemplated in the context of an audit. Often, disclosures are made in the audit or litigation phase of an IRS challenge. Once this occurs, the door can't be closed to discovery in a will or trust contest (and vice versa). Therefore, it may be important to consider whether a tactical or strategic decision to disclose internal memorandum or communications is contemplated. There may be valid (and important) reasons that counsel may wish to disclose internal memorandum and communications with the client in order to demonstrate the business purpose for a transaction or otherwise support a discount taken. Once waived, everything within (and potentially related to) those communications also will be deemed waived in other contexts. *See, e.g.,* United States v. Brown, 478 F.2d 1038 (7th Cir. 1973).

[59] *Eicholtz,* 331 Mich. at 671 (citing McKinney v. Kalamazoo-City Savings Bank, 244 Mich. 246, 253, 221 N.W. 156, 158 (Mich. 1928)).

disclosure of the confidential communication would damage the testator's reputation[60] or reveal "scandalous and impertinent matter."[61]

Where a testamentary instrument is alleged to be the product of undue influence or executed when the testator lacked the requisite capacity to do so, the executor may not wish to facilitate discovery because the outcome could be adverse to the executor's position, authority, or personal interests. Under such circumstances, the common law essentially *implies* a waiver of the privilege, especially when the litigation involves claims by individuals claiming through (as opposed to against) the testator.[62] In *Steven v. Thurston*,[63] where the claims were considered to be "through" the testator, the court noted:

> If the defendants are successful, they, rather than the plaintiff, will be the representatives of the testator. Here the privilege is being asserted not for the protection of the testator or his estate but for the protection of the claimant to his estate. The authorities uniformly hold that in this situation all reason for assertion of the privilege disappears and that the protection of the testator lies in the admission of all relevant evidence that will aid in the determination of his true will.[64]

Consequently, in cases where the dispute is among parties claiming "through" as opposed to "against" the testator, *generally* it is recognized that "it would be obviously unjust to determine that the privilege should belong to the one claimant rather than to the other."[65,66] Hence, under

---

[60] *See* Brunton v. Kruger, 2014 Il. App. (4th) 130421, 380 Ill. Dec. 366, 375; 8 N.E 3d 536, 545 (Ill. App. Ct. 4th Dist., 2014) (citing E.S. Stephens, *Waiver of Attorney – Client Privilege by Personal Representative or Heir of Deceased Client or by Guardian of Incompetent*, 67 A.L.R.2d 1268 § 1 (2009)). *See also* United States v. Yielding, 657 F.3d 688, 787, 2011 U.S. App. Lexis 20147, at *33 (8th Cir. 2011); *and Mayorga*, 302 A.D.2d at 11.

[61] Cohen v. Jenkintown Cab Co., 238 Pa. Super. Ct. 456, 463, 238 (1976 Pa. Super.), 357 A.2d 689, 693 (1990) (citing WIGMORE, *supra* note 55 §§ 2314, 2329).

[62] *See Stevens v. Thurston*, 112 N.H. at 289. *See also In re* Graf's Estate, 119 N.W.2d 478, 481 (N.D. 1963).

[63] *Id.*

[64] *Id.* at 119 (internal citations omitted).

[65] Runnels v. Allen's Admr., 169 S.W.2d 73, 76 (Mo. Ct. App. 1943).

[66] In *In the* Estate of Hebbeler, 875 S.W.2d 163; 1994 Mo. App. LEXIS 438 (Mo. 1994), the Missouri court applied the very same waiver theory to a dispute between competing parties, each of whom claimed rights under *inter vivos* documents. As a consequence, relatives and friends of the testator both were found competent to waive the privilege, because each was found to be claiming through the testator by virtue of the disputed *inter vivos* instruments.

circumstances where neither party to the litigation is a stranger to the estate and both parties are claiming under the testator, the privilege has been found to be inapplicable.[67,68]

In *Blackburn v. Crawfords*,[69] the U.S. Supreme Court reviewed the importance of the privilege and why, for policy reasons, it should generally remain applicable as to claims *against* the testator or his estate. Under such circumstances, the court indicated that if "the privilege did not exist at all, everyone would be thrown upon his own legal resources. Deprived of all professional assistance, a man would not venture to consult any skillful (*sic*) person, or would only dare to tell his counsel half his case."[70]

However, the *Blackburn* court went on to opine that when there's a contest *between* the heirs at law and a devisee (*claiming through or under* the testator), the attorney's testimony should be allowed when it will not affect a "right or interest of the client; and the apprehensions of it can present no impediment to a full statement to the solicitor."[71]

In the majority opinion, the *Blackburn* court importantly noted that the protections of the privilege could be waived, and that such a waiver could be either express *or* implied:

> We think it as effectual here by implication as the most explicit language could have made it. It could have been no clearer if the client had expressly enjoined it upon the attorney to give this testimony whenever the trust of his testamentary declaration should be challenged by any of those to whom it related. A different result would involve a perversion of the rule, inconsistent with its object, and in direct conflict with the reasons upon which it is founded.[72]

---

[67] *In re* Loree's Estate, 158 Mich.; Warner v. Kerr, 216 Mich. 139, 145–146, 184 N.W. 425 (Mich. 1921). *See also Lamb*, 124 Ill. App. 3d at 687.

[68] As recently as May 6, 2016, an Illinois appellate court found the privilege (as well as the attorney work-product doctrine) to be ineffective shields to discovery sought by prior beneficiaries from the estate planning attorney who was himself alleged to have been the perpetrator of undue influence in the formulation and amendment of his client's trust favoring a charity with which the attorney was actively involved. *Eizenga*, 54 N.E.3d.

[69] Blackburn v. Crawfords, 70 U.S. 175, 1865 WL 10735, 18 L. Ed. 186, 3 Wall. 175 (1865).

[70] *Id.* at 192, 193.

[71] *Id.* at 193.

[72] *Id.* at 193. But see Justice Clifford's dissent, where he indicates that the testimony of the attorney was properly excluded "as falling within the rule of privileged

While the dissent in *Blackburn*[73] argues against the creation of an implied waiver of the privilege in contests between heirs and devisees who claim through the testator, the cases that historically followed almost uniformly adopt the "implied waiver" concept under such circumstances.

In *Zook v. Pesce*,[74] the Maryland court explored the underlying rationale for an implied testamentary "exception" to the privilege. Relying in part upon *United States v. Osborn*,[75] the court in *Zook* opines, in pertinent part, that:

> [C]onfidential communications between attorney and client for the purpose of preparing the client's will . . . are privileged during the testator's lifetime and, also, after the testator's death unless sought to be disclosed in litigation between the testator's heirs, legatees, devisees, or other parties, all of whom claim under the deceased client.
>
> The rationale underlying this exception is that in the context of a contested estate, such disclosure "helps the court carry out the decedent's estate plan." Were a court to exclude such evidence, "the court administering the will might reach an erroneous conclusion about the decedent's donative intent." Thus, some states have elected to allow this exception to the attorney-client privilege based on the idea that "*the deceased client would presumably want his communications disclosed in litigation between such claimants so that his desires in regard to the disposition of his estate might be correctly ascertained and carried out.*"
>
> Happily for both parties in this case, Maryland recognized the wisdom of the testamentary exception about a century ago.

* * *

> . . . It may be laid down as a general rule of law, gathered from all the authorities, that, unless provided otherwise by statute, communications by a client to the attorney who drafted his will, in respect to that document, and all transactions occurring between them leading up to its execution, are not, after the client's death, within the protection of the rule as to privileged communications, in a suit between the testator's devisees and heirs at law, or other parties who all claim under him.[76]

---

communication; and I am also of the opinion that the suggestion of a waiver is utterly without foundation or just pretense." *Id.* at 195.

[73] *Blackburn, id.*

[74] *Zook*, 438 Md. at 242–244.

[75] *Osborn*, 561 F.2d at 1340.

[76] *Zook*, 438 Md. at 242–243 (emphasis added, internal citations omitted).

In further explanation of the "implied waiver" theory, the court in *In re Graf's Estate*[77] indicated that:

> [t]he recognition of a privilege does not mean that there are no exceptions to it. One such exception adopted by many of the courts is that such communications lose their confidential character after the death of the client and that such communications can be shown in litigation between parties, all of whom claim under the client. Thus, where the controversy is to determine who shall acquire the property of the deceased, and where all parties claim under him, . . . neither can set up a claim of privilege against the other with respect to the communications of deceased with his attorney.
>
> The courts which adopt this view do so on the theory that, in a controversy not adverse to the estate, between heirs at law, next of kin, devisees, legatees, and personal representatives, the claim that the communication was privileged cannot be heard. In such case, the interest of the deceased as well as that of the estate is that the truth be ascertained.[78]

Arguably, from a policy perspective, permitting the privilege to preclude the attorney's testimony in cases between persons claiming through (as opposed to against) the testator "would, in effect, allow the shield intended for the client to be misappropriated for the benefit of the very persons against whom the client may have had claims."[79]

Because of a strong policy bias in favor of upholding a testator's true intent and purposes, a number of states have via statute, court rule, or rule of evidence, codified the waiver of the privilege relative to communications relevant to an issue between parties, all of whom claim through the client, regardless of whether the respective claims are by testate or intestate succession or by *inter vivos* transaction.[80]

After the privilege is waived relative to the execution of a testamentary instrument, all communications relating to the preparation, execution,

---

[77] *In re* Graf's Estate, 119 N.W.2d at 481.

[78] *In re* Graf's Estate, 119 N.W.2d at 481, *relying in part on* Winters v. Winters, 102 Iowa 53, 71 N.W. 184 (IA 1897) (internal citations omitted).

[79] *In re* Estate of Colby, 187 Misc. 2d at 634.

[80] By way of example, and without limitation, see KAN. STAT. ANN. 60–426(b)(2). *See also* Godley v. Valley State Bank, 2000 WL 33676159 (Kan. June 21, 2000).

and subject matter of the instrument may not be considered privileged.[81] In addition, after the privilege is waived, the ". . . confidence is not apportionable *(sic)* by a reference to what the testator might have intended had he known or reflected on certain facts which now bear against the will; indeed, the privilege covering conversations about preparation or execution of the will or its subject property is not apportionable *(sic)* at all."[82,83]

WHEN THE CLAIM IS AGAINST THE TESTATOR, THE IMPLIED WAIVER THEORY GENERALLY WON'T APPLY

Other key elements to the analysis (and potentially critical to the outcome of whether an evidentiary, statutory, or implied waiver theory will be applied to negate the impact of the privilege) may entail (1) the claimant's relationship to the testator, and (2) the nature of the claim.

It is well established that "[a]lthough the privilege attaches to communications between a testator and the testator's counsel, the privilege may be breached upon the testator's death if litigation ensues between the testator's heirs, legatees, devisees, or any other parties claiming under the deceased client."[84] But waiver generally will not be implied "when it is sought to be invaded by parties claiming against the estate."[85]

Examples of claims "through" the testator would include claims regarding rights of inheritance that would be established pursuant to an

---

[81] *See* Hanson v. First Nat. Bank of Birmingham, 217 Ala. 426, 116 So. 127 (Ala. 1928).

[82] Paley v. Superior Court, 137 Cal. App. 2d 450, 462, 290 P.2d 617 (Cal. Ct. App. 1955), superseded in part on other grounds by implementation of subsequent rules of evidence in the state of California.

[83] Therefore, as previously alluded to, while the IRS might not be able to force production of truly privileged communications (because it likely would be considered a third party claiming against the estate), the executor might elect to waive the privilege or the privilege might be waived in the context of will or trust litigation that results in the door to discovery being opened for the IRS as an unintended consequence of the will or trust contest.

[84] Epstein, *supra* note 14, at 752.

[85] Epstein, *supra* note 14, at 755. *See also* Duggan v. Keto, 554 A.2d 1126 (D.C. 1989). But, the possibility remains that another premise for waiver may exist in such cases, such as the use of the attorney as a subscribing witness (as otherwise discussed in this book).

executed *inter vivos* instrument or by testate or intestate succession.[86] The fundamental premise as to why such claims should be exempt from application of the privilege is the "theory that claimants in privity with the estate claim through the client, not adversely, and the deceased client presumably would want his communications disclosed in litigation between such claimants so that his desires in regard to the disposition of his estate might be correctly ascertained and carried out."[87]

Citing in part the U.S. Supreme Court case *Glover v. Patten*[88] (and other sources), the court in *Fletcher v. Superior Court*[89] identified that:

> "[a]n exception to the application of the privilege on behalf of a deceased client has long been recognized when the dispute is between various parties claiming 'through' or 'under' the client, as opposed to a dispute between the estate and a 'stranger.' In *Glover v. Patten*[90] the United States Supreme Court held that 'in a suit between devisees under a will, statements made by the deceased to counsel respecting the execution of the will, or other similar document, are not privileged. While such communications might be privileged, if offered by third persons to establish claims against an estate, they are not within the reason of the rule requiring their exclusion, when the contest is between the heirs or next of kin." This analysis presupposes that the privilege to which the exception applies is only for communications between the decedent and the decedent's attorney.[91]

As a consequence, the implied waiver exception to the privilege has been applied to cases involving lost wills,[92] lack of capacity, or undue influence,[93] but deemed inapplicable to claims for breach of contract to create mutual wills, otherwise make a will or leave a bequest, or for creation of a constructive trust to compensate for services rendered during the testator's

---

[86] *See* Fletcher v. Superior Court, 44 Cal. App. 4th 773, 778 (Cal. App. 1996). *See also* Petition of Stompor, 165 N.H. 735, 738, 739, 82 A.3d 1278 (2013).

[87] *Fletcher, id.* at 779 (internal citations omitted).

[88] Glover v. Patten, 165 U.S. 394, 406, 17 S. Ct. 411, 416, 41 L. Ed. 760 (1897).

[89] *Fletcher,* 44 Cal. App. 4th at 779.

[90] *Glover,* 165 U.S.

[91] *Id.* (internal citations omitted).

[92] *See* Clark v. Turner, 183 F.2d 141, 87 U.S. App. D.C. 54 (D.C. 1950).

[93] *See Brunton,* 380 Ill.; *In re* Everett's Will, 105 Vt. 291, 166 A. 827, 830 (Vt. 1933); *and Eicholtz,* 331 Mich.

life.[94] This is because the former causes of action have been categorized as those that claim "through" the testator, with the latter being characterized as actions "against" the testator.

Interestingly, when the claim relates to whether the claimant could be an heir at law (despite not having received a bequest under a will), the privilege (on at least two occasions) did not preclude inquiry into confidential communications between the client and his attorney as to the nature of the purported heir's familial relationship.[95]

THE USE OF THE ATTORNEY AS WITNESS TO EXECUTION OF THE INSTRUMENT MAY CONSTITUTE AN EXPRESS WAIVER

Importantly, a number of courts have held that where the privilege might otherwise have precluded the attorney's testimony (because the claim was against as opposed to through the testator), the use of the attorney as a subscribing witness to the execution of the instrument may nonetheless constitute a waiver of the privilege by the client.[96] Essentially, the use of the attorney as a subscribing witness takes the analysis outside the confines of an "implied" waiver and places it in the category of an "explicit" waiver. Consequently, even claims "against" as opposed to "through" the testator (or adverse to the estate) might be supported by the testimony of the attorney who acted as a subscribing witness.[97]

---

[94] *See* Estate of Queener v. Helton, 119 S.W.3d 682 (Tenn. Ct. App. 2003). *See also* DeLoach v. Myers, 215 Ga. 255, 109 S.E. 777 (Ga. 1959).

[95] Johnson v. Antry, 5 S.W.2d 405 (Mo. 1928). In this case, the attorney was permitted to testify as to his client, the testator's, declarations that the claimant was treated as his adopted child despite a lack of formal adoption proceedings, and that he had done so since the child's minority. *See also Blackburn* 70 U.S., where the attorney was permitted to testify that the claimant was not the testator's wife. *But, see In re* Marden's Estate, 355 So.2d 121 (Fla. 3rd Dist. 1978), *cert. denied,* 361 So.2d 833 (Fla. 1978), where the testimony of the testator's estate planning attorney was held to not be subject to the privilege, but the testimony of an attorney who represented the testator in matters unrelated to the preparation of the will was precluded under the privilege with regard to establishing claimant as the testator's common-law spouse.

[96] *See* Denver Nat. Bank v. McLagan, 133 Colo. 487, 491, 298 P.2d 386, 66 A.L.R.2d 1297 (Colo. 1956); *Eicholtz,* 331 Mich., *relying on In re* Heiler's Estate, 288 Mich. 49, 284 N.W. 641 (Mich. 1939). *See also* Brown v. Edwards, 640 N.E.2d 401 (Ind. App. 1st Dist. 1994); *and* Vaughn v. Vaughn, 217 Ala. 364, 116 So. 427 (Ala. 1928).

[97] *Brown,* 640 N.E.2d at 406.

In *Pence v. Waugh*,[98] the Indiana court reasoned that:

> Clearly, it must be presumed, that the testator meant that his witness should be competent to make proof for the probate of the will, and that he intended by his selection, to waive the privilege in that regard, and it is no less clear that the desire and interest of the testator were as strong to support his will against contest, and that his selection, for that reason, was with like intention.[99]

Consistent with the concept that use of the attorney as a subscribing witness constitutes a waiver, courts have held that whatever the attorney learned in the course of witnessing the document is not privileged.[100] As a result, a waiver of the privilege in a claim "against" the testator has been found to occur when the attorney acts as a subscribing witness.

In *Brown v. Edwards*,[101] where the claim was against the estate (as it represented a breach of contract claim relative to the mutuality of wills), that court held:

> By choosing their attorney and his assistant to witness the wills, Velma and Warren implicitly requested that they defend the 1974 testamentary scheme against attack, regardless of any confidentiality which previously may have attached to the conversations among the four. That is, at the time, Velma and Warren intended that Lake and Ball should be competent to divulge the scope of their testamentary intent with regard to the 1974 wills if the mutual and reciprocal nature of the wills were ever questioned. The trial court properly decided that the testimony was admissible without violation of the attorney-client privilege.[102]

---

[98] Pence v. Waugh, 135 Ind. 143, 154, 34 N.E. 860, 863 (Ind. 1893).

[99] *Id.* at 864.

[100] *Eicholtz*, 331 Mich., *relying on In re* Heiler's Estate, 288 Mich. *See also Hanson*, 217 Ala. at 426; *and DeLoach*, 215 Ga. at 260, which reflected that "[a]lso a witness to a will although attorney for the testator, is permitted to disclose everything which he knew concerning his attestation and the circumstances surrounding and leading up to it."

[101] *Brown*, 640 N.E.2d at 406.

[102] *Id.*

As further explanation for exempting the privilege's application when the attorney acts as a subscribing witness, the court in *Vaughn v. Vaughn*[103] held that:

> The necessities of the case require that an attorney, who attests the execution of a will, be released from the general rule of privileged communication, to the extent that he is free to perform the duties of the other relation in which he is thus placed by the testatrix; and he may testify to all matters relevant to the issues presented by the attempt to probate the will, its execution and the mental status of the testatrix at the time, etc.[104]

Once the privilege is deemed "waived" (because of the client's use of the attorney as a subscribing witness), the potential for testimony by the attorney as to all matters leading up to the execution, including statements by the testator, his mental condition, facts relating to undue influence, and other matters affecting the validity of the instrument may be found to have been waived.[105]

In the Michigan case *In re Estate of Ford*,[106] the court held that:

> . . . even if he had been testatrix's attorney with respect to some aspects of the will, because witnesses to a will may properly be called upon to prove the will, disclosures made by the testatrix to a person functioning as a witness are necessarily intended to be disclosed to third parties and, therefore, are not confidential communications protected by the attorney-client privilege. Mr. Holland was therefore not precluded by the attorney-client privilege from offering evidence concerning Mrs. Ford's intention and understanding, her soundness of mind, and whether she was operating under the undue influence of any person.[107]

Consequently, once the privilege has been deemed waived (by virtue of the attorney acting as a subscribing witness), discovery of pertinent but

---

[103] *Vaughn*, 217 Ala. at 364.
[104] *Id.* at 365, 366 (internal citations omitted).
[105] *Denver Nat. Bank*, 133 Colo. at 487.
[106] *In re* Estate of Ford, 206 Mich. App. 705, 522 N.W.2d 729 (1994).
[107] *Id.* at 708, 709 (internal citations omitted).

otherwise confidential communications between the client and the attorney may occur, even if such communications occurred post-execution.[108]

While the "subscribing witness" waiver of the privilege emanates from common law, some states have codified the concept. In Oklahoma (as in Kansas), where such codification has occurred, the rationale behind the statute has been explained:

> The reason for the rule is obvious. One who makes a will does so with the knowledge that upon his death it will be published, and that in order to do so the testimony of witnesses as to the facts and circumstances in connection with its preparation and execution may be required in order to establish the fact that it expresses his wishes; that the making thereof was his free and voluntary act, and that he was competent to dispose of his property. He therefore waives the protection of the statute, and impliedly consents that his attorney, who attests the execution thereof, may testify. The same rule would apply to the other attesting witnesses, the wife and secretary of the attorney. The trial court did not err in permitting these witnesses to testify.[109]

But what if the contest represents a claim "against" as opposed to "through" the testator, and the testimony sought is that of a subscribing witness attorney to a will that has been revoked? This very situation was explored in *Lennox v. Anderson*.[110] The *Lennox* court explored the impact of the attorney acting as a subscribing witness of an instrument that was subsequently revoked. Premised upon the revocation of the instrument, the court held that the privilege remained intact as against the claims of a party adverse to the estate:

> The general rule is: "Where a testator requests the attorney who drafted the will, and with whom he has consulted in regard thereto, to sign the will as an attesting witness, and the attorney does so, his testimony with reference to the transaction and communications between him and the testator at the time are not inadmissible as privileged."[111] The reason is that "The testator, by his act, has in effect consented that, whenever the will shall be offered

---

[108]   *See Saliba*, 202 Ga.

[109]   *In re* Wilkins' Estate, 199 Okla. 249, 250, 185 P.2d 213, 216 (Okla. 1947) (internal citations omitted).

[110]   Lennox v. Anderson, 140 Neb. 748, 1 N.W.2d 912 (Neb. 1942).

[111]   *Id.* (citing 64 A.L.R. 192).

for probate, the attorney may be called as a witness and testify to any facts within his knowledge necessary to establish the validity of the will." By his act, the testator waives the privileged communication. The foregoing rule prevails, "notwithstanding statutory provisions that an attorney cannot, without the consent of his client, be examined as to any communication made by the client to him."[112] It will be noted that the foregoing rule applies to a situation distinctly different from that appearing in the instant case. Here, the conversation had by the attorney and client at the time of the execution of the will and the will itself are offered as corroborating evidence in an action by the beneficiary of the will to establish an oral contract. In the instant case the will offered in evidence had been revoked by the testator. When a person employs an attorney to have a will drawn and confides in the attorney as to the disposition of his property, it is the client's desire that during his lifetime they will be kept a secret, and a confidential relation exists. The attorney is not privileged to give the will publicity in any form. This confidential communication is temporary. After the testator's death, the attorney is at liberty to disclose all that affects the execution and contents of the will. The privilege has been waived by the testator, especially so when the scrivener of the will is a witness to it. So, in the instant case, when Charles J. Sanders consulted counsel about the making of a will, he never intended it to be published. He subsequently revoked the will and made a different disposition of the property. The effect of this act is: "While a testator waives the seal of confidence by requesting his attorney to witness his will, it seems that he may annul such waiver by revoking the will, so that the attorney will not thereafter be permitted to testify as to its execution and instructions given by the testator respecting the will."[113] The reason for the above rule is that the right of secrecy belongs to the client, not to the lawyer who drafted the will.[114]

The resurrection of the privilege in *Lennox* emphasizes the disparate treatment in certain jurisdictions that might be afforded to executed documents witnessed by the attorney in the context of a claim "against" as opposed to "through" a testator.

---

[112] *Id.*

[113] *Id.*

[114] *Id.* at 754–756 (emphasis added; except where noted, internal citations omitted).

WILL THE WAIVER APPLY TO ALL INSTRUMENTS?

Theories that "imply" a waiver or otherwise deem there to be an "exception" to the privilege that extends to documents that have been revoked, superseded, or never executed by the testator vary by jurisdiction and tend to be fact-dependent and claim-dependent. In an undue influence case, the fact that the testator met with multiple attorneys and made potentially differing statements of intent may be of significant importance.

Hypothetically, a client (long-standing or otherwise) discusses creation or modification of an existing plan with attorney Mr. Good ("Good"), but Good finds indicia of undue influence or lack of sufficient capacity. Good does what he should and exercises independent judgment. As a result, Good recommends testing and a consultation with a medical professional. Good also attempts to slow the process to see whether consistent instructions and rationale for the change in disposition are provided by the client in a confidential setting. Good creates and maintains careful and thorough notes of his observations and communications with the client. However, the influencer, Mr. Bad ("Bad"), sensing that his goals might not easily be attained under the auspices and guidance of Good (because Good is actually exercising professional judgment for the protection of his client), takes the testator "on the road" until Bad is able to find an attorney who (for lack of experience or other reasons) facilitates implementation of what amounts to Bad's testamentary plan and desires. Will discovery of Good's communications and files relating to an incomplete testamentary instrument be discoverable? Unfortunately, the answer (depending upon the jurisdiction and facts) is . . . maybe!

As already indicated, claims of undue influence generally will result in the privilege being deemed inapplicable. The general policy is that "if an heir challenges the will by alleging undue influence, it is in the interest of the estate that the "validity of [the] will *** be determine in the fullest light of the facts."[115]

This waiver may be implied not only in the context of privileged communications with the testator's attorney but also for communications conducted with the testator's accountant for the very same policy reasons enunciated earlier.[116] Despite the well-established and generally universally

---

[115] *Brunton*, 380 Ill. Dec. 366, 376; 8 N.E.3d 536, 546.

[116] *Id.* It may also be important to note that the mere presence of the client's accountant, where their participation is "necessary, or at least highly useful, for the effective consultation between the client and the lawyer" may not result in inapplicability of the privilege. See United States v. Kovel, 296 F.2d 918, 922, 96 A.L.R.2d 1169, A.F.T.R.2d 36662,-1 USTC P 9111 (C.A.N.Y. 1961).

accepted policies behind the waiver of the privilege in litigation between parties claiming through (as opposed to against) the testator, some jurisdictions apply a narrow waiver approach and others extend the waiver to even unexecuted documents.

In *In re McCulloch's Will*[117] and in *Ex Parte Hurin*,[118] at least two jurisdictions held that once a subsequent will is submitted for probate, the privilege as to communications between the attorney and his client relative to prior wills, which were thereby superseded, is reinstated. Consequently, the attorney in the revoked will was precluded from testifying as to his communications with the decedent. In juxtaposition, in *Green v. McClintock*,[119] an attempt to limit waiver of the privilege to the last testamentary instruments executed was thwarted. In *Green*, the court recognized that a change in a previously established estate plan could itself constitute proof of undue influence. As a consequence, in *Green*, the Maryland court not only permitted testimony from the attorney who drafted the prior estate planning documents with regard to communications during the period leading up to execution but also permitted his testimony relative to post-execution discussions held years later because they were found to help clarify the testator's donative intent.

In *Gould, Larson, Bennet, Wells, and McDonnell, P.C. v. Panico*,[120] a Connecticut court, relying upon common law in a factual scenario partially akin to the "Mr. Good" hypothetical outlined earlier answered the question as to whether the privilege should be pierced when the representation does not result in an executed document with a resounding *no*. In *Gould*, the court concluded that the exception to the privilege does not apply where the discussions held with the attorney do not result in the culmination of an executed will. In *Gould*, the law firm had previously prepared a will for the testator, and the will was executed. Approximately a decade later, another attorney from the firm met with the testator about preparing a new will or codicil. Within two weeks of that meeting, the testator met with two other attorneys (from different firms), the last of which created a will that was executed by the testator. Contestants to the will that ultimately was executed by the testator sought discovery of the communications between the testator and the associate from the testator's original estate planning firm. The court recognized that the principal reason behind holding the privilege

---

[117] *In re* McCulloch's Will, 263 N.Y. 408, 189 N.E. 473, 91 A.L.R. 1440 (N.Y. 1934).

[118] *Ex Parte* Hurin, 59 Ohio App. 82, 12 Ohio Op. 377, 17 N.E.2d 287 (Ohio 6th Dist. 1938).

[119] Green v. McClintock, 218 Md. App. 336, 97 A.3d 198 (Md. 2014).

[120] *Gould*, 273 Conn. 315, 869 A. 2d 653, 2005 Conn. LEXIS 111 (2005).

inapplicable to communications between the testator and his attorney (in a suit between parties claiming through the testator) was because the privilege was designed for the protection of the testator. Providing discovery of such communications generally is in the testator's interest in a controversy between parties claiming under him because it promotes "a proper fulfillment of his will."[121] The court further recognized the importance of such testimony in undue influence cases when it reflected that:

> . . . if the will does not reflect the decedent's actual intention, but rather that of another who induced him by undue influence to make the will, it cannot be said that the decedent would want such a will established as his own. If the law protected the communications, it would foster that which it abhors, namely, deceit and fraud.
>
> Therefore courts have recognized that an attorney who prepared a will can be required to disclose all that he knows concerning the testator's state of mind. "The attorney may know by whom and to what extent the testator was influenced. Again, he may know that the testator was not influenced at all, and may further know the very reasons that controlled him in doing what he did in making the will. In the first instance, should the person causing the will to be made be protected by the privilege? And in the latter, case, should the one who claims undue influence be permitted to invoke it and thus make certain circumstances to which he points and which may be easily explained to stand as the real truth?

* * *

> 'It may be laid down as a general rule of law, gathered from all the authorities, that, unless provided otherwise by statute, communications by a client to the attorney who drafted his will, in respect to that document, and all transactions occurring between them leading up to its execution, are not, after the client's death, within the protection of the rule as to privileged communications, in a suit between the testator's devisees and heirs at law, or other parties who all claim under him.' This rule is well settled law in many jurisdictions.[122]

---

[121] *Id.* at 324.

[122] *Id.* at 324, 325 (internal citations omitted).

Yet, despite recognizing both the importance and the policy reasons behind the *implied waiver* of the privilege, the court (in *Gould*) refused to apply the waiver of the privilege to a situation where the communications did not result in the preparation and execution of an instrument. Consequently, the Connecticut court narrowed the application of the implied waiver theory previously accepted and applied in *Doyle v. Reeves*[123] (another Connecticut decision).

Gast v. Hall,[124] an Indiana decision that cites *Gould*, represents yet another instance when one might have assumed, in the interest of the pursuit of truth and justice and upholding the testator's true desires, that attorney testimony would have been permitted, but the opposite occurred. In *Gast*, the testator was himself embroiled in will contest litigation. The opposing party, who was contesting the testator's interest in the original will contest, became the "devisee" of the testator's will. At one point during the pending litigation, the testator's historically negative view of the devisee inexplicably and drastically changed. The testator's longtime attorney became so concerned about the change in testator's perspective that he sought and obtained the appointment of a guardian ad litem to protect the testator's interests in the pending litigation. Within days of the guardian ad litem's appointment, the devisee literally found testator a new estate planning attorney and drove testator (unbeknownst to the testator's longtime attorney, who was then actively representing the testator in the original will contest) to a new attorney, which (while the original will contest was still pending) resulted in the creation and execution of a new will for the testator that left everything to the devisee. The testator died two months later. The court held that because the testimony sought from the testator's (longtime estate planning and) litigation attorney related to communications between the attorney and the testator in the context of the litigation (which included such things as comments made by the testator during the course of the litigation and difficulties the testator began to have in understanding the importance of key issues relating to the original will), the communications remained subject to the privilege because they did not occur in the context of the attorney's preparation of an estate plan for testator, but rather, occurred during pending litigation. Therefore, despite the communications being extremely relevant to the claim of undue influence and involved parties claiming "through" the testator, the privilege was applied

---

[123] Doyle v. Reeves, 112 Conn. 521, 12 A. 882 (Conn. 1931).
[124] Gast v. Hall, 858 N.E.2d 154 (Ind. Ct. App. 2006).

to preserve the confidential nature of the communications and preclude the attorney's testimony.[125]

In Oregon, a different result might have occurred. In *Tanner v. Farmer*,[126] the court was faced with a challenge to *inter vivos* gifts that took place days before the testatrix's death. When the testatrix died, several intended transactions were in the works, but they had not been completed. One such transaction was the creation of a will; another was the institution of divorce proceedings. The testatrix's surviving spouse challenged gifts to the testatrix's nephew and sought recoupment. Under the circumstances presented, the court held that the privilege did not apply to communications between the testatrix and her attorney with regard to the planned will and divorce proceedings, where (as here) all claimants were parties claiming through (as opposed to against) the testatrix.[127]

In *In re Everett's Will*,[128] where undue influence was alleged to have commenced shortly after the testator and his second wife met, the court held that discovery of attorney-client communications relating both to executed and to unexecuted documents was permissible. In this case, the Vermont Supreme Court recognized the need for liberal discovery rules in undue influence cases. The court indicated that, among many factors to be considered in an undue influence case, one is the "normality" of the will's disposition. In this regard, the court indicated that:

> [f]urthermore, the normality of the will's dispositions, with reference to the natural and uninfluenced desires of the testator, must be investigated. That influence is 'undue,' implies in part that the testamentary disposition in controversy deviates from that which the testator under the influence of his ordinary inclinations would have made. If the tribunal can ascertain his normal tendencies and plans, a standard is found by which to test the dispositions in issue. If these harmonize with this normal standard, the charge of undue influence can have little or no support; if they diverge abnormally, there is then some inducement to examine further into the nature of the influence producing this divergence. Accordingly, to establish this normal tendency or inclination, the testator's condition

---

[125] Gast v. Hall, 858 N.E.2d 154 (Ind. Ct. App. 2006).

[126] *Tanner*, 243 Or. at 431, 435.

[127] *Id.* (citing UNIF. R. EVID. 26(2)(b) (1954); Bergsvik v. Bergsvik, 205 Or. 670, 685, 291 P.2d 724 (Or. 1955); *and* CHARLES TILFORD MCCORMICK, MCCORMICK ON EVIDENCE § 98 at 199, 200 (1954)).

[128] *In re* Everett's Will, 105 Vt. at 835, 836.

of mind before and after the time in issue not only may be but must be examined; his state of affection or dislike to specific persons, and his general testamentary attitude towards them, will help to form the standard of his normal dispositions. For this purpose, his utterances indicating the state of his affections and intentions, and in particular his other testamentary acts or expressions, if any, whether prior or subsequent, may all be considered; the evidential principles already noted . . . sufficing equally for this purpose. This use of such evidence is also universally sanctioned.[129]

In *Petition of Stompor,* the New Hampshire court (also citing decisions from New York and Oregon) found that adoption of a Rule 502(d)(2) exception essentially waived the privilege with regard to attorney-client communications, whether or not they culminated in executed estate planning documents, and that this exception is not limited to the last documents executed.[130] Besides the direct implications of a Rule 502(d)(2) adoption, the court reviewed the rationale behind that rule, when (relying in part on the U.S. Supreme Court case *Swidler & Berlin v. United States*[131]) it stated that:

> . . . "all reason for assertion of the privilege disappears" when the privilege is being asserted not for the protection of the testator or his estate but for the protection of a claimant to his estate. This is so because the best way to protect the client's intent lies in the admission of all relevant evidence that will aid in the determination of his true will. As the United States Supreme Court has noted, "[t]he general rule with respect to confidential communications is that such communications are privileged during the testator's lifetime and, also, after the testator's death unless sought to be disclosed in litigation between the testator's heirs"; "[t]he rationale for such disclosure is that it furthers the client's intent."[132]

Similarly, in *In re Graf's Estate,*[133] where the testator consulted with an attorney about preparation of a will, but then executed a will prepared by an

---

[129] *In re* Everett's Will, 105 Vt. at 830.
[130] *Stompor,* 165 N.H. at 735.
[131] Swidler & Berlin v. United States, 524 U.S. 399, 405, 118 S. Ct. 2081, 141 L. Ed.2d 379 (1998).
[132] *Stompor,* 165 N.H. at 738, 739 (internal citations omitted).
[133] *In re* Graf's Estate, 119 N.W.2d at 478.

attorney some 300 miles away from testator's residence (in the community where the proponent of the will resided), the North Dakota court held the privilege inapplicable as a bar to the testimony of the attorney who drafted the will proffered for probate as well as that of the attorney with whom the testator consulted (but which did not culminate in the preparation of estate planning documents). In this case, the court's rationale was essentially summarized as follows:

> [T]he confidential nature of communications between attorney and client is not recognized, and this privilege no longer is applicable, in litigation which occurs after the client's death, which litigation is between parties, all of whom claim under the client. Where the litigation is to determine who shall take the property of the deceased and all parties claim under the client, neither party to the litigation can claim that such communications are privileged. Between persons claiming under the deceased client and others who are not heirs, next of kin, legatees, or devisees of the testator, the privilege still would survive.
>
> The reason for this exception to the general rule of holding communications between attorney and client as privileged, is sound. In controversies between heirs at law, devisees, legatees, or next of kin of the client, such communications should not be held as privileged because, in such case, the proceedings are not adverse to the estate. The interest of the estate as well as the interest of the deceased client demand that the truth be determined.[134]

IS THE PRIVILEGE SUBSTANTIVE OR PROCEDURAL?

Whether a court deems the privilege substantive or procedural in nature may well impact whether the privilege will permit or bar testimony in a given case. If the privilege is addressed specifically in an instrument, it may be deemed a substantive provision. If one is relying on a rule of evidence, such rules tend to be procedural in nature and may subject the determination to the rule of the jurisdiction where the proceeding takes place.

---

[134] *Id.* at 481.

One treatise on the privilege recognized that:

> [u]nfortunately, the reported opinions are substantially incon-
> sistent both in the way they identify factors, and in the way identi-
> fied factors are employed.
>
> To identify the most interested state, courts generally use
> some combination of five factors: place where the trial will occur;
> place of discovery for which a privilege has been asserted; loca-
> tion of the origin of the attorney-client relationship; place of
> communication; location of events leading to cause of action; and
> locations of domiciles, places of incorporation, or places where
> the parties do business.[135]

While another treatise propounds that whether the communication
should be treated as a privileged communication, the privilege primarily is
affected by where the communication took place.[136]

If the privilege is deemed procedural in nature, the statutes, court
rules, rules of evidence, and common law in the jurisdiction where the
administration or the litigation takes place may be determinative in how
the privilege is applied.[137] If the privilege is deemed substantive or an otherwise integral part of the representation out of which the privilege arose,
it is possible that the communication will be governed by the laws of the
state where the communication took place. Because the answer may not be
definitive, the receipt of a subpoena by the estate planning attorney may
cause considerable angst.

While a review of the cases reflects some commonality of themes and
policies, it is clear that the application and waiver of the privilege can vary
depending upon the parties, claims, and jurisdiction(s) involved. Because

---

[135] PAUL R. RICE, ATTORNEY-CLIENT PRIVILEGE IN THE UNITED STATES § 12:18 at
1260–1263 (2013) (internal citations and internal footnotes omitted).

[136] EPSTEIN, *supra* note 14, at 761.

[137] In Huber v. Noonan, 2018 WL 5262368 (10/23/2018), an unpublished Pennsylvania Superior Court case, the court held that "the Privilege was procedural in
nature and therefore because Florida had more significant contacts and greater
concern for the primary and principal litigation, . . . Florida law should also control
the matter of attorney-client privilege" at *7 (citing Griffith v. United Air Lines, Inc.,
416 Pa. 1, 203 A.2d 796 (1964) and Carbis Walker LLP v. Hill, Barth and King, LLC,
930 A.2d 573 (Pa Super 2007)).

the estate planner's testimony and files often are of key importance to rebutting a presumption of undue influence or may otherwise influence the outcome of a challenge based upon claims of lack of capacity or undue influence, preservation of the attorney's ability to testify or produce his records may be of great importance to fulfilling the testator's true estate planning desires and intent.[138,139]

---

[138] As already alluded to in this book, recognizing that the privilege may be explicitly or impliedly waived, the creation and maintenance of detailed contemporaneous notes regarding the estate planner's observations as well as the decedent's intentions, desires, and reasoning may be extremely important.

[139] For practical recommendations about how one might address the privilege proactively, see Bloomberg BNA & Sandra D. Glazier, Esq., *Testimony from Beyond the Grave: The Gravamen of the Attorney-Client Privilege in Will and Trust Contests*, 57 TAX MANAGEMENT MEMORANDUM (2016).

CHAPTER 12

Video Recording, Electronic Wills, and Remote Witnessing and Notarization[1]

VIDEO RECORDING

Often, the question arises as to whether videotaping the execution of important estate planning instruments will be helpful or harmful. The easy answer is . . . it depends. Video recording vulnerable adults has the potential to undercut the estate planner's own perceptions of the client's capacity. This is because it will permit others to view the client, likely over a smaller segment of time and without the benefit of other insights obtained by a diligent estate planner, which may result in the viewer (be it a judge or a jury) imposing their own assessment on these issues. In addition, individuals often feel they do not look good when recorded, and this may have the effect of limiting self-generated engagement while being recorded. Counsel may not be adept at asking the types of open-ended questions that might be necessary to truly reflect that the plan is one originated by the client (as opposed to another who has engaged in efforts to influence the plan).[2] To have

---

[1] Adapted in part from an article previously published by BNA: Bloomberg BNA and Sandra D. Glazier, Esq., *Electronic Wills: Revolution, Evolution, or Devolution*, 44 TAX MANAGE. ESTATES GIFTS TRUSTS J. 34-50 (2019).

[2] Leading questions may elicit agreement with propositions that may not be true. By using leading questions (especially if premised upon information supplied by someone other than the grantor/testator), the attorney may be unintentionally buttressing tactics utilized by an undue influencer to create false narratives and memories and thereby unwittingly assist in supplanting the will of the grantor/testator.

the client carry off a good video recording, the preparation required may necessitate coaching and multiple recordings, which will create additional questions about the true voluntary nature of the process. Such activities are almost certain to engender questions about how many times the planner felt it was important to video record an execution and why the recording was done in this particular instance. When deciding whether to record the execution, consider the client's vulnerabilities and assess how they might be viewed by others who are unfamiliar with the individual. It is entirely possible that the recording will support a challenger's contentions that the client was extremely vulnerable and therefore susceptible to undue influence, or even that the client lacked sufficient capacity to engage in the transaction.

A review of several appellate decisions from different jurisdictions demonstrates that "video recording a will (or trust) execution ceremony provides evidence in the event of future will (or trust) contests, which can be good or bad."[3] Regardless of what is being executed (will, trust, power of attorney, beneficiary designation, deed, or joint ownership agreement), it is important that the video demonstrate, at a minimum, that the individual (1) had the requisite capacity to engage in the transaction,[4] (2) can provide pertinent information without prompting, (3) understood the nature and effect of the instrument, and (4) to the extent possible, voluntarily created and engaged in actions to implement the plan. When the instrument reflects a significant change from a historical plan, an explanation generated by the individual as to his rationale for the change also is helpful.

Some cases where videotaping of the estate planning documents may have played a role in the outcome of a case in which undue influence was alleged reflect how a video can support the validity or invalidity of the action taken. In many of these cases, the video generally supported other evidence that might have, by itself, been sufficient to support the fact finder's conclusion. Essentially, the video corroborated witness testimony or other evidence that was introduced. Consequently, even when one decides to videotape the execution of documents, it remains important to not forego taking other appropriate steps that are generally associated with the formalities of execution, and to not use leading statements as part of the process.

See Dominic J. Campisi, Evan D. Winet, & Jake Calvert, *Undue Influence: The Gap Between Current Law and Scientific Approaches to Decision-Making and Persuasion*, 43 ACTEC L. J. 368 (2018).

[3] Gerry W. Beyer, *Will Execution Ceremony: Should It Be in Pictures*, 45 ESTATE PLAN-NING J, 1 (2018).

[4] *See* chapter 2.

Examples of Video Recording That Helped Invalidate Instruments

- *Trautwein v. O'Brien*[5] represents an example of where videotaping the execution of a will likely undercut the attorney's own testimony and opinion of the testator's capacity. In *Trautwein*, the appellate court found that:

  > [t]he most compelling evidence presented on the issue of testamentary capacity in the trial court was a videotape of the testator at the execution of the purported will. That tape discloses a man near the end of his life suffering the debilitating effects of a series of severe strokes; a man who at times appears totally detached from the proceedings. Viewing the tape clearly reveals the testator's inability to comprehend all that was going on about him. Certainly, one would seriously question his ability to dispose of several million dollars in estate assets by means of a complicated will and trust arrangement. Further, it is apparent from the tape that the whole proceeding was directed and controlled by the decedent's attorney. [Decedent's] total participation was prompted by the use of leading questions. The tape further shows that the decedent lacked an accurate understanding of the extent of his property and holdings, his estimates ranging from five to eight million dollars.[6]

  In addition, the appellate court found that the tape supported evidence of the decedent's susceptibility to undue influence due to the vulnerabilities depicted in the video. As a result of both of the court's findings, the trial court's grant of summary disposition in favor of the beneficiaries (individuals upon whom the decedent had been dependent upon for care, and who benefited under the revised plan) was found to constitute reversible error.

- The *Estate of Seegers, Deceased*,[7] is an example of where a video recording of a will execution by family members present but not involved in the will execution helped support the testimony of contestants in overturning the validity of a proffered will. In October 1984, the

---

[5] Trautwein v. O'Brien, 1989 WL 2149 (Ohio Ct. App. 10th D., 1989).

[6] *Id.*

[7] Estate of Seegers, Deceased, 733 P.2d 418, 1986 Okla. Civ. App. 21 (Okla. Ct. App. – Div. 4 1986).

91-year-old decedent made a will. The attorney who prepared the 1984 will had a historical relationship with the decedent's nephew ("Combrink"). The attorney obtained information regarding the terms to contain in the will from Combrink (who, as her conservator, held a confidential relationship with the decedent). The importance of the video was multifaceted. The appellate court opined that once the presumption of undue influence was established, the party who sought to benefit under the proposed will had the burden to rebut the presumption by "showing that the confidential relationship had been severed or that the party making the disposition had competent and independent legal advice in the preparation of the will."[8] Other relatives who had been asked to leave the room when the attorney began to meet with the decedent videotaped the will execution from an adjacent room. They testified that when the decedent attempted to read the will (which had been brought by the attorney for the decedent's execution without provision of a prior draft to facilitate review), the attorney informed the decedent that it was the same as a prior will (except for the addition of the name of a niece-in-law). Because of the decedent's poor eyesight, she needed to read documents slowly. When she attempted to read the document, the attorney hastened her attention to the signature page, instructed her to sign, and indicated that he would answer any questions she had after she executed the document. The decedent signed the will. The video recording was 17 minutes long, which duration demonstrated the short time devoted to permitting the decedent to gain an understanding of the contents of the will. The attorney's instructions, coupled with the decedent's willingness to sign without having her questions addressed, "were indicative of the susceptibility of [decedent] to undue influence exerted by [Combrink] with the aid and assistance of" the attorney.[9] Ten days following the execution of the October 1984 will, the decedent became ill and required hospitalization. Following hospitalization, she was transferred to a nursing home, where she died on April 1, 1985. In January 1985, Combrink again informed the attorney of changes that he represented that the decedent desired. Combrink testified that he tried to talk the decedent out of making the changes, but she nonetheless desired to proceed. Those changes represented a significant deviation from the decedent's historical plan. Combrink testified that

---

[8] *Id.*, at 423 (citing White v. Palmer, 498 P.2d 1401, 1406 (Okla. 1971)).
[9] *Estate of Seegers,* 733 P.2d at 422.

he told the decedent the change would cause a "hassle," but he didn't explain that the change would result in the niece, who had video-taped the prior will execution, and her siblings not receiving the same bequests as other nieces and nephews, or that he thought it was wrong to remove those beneficiaries. Nor did Combrink ask the decedent her rationale for making the change. The attorney informed the decedent that the omitted nieces and nephews had been removed from the will, and that the decedent's sister would receive less than an intestate share, but didn't explain that the nieces and nephews would get nothing if the decedent's sister predeceased her. Combrink arranged for the witnesses to the will and was present in the nursing home (but not in the decedent's room) when the 1985 will was signed. The court focused on the conduct of the attorney and Combrink, as well as on the significant change reflected by the 1985 will from the one signed less than four months earlier. The court concluded that there was a *prima facie* showing of undue influence. Also of significance was the court's recitation of the requirement that a decedent have competent and independent legal advice.

Here it appears that the importance of the video recording was to demonstrate the lack of independent counsel necessary to help insulate and protect the instrument from the effects of the presumption of undue influence. This may be largely because "independent advice has been held to mean the testator had the benefit of conferring fully and privately about the consequences of his intended will with a person who is not only competent on such matters, but who was so disassociated from the interest of the beneficiary named there as to be in a position to advise with the testator impartially and confidentially."[10]

- In *In re Estate of Smith*,[11] multiple video recordings were available that established that the decedent had sufficient capacity to execute each of the wills. Despite the fact that the videos reflected decedent's capacity and statements that decedent wanted his estate to go to Mr. Irving (his attorney) and Mr. Irving's wife, the court held that the video was not sufficient to rebut the presumption of undue influence that existed under the facts and circumstances presented. Here, the decedent was 99 years old and had no close relatives. There was evidence that the decedent continued to consider Mr. Irving to be at least one of his attorneys. Mr. Irving had begun assisting

---

[10] *Id.* at 423 (citing White v. Palmer, 498 P.2d 1401, 1406 (1971)).
[11] *In re* Estate of Smith, 827 So. 2d 673 (2002).

the decedent with financial matters. Mr. Irving was aware, through services he rendered as the decedent's attorney, that the decedent had made gifts and left bequests to non-family members under prior instruments. The decedent had frequently visited Mr. Irving at his law office, and Mr. Irving began to visit the decedent at her residence. At the time the contested will was prepared, Mr. Irving had previously acted as the decedent's attorney, had control over much of the decedent's assets, and was aware that the decedent wished to leave him a bequest. Mr. Irving had referred decedent to another attorney because he knew he could not prepare a will under which he himself (or his wife) would be named a beneficiary. Mr. Irving and the attorney who prepared the contested will, Osborne, were friends. Mr. Irving referred decedent to Osborne. Mr. Irving provided the video equipment for the recording of the execution ceremony. While the videos reflect that decedent, after being asked by Osborne, confirmed that he wanted Mr. and Mrs. Irving to receive the bulk of his estate, the videos also reveal that the decedent did not, on his own, tell Osborne how he wanted to dispose of his estate, other than that he didn't want relatives to take it. Additionally, the videos do not reflect Osborne providing decedent with any advice, nor did the decedent provide an explanation, in his own words, as to why he wanted the Irvings to receive the bulk of his estate. While Mr. Irving was not present during the execution of documents, given his fiduciary relationship with decedent (which was not severed at the time the will was executed), he could have told decedent anything prior to the time decedent met with Osborne. Therefore, while the video clearly established capacity and there was no direct evidence of undue influence, the absence on the video of any self-generated explanations as to why decedent wanted the Irvings to inherit the bulk of his estate, and the lack of advice on the video, resulted in the video being deemed insufficient evidence to rebut the presumption that the bequests were the result of undue influence.

Examples of Video Recording That Helped Validate Instruments

- In *Noland v. Noland*,[12] a significant amount of testimony was presented that reflected that decedent suffered significant cognitive impairments, which negatively affected his memory, ability (at times) to

---

[12] Noland v. Noland, 330 Ark. 660, 956 S.W.2d 173 (1997).

identify members of his family, and behavior. The trial court and the court of appeals invalidated estate planning instruments and deeds premised upon such evidence. Nonetheless, because individuals can experience lucid intervals, a video recording taken by one of decedent's sons, who was present in the attorney's office when the documents execution took place, was instrumental in convincing the Arkansas Supreme Court justices that the decedent had the requisite capacity, and that the instruments weren't the product of undue influence. The 45-minute video recorded the attorney interviewing decedent regarding his estate planning desires (including the use of non-leading questions relative to key elements of the plan and the extent of decedent's assets). The court found that the video demonstrated on that particular date that decedent was able to identify his four children and express his desire that all of his children receive equal shares of his property. The video also reflected decedent's explanation that he didn't previously understand the implications of a deed he had executed and consequently that the deed didn't accurately reflect his estate planning desires. The video supported the attorney's own conclusion that, on the operative date, decedent possessed the requisite mental competency to execute a trust and deed (that changed the dispositive provisions of decedent's plan to treat his children in an equal fashion to the largest extent then possible), and that decedent exercised his own free will in doing so.

- In *In re Robertson Estate*,[13] a video supported the admission of the decedent's will and codicil and supported that these instruments were (1) not the product of undue influence, and (2) executed when the decedent had the requisite capacity. Despite evidence that established that decedent (who was a 90-year-old widow) was aged and frail, lived with her granddaughter following an illness, the granddaughter (who stood in a confidential relationship with the decedent) benefited under the will and codicil to the exclusion of two of the decedent's two grandsons, who were cousins of the granddaughter who survived the decedent, the will and codicil were admitted to probate. It appears that the video may have played an important supporting role to other evidence introduced during the trial. In this case, the decedent's attorney obtained the video recording (and the decedent selected that attorney without the granddaughter's involvement). In addition, the will

---

[13] *In re* Robertson's Estate, 372 So. 2d 1138 (1979).

was witnessed by the decedent's treating physician. The evidence (including the video) reflected that the decedent's mind at the time the will was executed was unimpaired and that the decedent understood the extent of her estate and objects of her bounty. No evidence was introduced that indicated she was any less competent when the codicil was executed. Nothing reflected that the grand-daughter procured the instruments or knew of their content or was involved in any way in the formulation of the plan or convey-ance of information to the attorney or present when the decedent conveyed information regarding her desire to make a will. Import-ant to the outcome of this case also appears to be the use of the decedent's physician as a witness to the execution, and a finding that the granddaughter who benefited under the will and codicil had not procured the instruments (in addition to the fact that a presumption of undue influence, under Florida's standards, was not established).

- In *In re Estate of Clinger*,[14] a video recording of an earlier 2001 will (which contained similar dispositive provisions to a challenged 2011 will) was admitted into evidence. The video of the earlier will provided the jury with a direct opportunity to assess the decedent's testimentary capacity as of 2001 (but not the voluntariness of the instrument, or whether it was or was not the product of undue influence). The jury asked to view the video during its deliberation. Therefore, it is likely that the video played a supportive role in the jury's finding that the decedent had sufficient capacity and that the 2011 will was not the product of undue influence.

- In *Holliman v. Johnson*,[15] the trust opponents challenged an irrevo-cable trust and the execution of deeds intended to correct a prior transfer of property into a joint tenancy that disfavored the dece-dent's daughters. The challenge alleged lack of capacity and undue influence. The challenger's expert, a certified legal nurse consul-tant, testified that a review of the medical records reflected that decedent's short-term and situational memory were impaired, as were her eyesight and hearing. Contestants also claimed that a video of the execution demonstrated that decedent's hearing impair-ments impeded her ability to understand the transaction. The court

---

[14] *In re* Estate of Clinger, 292 Neb. 237, 872, N.W.2d 37 (2015).
[15] Holliman v. Johnson, 2016 Ark. App. 39, 480 S.W.3d 903 (Ark. Ct. App. Div. II, 2016).

had the benefit of watching the 20-minute video of the execution of the trust and deeds, and this probably had bearing on the trial court's determination. In the video, the decedent acknowledged the attorney's verbal listing of her assets. Evidence external to the video reflected that decedent directed her daughter to contact the lawyer to prepare the trust and related documents. The distribution of the assets under the trust was the same as under the prior will. The proponent's expert testified that the videotape reflected that the decedent was engaged and had understanding. In the video, decedent spontaneously asked the attorney what would happen if one of her sons refused to act as a trustee. The appellate court affirmed the trial court's determination that the trust and deeds were valid.

Recommendations for Video Recording

In any case, where there is a vulnerable person and there is the potential for controversy, videotaping, if done properly, can corroborate the actions taken leading up to and occurring during the execution ceremony. It may be important that the video capture the following:

- A discussion involving the individual reflecting when he received a copy of the instruments and when and whether anyone met with him to read or explain in sufficient detail the important provisions of the instruments or actions contemplated under the instrument.
- Those elements necessary to establish sufficient capacity.
- A statement generated by the individual reflecting why he is engaging in the transaction and any rationale he may have for making a change.
- Indications by the individual regarding the voluntary nature of the transaction.
- A discussion of any health conditions suffered by the individual or medications taken may be appropriate. In some cases, the presence of the signer's physician or a mental health professional may be desirable, or include a discussion regarding a recent mental health examination.
- It may be helpful to have any video recording conducted by an experienced videographer, preferably in a quiet setting such as an office or residence. Arrange for the video to be conducted in a thoughtful manner so that the individual is made aware, in advance, of the format, who will be present, and the purpose of the video recording.

ELECTRONIC WILLS, VIRTUAL WITNESSES, AND NOTARIZATION

With the advent of electronic will statutes that permit virtual witnesses and remote notarizations that may require, to some extent, video recording, the issue of even how to facilitate the execution and witnessing of documents may become a strategic decision that the planner should consider, especially when a vulnerable adult is involved.[16]

So far, Nevada, Indiana, Florida, and Arizona have electronic will statutes. Other jurisdictions, including California, New Hampshire, Texas, Virginia, and Maryland, have or are considering adopting their own versions of an electronic wills act. The National Conference of Commissioners on Uniform State Laws has also promulgated an Electronic Wills Act that states may consider when analyzing whether to adopt an electronic will statute.[17]

Other considerations relate to the admissibility of the recording. Some states have adopted statutes regarding the admissibility of such recordings and the purposes for which they may be admitted as evidence.[18] But, even if the recording is admitted for one purpose but not for another, can the bell be unrung once the trier of fact has viewed the video?

In Nebraska, the Supreme Court held that while a video recording of a will execution was admissible, special instructions should nonetheless be given to the jury.[19] Those instructions informed the jury that the tape should be considered only for purposes of demonstrating capacity and state of mind. The tape should not be considered for purposes of demonstrating the absence of undue influence, because responses to questions about whether the instrument was freely and voluntarily done would be hearsay if offered to prove the truth of the matter asserted.

In the context of undue influence, electronic wills may themselves put vulnerable adults at risk. Removing attorneys from the process by placing vulnerable adults in the potential position of executing documents (perhaps created by malfeasant family members or care providers) where there is only limited interaction before witnesses or a notary (who may know nothing about the plan or who might not have the sufficient wherewithal

---

[16] For a more expansive discussion of electronic wills, see Glazier, *Electronic Wills*, *supra* note 1.

[17] Uniform Law Commission, *Electronic Wills Act*, https://www.uniformlaws.org/viewdocument/final-act-with-comments-130?CommunityKey=a0a16f19-97a8-4f86-afc1-b1c0e051fc71&tab=librarydocuments.

[18] ARIZ. REV. STAT. § 14-2524; IND. CODE § 29-1-21.5.

[19] *In re* Estate of Clinger, 292 Neb. at 237.

to adequately assess capacity) doesn't necessarily provide a benefit, even if it provides greater convenience. However, the converse may also be true. Individuals have always been free (in most states) to create holographic wills or to sign hard copies of documents created on a computer and printed out for their execution. When such documents represent the intention of the testator but are created under circumstances where a presumption of undue influence may arise, the absence of counsel can result in the instruments being set aside.

Attorneys who are involved in identifying, planning for, or litigating undue influence are (or should be) aware that the lack of independent counsel can constitute a "suspicious circumstance" that may undercut the enforceability of wills of vulnerable adults when concerns exist that the same may be the product of undue influence. Unfortunately, the public generally is not aware of the importance of independent competent counsel in defending the enforceability of a will that they might create. They also may not be aware of the staggering statistics regarding the prevalence of undue influence.

As we fashion new laws to address the public's apparent desire for low-cost options and easy access, it might be helpful to require the inclusion of a notification that alerts the public of the potential importance of obtaining competent independent legal counsel in the creation and execution of testamentary instruments.

Generally, the receipt of independent competent legal advice may enhance the likelihood that a testator's estate plan will withstand attack. Such advice needs be more than just perfunctory. The provision of professional legal advice and services, in contrast to serving as a mere scrivener, requires the "interpretation and application of legal principles to guide future conduct or to assess past conduct."[20] A scrivener is merely someone who transcribes or memorializes what others tell him or her.[21] Acting as a mere scrivener does not constitute the rendition of legal advice.[22] Importantly, in some states, a lack of independent counsel can even heighten the burden required to rebut a presumption of undue influence once that presumption has been found to exist.[23]

---

[20] Alomari v. Ohio Dep't of Pub Safety, 626 F. App'x 558, 570 (6th Cir. 2015).

[21] *See* People v. Lee, No. 306192, 2012 WL 6097316, at *2 (Mich. App., Dec 6, 2012) (one who transcribes results generated by a machine is a scrivener).

[22] State v. Beaudry, 53 Wis. 2d 148; 191 N.W.2d 842 (1971).

[23] Haynes v. First Nat. State Bank of New Jersey, 87 N.J. 163, 432 A.2d 890, 23 A.L.R.4th 347 (1981).

Given potential issues relating to the rendition of legal services without a license, it is likely that many of the online services will be little more than form providers or scriveners. While this might work for some, it may leave vulnerable adults at greater risk of undue influence. Because some states do not recognize a "probable cause" or "good faith" exception to the application of no-contest clauses, perhaps statutes that permit electronic wills should prohibit the inclusion of a no-contest clause in such instruments. If the statute does not prohibit the use of a no-contest clause, perhaps it should at least reflect that the instrument may be attacked if there exists "good faith" or "probable cause," particularly in those states that do not otherwise apply such exceptions to the enforcement of no-contest clauses.

Index

Note: Page numbers with n indicate footnotes.

Attorney work-product doctrine,
140–141, 141n17
Audit, waiver of attorney-client privilege
and IRS, 149n58
Authority, as tactic of undue influence,
67–68

B
"Baby boomer generation," 3
Bates-stamped document pages, 128
Baxter v. Baxter, 144–145n36
Bednarz Trust, In re, 126–127n5,
146–147n43
Beneficiary
lawyers as, 94–101
risk factor for undue influence and
conduct of, 62
Blackburn v. Crawfords, 151–152,
156n95
Black's Law Dictionary, 25
"Blueprint" for addressing elder
abuse, 8n29
Blum, Bennett, 30, 65, 66
Booher v. Brown, 147
Brown v. Edwards, 157
Burden of proof, presumption of
undue influence and, 81, 90–91
Bursting bubble approach, 101

C
California
definition of undue influence in,
51–53
Due Process in Competency
Determination Act, 66
lawyers as beneficiaries and
presumption of undue influence
in, 97–98
presumption of undue influence
in, 81
Campbell, id., 84n25
Capacity, 39–46
contractual, 42
definitions of, 39–40
donative, 42, 43–46
fraud and duress and, 69
levels of dementia and, 40–41
powers of attorney and, 46

practice guidelines when may be
issue, 32–34
presumption of sufficient, 79
probable cause exception and, 107
proxy and, 44–46
testamentary, 27–28, 42–43
Capacity inquiry, 135
Caregiver, defined, 5–6
Caro v. Meerbergen, 149n57
Challenger, longitudinal perspective in
undue influence case, 124–125
Chronology, importance in undue
influence litigation, 128
Circumstantial evidence. *See also*
Evidence
probable cause and, 119
undue influence cases and, 56–59,
123, 139n12
Clients. *See also* Attorney-client
privilege
assessing capacity of, 12–14
if attorney believes diminished
capacity is present, 15–17
attorney responsibility to, 35
communications with client with
diminished capacity, 11–12
identifying who is a client, 10
with sufficient capacity but
vulnerable to exploitation, 34–37
Clifford, Nathan, 151–152n72
Clinical Dementia Rating
(CDR) Dementia Staging
Instrument, 41n11
Coercive persuasion, duress *vs.,*
76–77
Cognitive impairment. *See also*
Dementia
informed consent and, 134
risk of undue influence and, 61, 130
Commitment and consistency, as tactic
of undue influence, 67
Communication
with client who has diminished
capacity, 11–12
defining privileged, 140–145
determining whether is privileged,
139–140
Competency, undue influence
and, 48